IMAGES
of America

LAKE MATTAMUSKEET

NEW HOLLAND AND HYDE COUNTY

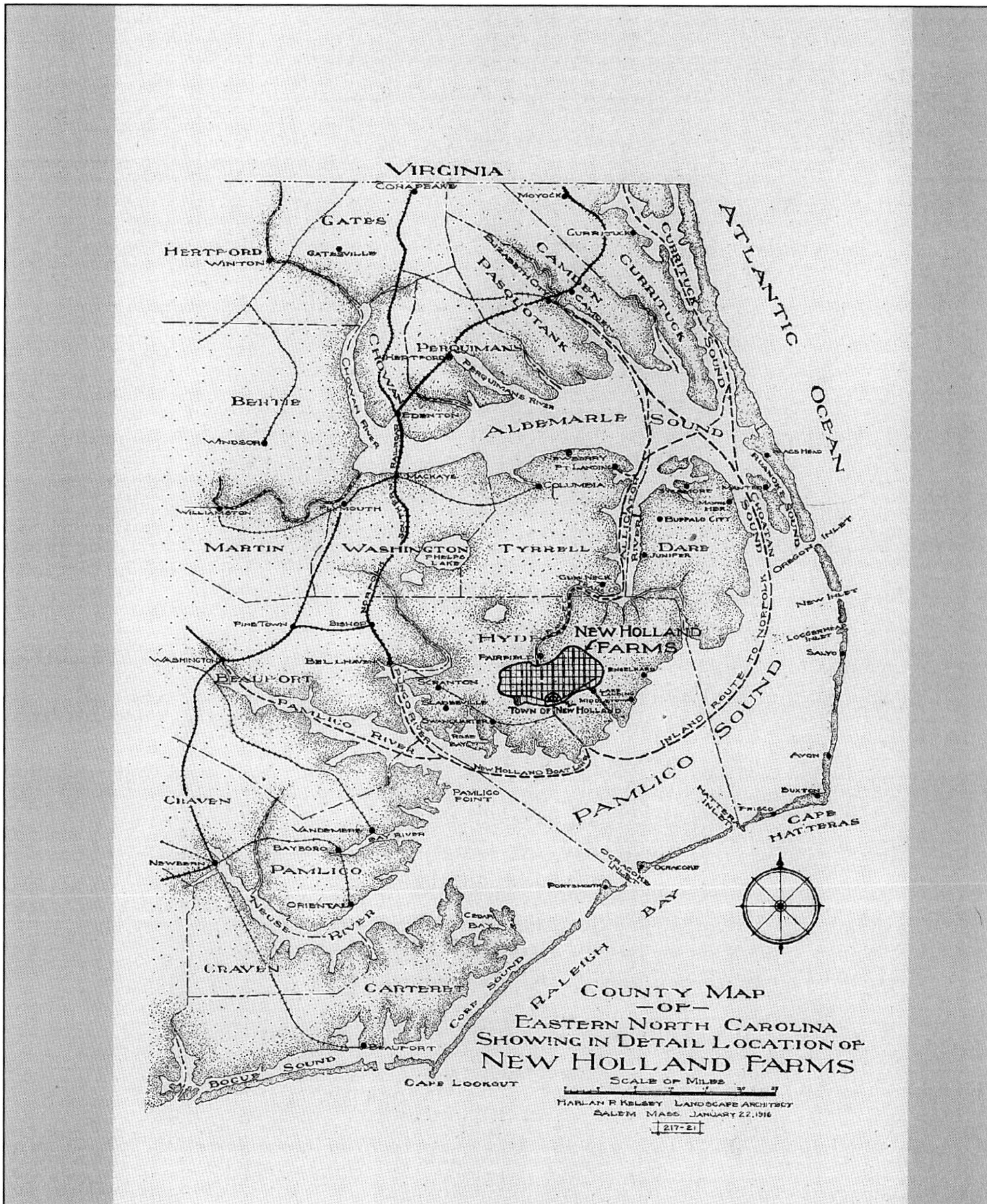

This 1916 map showing the location of Lake Mattamuskeet in Hyde County, North Carolina, appeared in a New Holland Farms, Inc. brochure promoting land sales in the reclaimed lake bed. (Courtesy of Ercell Gibbs.)

Cover Photograph: Probably the earliest surviving view of this structure, this photograph shows the Mattamuskeet Drainage District's pumping plant *c.* 1916. Today, the Mattamuskeet Lodge is situated on this site, which remains a popular photographic view. (Courtesy of Elizabeth Butt.)

IMAGES
of America

LAKE MATTAMUSKEET

NEW HOLLAND AND HYDE COUNTY

Lewis C. Forrest

ARCADIA
PUBLISHING

ISBN 978-0-7385-0271-7

Published by Arcadia Publishing
Charleston, South Carolina

Printed in the United States of America

Library of Congress Catalog Card Number: 99-067060

For all general information contact Arcadia Publishing at:
Telephone 843-853-2070
Fax 843-853-0044
E-mail sales@arcadiapublishing.com
For customer service and orders:
Toll-Free 1-888-313-2665

Visit us on the Internet at www.arcadiapublishing.com

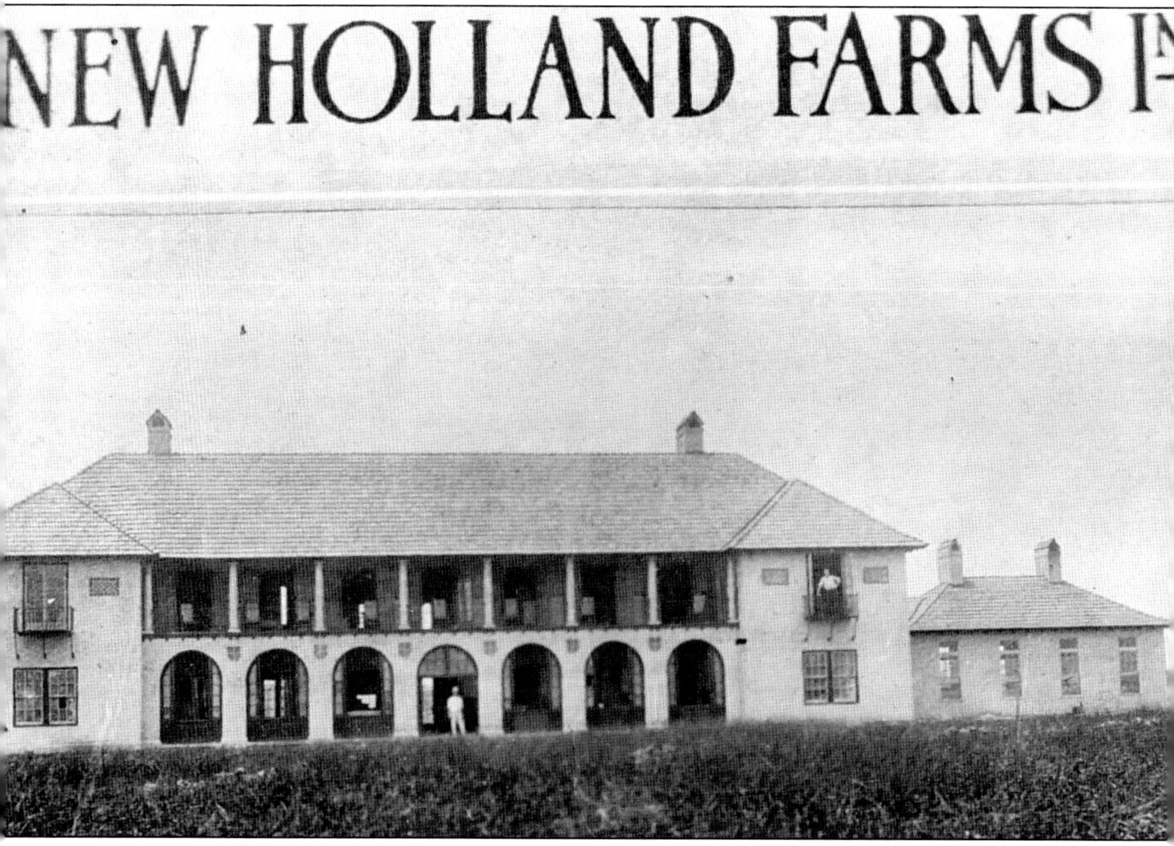

The New Holland Inn was built by New Holland Farms, Inc. around 1916 to the specifications of Douglas Nelson Graves. (Courtesy of Carolyn Ponzer Taylor.)

Contents

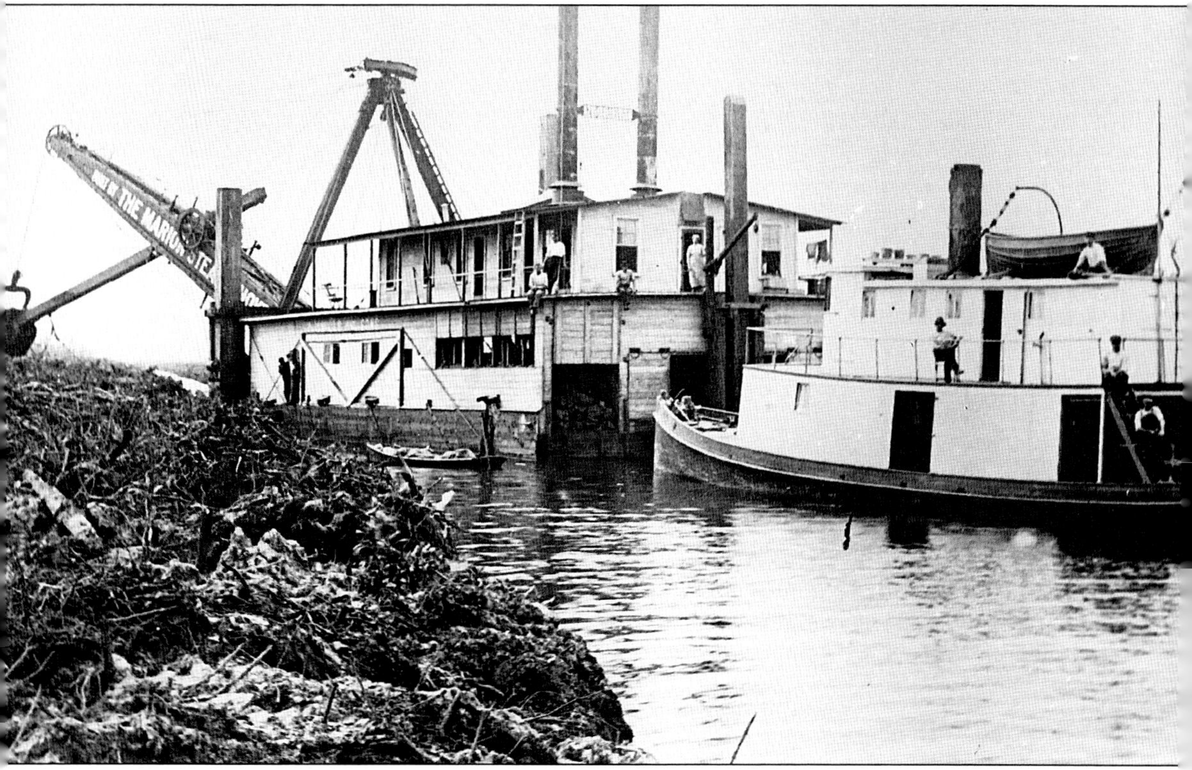

A dipper dredge is at work preparing the network of 130 miles of canals excavated to drain Lake Mattamuskeet. (Courtesy of Virginia Pugh.)

ACKNOWLEDGMENTS

The Mattamuskeet Foundation, Inc. is indebted to the people of Hyde County for their support of the efforts to preserve the New Holland story of Lake Mattamuskeet. The people and organizations that have generously loaned photographs for this book are identified in the captions. A team of volunteers from Hyde and Beaufort Counties provided special assistance for this publication and receive special recognition on page 127. The Mattamuskeet Foundation is especially grateful for the ongoing support of its members, patrons, and institutional partners.

Special appreciation is extended to the Mattamuskeet National Wildlife Refuge and to Donald E. Temple, manager. Access to the refuge is essential to the preservation and interpretation of the history of Lake Mattamuskeet. The entire refuge staff is to be commended for their cooperative spirit in working with all the community groups that seek to preserve and expand the use of Mattamuskeet Lodge and the refuge lands for the benefit of everyone.

INTRODUCTION

Lake Mattamuskeet is the largest natural lake in North Carolina. There are no underground springs or headwaters feeding into the huge lake; it is a wetlands depression that fills with rainwater and the natural runoff from the land around it. The lake's bed is the lowest point in Hyde County at 3 to 5 feet below sea level. Lake Mattamuskeet is one of a number of Carolina Bay lakes of disputed origin. A Native American legend attributes its formation to a fire that burned for 13 moons. Scientists cite the possibility of a prehistoric meteor shower or underground peat fires in speculating about how the lake was formed.

Lake Mattamuskeet is one of the most beautiful natural resources in North Carolina, located on the East Coast halfway between Maine and Florida. The lake is prominently located near the center of Hyde County, on the mainland just west of North Carolina's Outer Banks. Ocracoke Island, the site of the first landing of English explorers on American soil, is an important part of Hyde County.

Since 1934, the U.S. government has owned Lake Mattamuskeet, which makes up most of Mattamuskeet National Wildlife Refuge. The lake is a favorite wintering spot for migratory birds in the Atlantic Flyway. Hyde County is blessed with an abundance of wildlife. Surrounded by water, many of Hyde County residents make their living fishing, but farming has always been the largest industry in the county.

At the beginning of the 19th century, the State of North Carolina owned most of Lake Mattamuskeet. In 1825, the North Carolina Legislature vested title to Lake Mattamuskeet to the State Literary Board of North Carolina along with the authority to improve the lands and sell them to support the cause of public education. In 1837, the State Literary Board contracted the excavation of a 7-mile canal from the lake to the Pamlico Sound at Wysocking Bay, using slave labor from Hyde County's plantations. When opened to the lake, the water above sea level flowed by gravity through this canal into the sound, reducing the size of the lake from 120,000 to 55,000 acres. Over the next 75 years, other canals from the lake further reduced the lake to just under 50,000 acres.

On Friday, March 5, 1909, the North Carolina Legislature passed Public Law 509 authorizing the North Carolina State Board of Education and Hyde County landowners to establish the Mattamuskeet Drainage District to drain Lake Mattamuskeet. The parties hoped to better the economic conditions of Hyde County by reclaiming the rich 50,000-acre lake bed for farming and providing drainage to an additional 50,000 acres of rich farmlands privately owned outside of the lake. The law stated that a board of three commissioners would manage the affairs of the Mattamuskeet Drainage District. The state would have two representatives on the board, and the landowners outside the lake would have one.

The creation of the Mattamuskeet Drainage District set in motion a plan that eventually drained and reclaimed Lake Mattamuskeet three times—in 1916, in 1920, and in 1926. The third time, the drainage system kept the lake and adjacent farmlands relatively dry for more than five years.

Since the lake bed was below sea level, the district had to excavate canals to carry the fresh water to the Pamlico Sound and construct a pumping plant to lift the water from the lake bed into that canal system. The parties patterned the engineering design for the drainage project after the successful 1853 drainage of Haarlem Lake in Holland. The plan called for 87 miles of navigable canals and a steam-powered pumping plant capable of moving 800,000 gallons of water per minute. Modifications to the plan extended the canals to 130 miles, and the pumping plant proved capable of moving 1,200,000 gallons of water per minute. This was the largest pumping plant in the world, and the district was the largest pump-supported land reclamation project in America.

Before installation of the drainage system began, a group of private investors offered to buy the lake from the North Carolina State Board of Education and assume the commitments made by the state to the district. The state accepted the offer and, on January 14, 1911, sold Lake Mattamuskeet, consisting of 48,830 surveyed acres, to the Southern Land Reclamation Company for $99,660 or $2.04 per acre. The new owners exercised their rights to have two representatives on the drainage board and thereby took control of the drainage plan. In 1915, this corporation changed its name to New Holland Farms, Inc. These same owners laid out a town adjacent to the pumping plant site and called it "New Holland." From that time forward, the drainage project was called the "New Holland Project."

Over the next 23 years, private ownership of the lake changed hands twice with each of the subsequent owners continuing to control the drainage project and further their business interests. Economic conditions brought on by the Great Depression forced the third and final private owners to abandon the land reclamation project. A decision in the fall of 1932 to sell the lake led to the U.S. government buying the property. A new survey showed the property actually consisted of 49,925 acres for which the government paid $311,943, or $6.25 per acre.

This book tells the story of the lake drainage project and the early years of the Mattamuskeet Migratory Waterfowl Refuge. It includes the history of Company 424 of the Civilian Conservation Corps (CCC), which had 200 enrollees and was first known as Swanquarter Camp, located on Bell Island, and later relocated to New Holland and renamed Mattamuskeet Camp. This pictorial retrospective also relates some of the rich hunting and fishing history of Lake Mattamuskeet and highlights recent efforts to preserve and interpret the fascinating story of New Holland.

The Mattamuskeet Foundation, Inc.
Lewis C. Forrest, Ed.D.

One

The Plan to Drain Lake Mattamuskeet

Interest in draining Lake Mattamuskeet for farming purposes dates back to the 1700s. From 1664 to 1775, colonial governors appointed by the King of England ruled the Carolinas. Josiah Martin served from 1771 to 1775 as the last colonial governor of North Carolina.

In 1773, the Provincial Congress passed a bill to cut a large canal from Lake Mattamuskeet to the Pamlico Sound in order to drain the lake. At that time, the lake was from 6 to 9 feet deep and covered 110,000 acres. Governor Martin vetoed the bill. After the American Revolution, in 1789, Governor Samuel Johnson appointed a drainage board for the purpose of draining the wetlands of Hyde County (including Lake Mattamuskeet) to make them suitable for farming. Disputes over right-of-ways for the drainage canals prevented this board from accomplishing its assigned task.

By the beginning of the 20th century, farmers had been farming the rich land adjacent to the lake without fertilizer for more than 200 years with record yields. Hyde County received an average of 60 inches of rainfall each year. To take advantage of the rich soil, landowners had to devise ways to drain the land and prevent the flooding of their crops.

Under the authority of the 1909 legislation, the three-member board of commissioners of the Mattamuskeet Drainage District met for the first time on January 28, 1911, and elected officers. They established some operating policies at that meeting and then began planning how they would drain the lake.

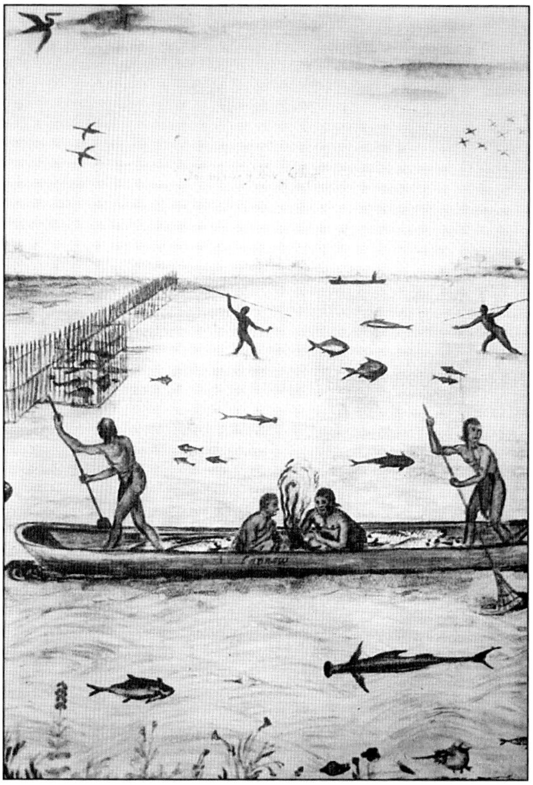

Before white settlers began moving into eastern North Carolina, Native Americans fished the waters of Lake Mattamuskeet and hunted waterfowl for food. In the late 16th century, they knew the lake in the Algonquian tongue as "Paquippe." The lake was deep enough for them to paddle their dugout juniper canoes, some as long as 35 feet, across the lake. (Used by permisson. © the British Museum, British Museum Press.)

This is the Algonquian village of "Pomeiock" as captured in watercolors by John White during his visit on July 12, 1585. Pomeiock was on the land that is today Hyde County, North Carolina, southeast of "Paquippe" (Lake Mattamuskeet) and west of modern Engelhard. The exact location of the village has not been found, but it was probably within today's Lake Landing Historic District. (Used by permisson. © the British Museum, British Museum Press.)

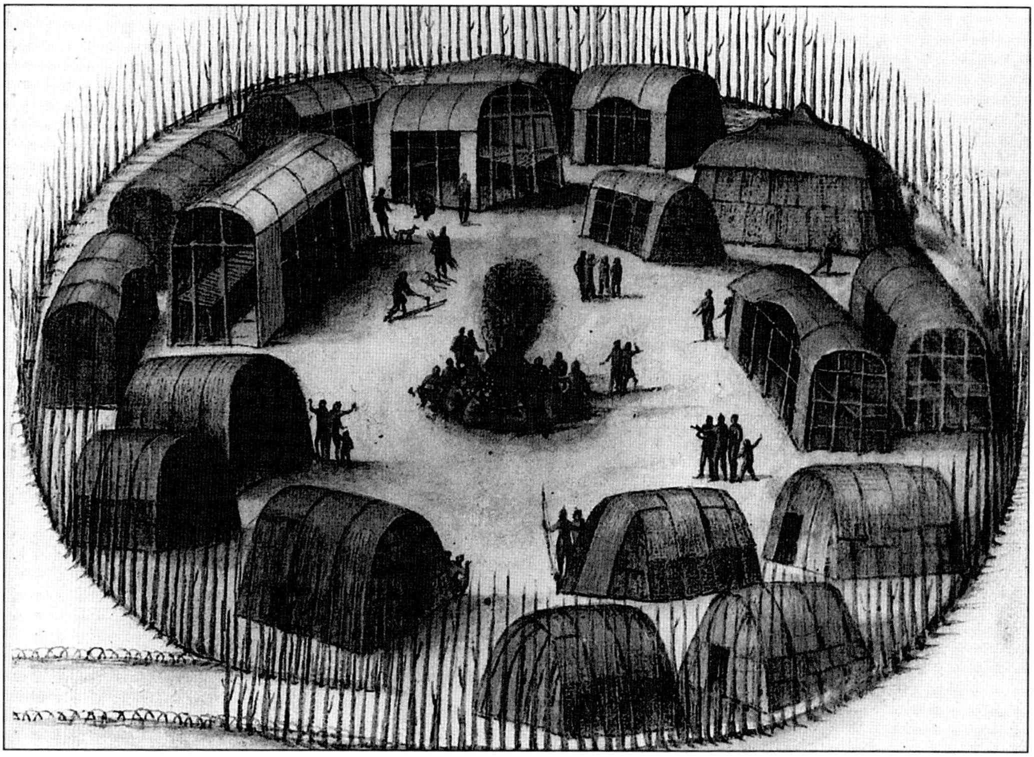

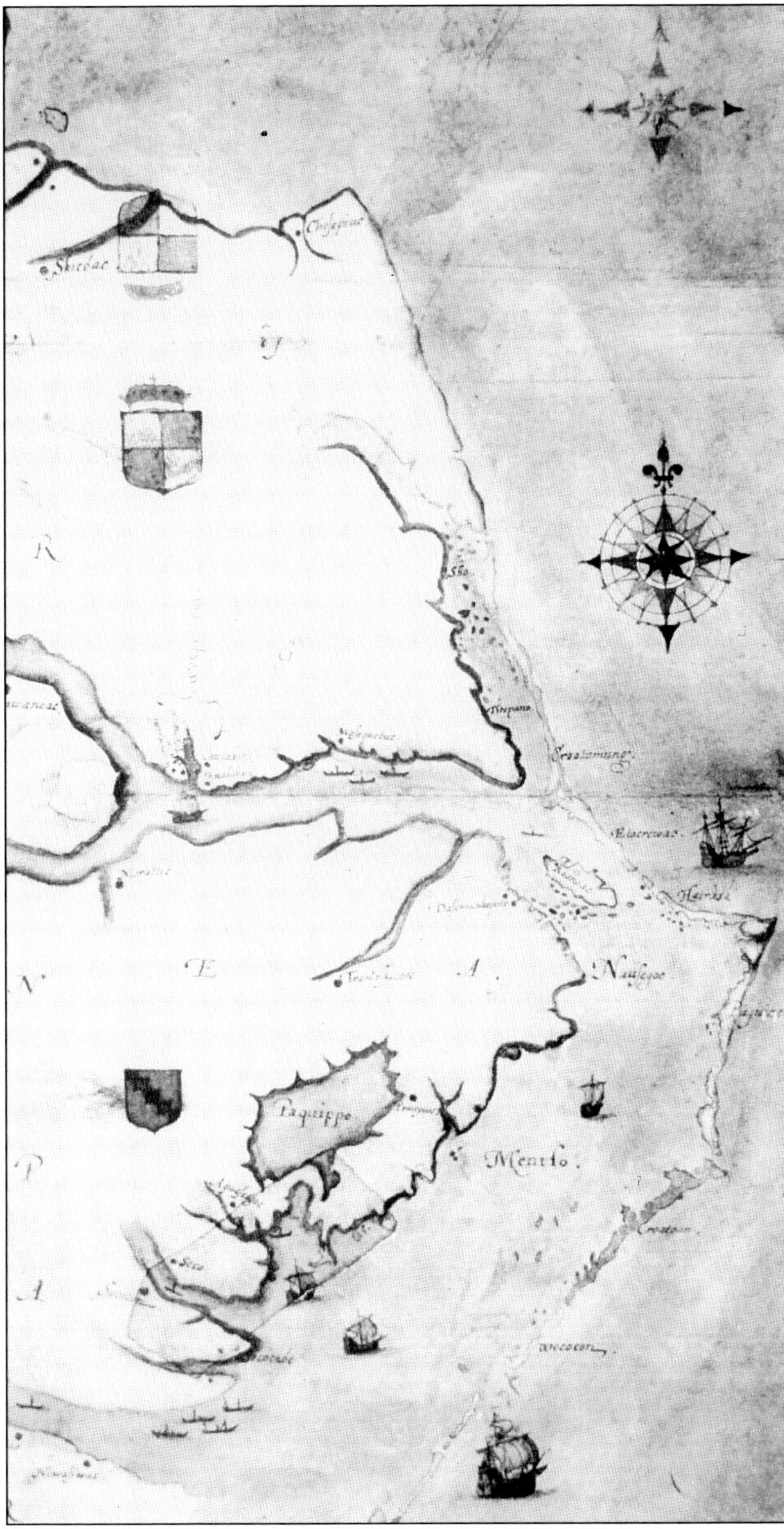

English artist John White visited "Paquippe" on only one occasion, accompanied by 60 of his countrymen, during July 11–12, 1585. White never saw the north or west shores of the lake, yet his map is amazingly accurate. Apparently, his Native American friends helped him draw the map. (Used by permisson. © the British Museum, British Museum Press.)

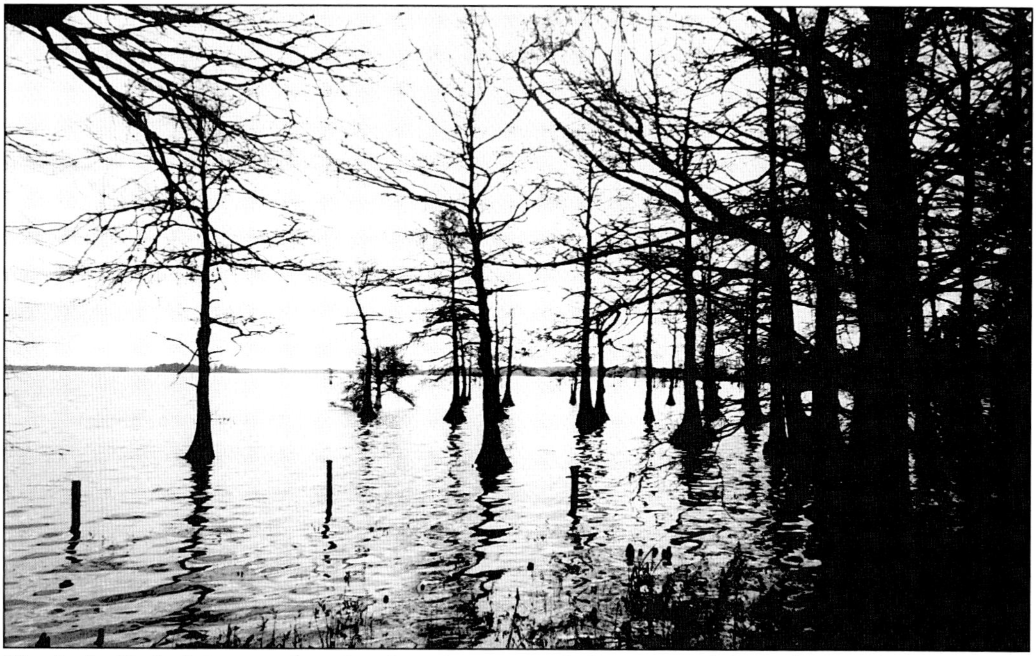

The bed of Lake Mattamuskeet has long been regarded as some of the richest soil in the world, having received nutrients from thousands of surrounding acres that have drained naturally into it for years. Soil experts have compared it to the rich land in the Yazoo, Mississippi delta region and the famous Nile River delta in Egypt. (Courtesy of Lewis Forrest.)

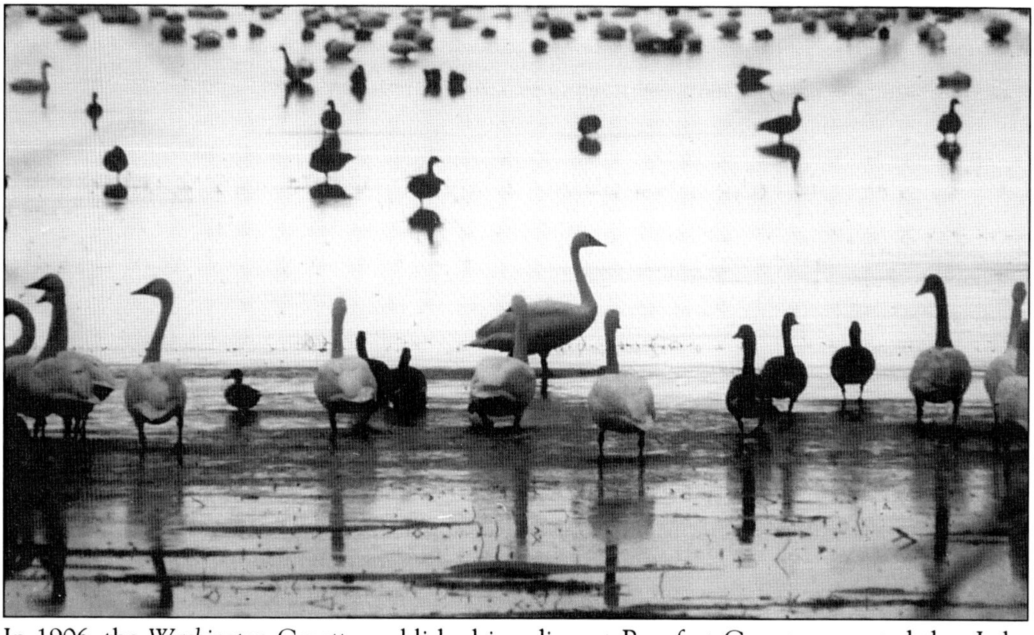

In 1906, the *Washington Gazette*, published in adjacent Beaufort County, reported that Lake Mattamuskeet was full to overflowing and stated that "There is an abundance of geese and ducks. Northern hunters are in the neighborhood, ready for sport." In 1910, an article appeared in the *New York Sun* acclaiming Lake Mattamuskeet as a wonderful place for hunters and sportsmen to visit. (Courtesy of Cliff Hollis.)

Lake Mattamuskeet is the home of more than 800 species of wildlife, including more than 200 species of birds. This Great Egret stands guard over the lake as though she is daring man to drain it again and disturb the natural habitat of so many harmless creatures. (Courtesy of Cliff Hollis.)

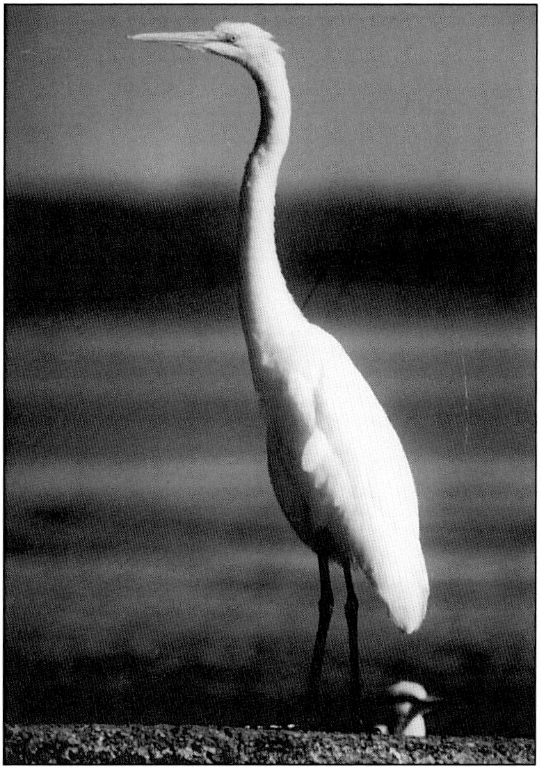

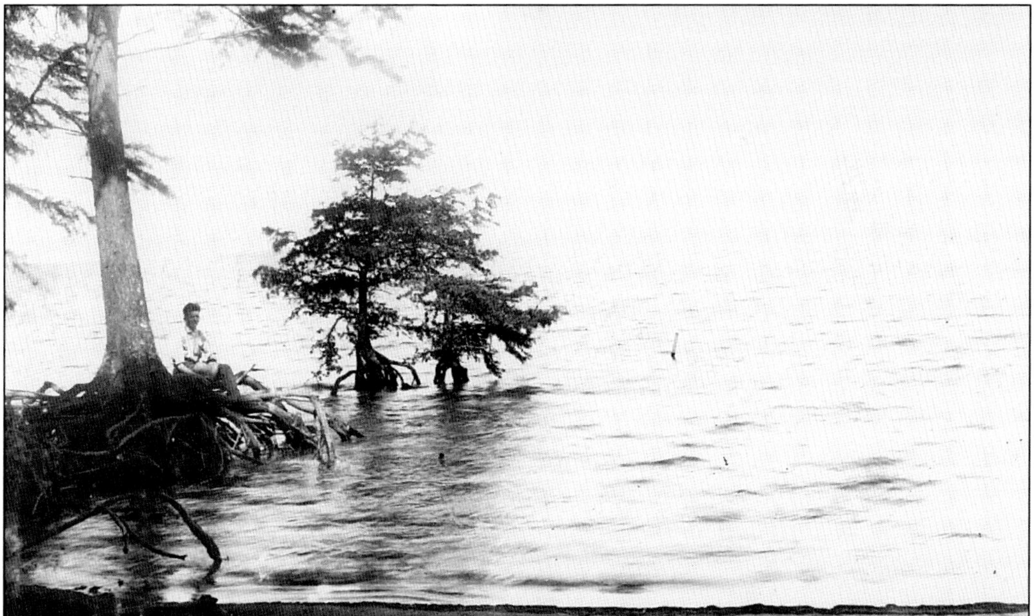

Sitting on the shore of Lake Mattamuskeet and looking across its vastness, it is hard to believe that all of the water could be pumped out to reclaim the rich bed as a place to live and farm. In 1909, Lake Mattamuskeet was approximately 18 miles long and 7 miles wide with the deepest point in the lake bed being 3.9 feet below sea level. (Courtesy of Louis Martin.)

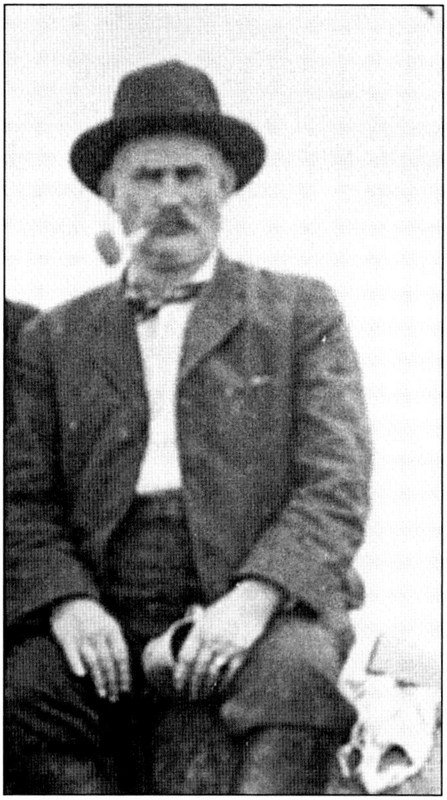

During 1909 and 1910, John Philetus Kerr (pictured here) and Charles Aurelius Webb, both from Asheville, and their friend Julian Smith Mann from Hyde County were considering how they could purchase Lake Mattamuskeet, drain it, and sell the land for a sizable profit, as well as increase the value of lands around the lake that would be reclaimed by the drainage. (Courtesy of Julian Mann III.)

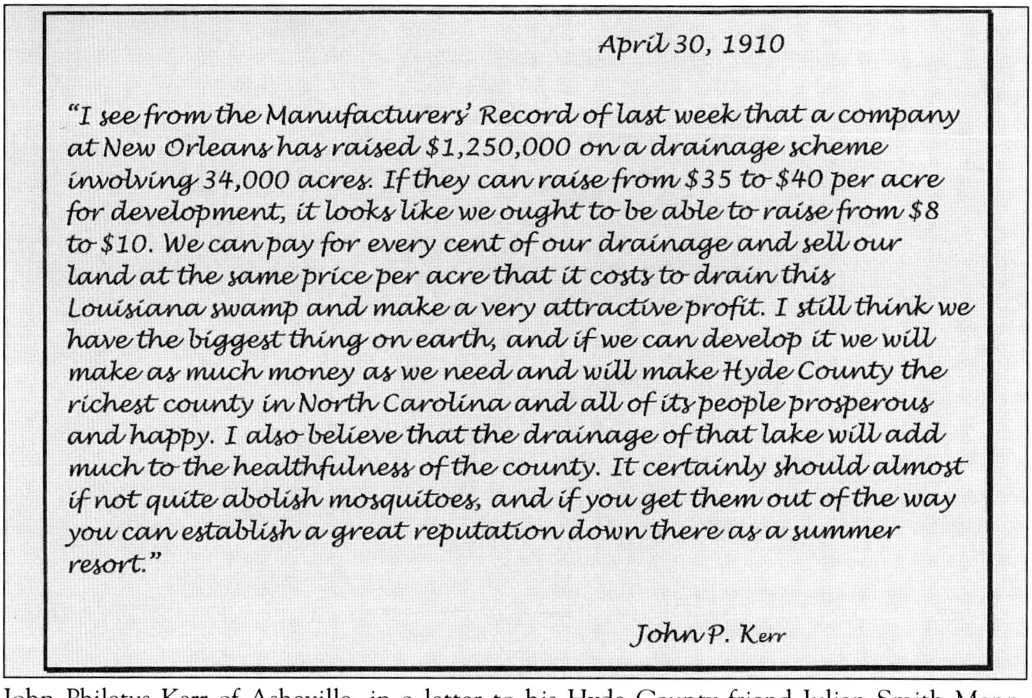

April 30, 1910

"I see from the Manufacturers' Record of last week that a company at New Orleans has raised $1,250,000 on a drainage scheme involving 34,000 acres. If they can raise from $35 to $40 per acre for development, it looks like we ought to be able to raise from $8 to $10. We can pay for every cent of our drainage and sell our land at the same price per acre that it costs to drain this Louisiana swamp and make a very attractive profit. I still think we have the biggest thing on earth, and if we can develop it we will make as much money as we need and will make Hyde County the richest county in North Carolina and all of its people prosperous and happy. I also believe that the drainage of that lake will add much to the healthfulness of the county. It certainly should almost if not quite abolish mosquitoes, and if you get them out of the way you can establish a great reputation down there as a summer resort."

John P. Kerr

John Philetus Kerr of Asheville, in a letter to his Hyde County friend Julian Smith Mann, shared his dream for the Mattamuskeet Lake drainage project. (Courtesy of Julian Mann III.)

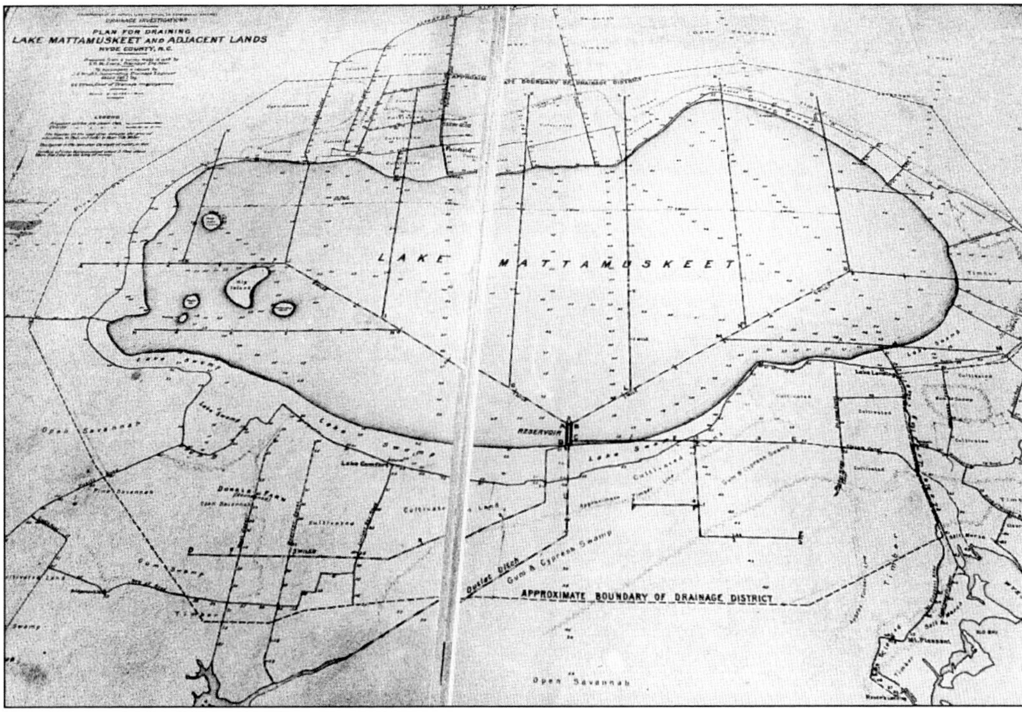

In 1908, under the supervision of J.O. Wright, the chief drainage engineer of the U.S. Office of Drainage Investigations, S.H. McCrory, surveyed the lake and produced a map entitled "Plan for Draining Lake Mattamuskeet and Adjacent Lands." While accepted in principle, the plan underwent some modifications before being implemented. This map is at the North Carolina Division of Archives and History. (Courtesy of Cliff Hollis.)

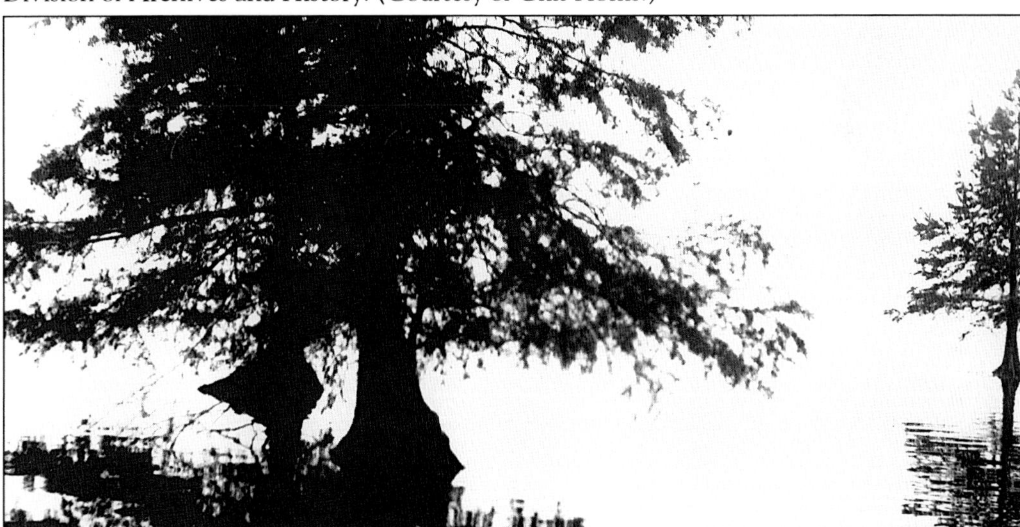

W. Edward Hearn, Bureau of Soils, U.S. Department of Agriculture, surveyed the soil in Lake Mattamuskeet in 1909 and reported on May 16, 1910, "These lands when drained and reclaimed would be as productive as any in the State" and "it is not likely these soils will require much, if any, fertilizer during the first few years." (Courtesy of the North Carolina Division of Archives and History.)

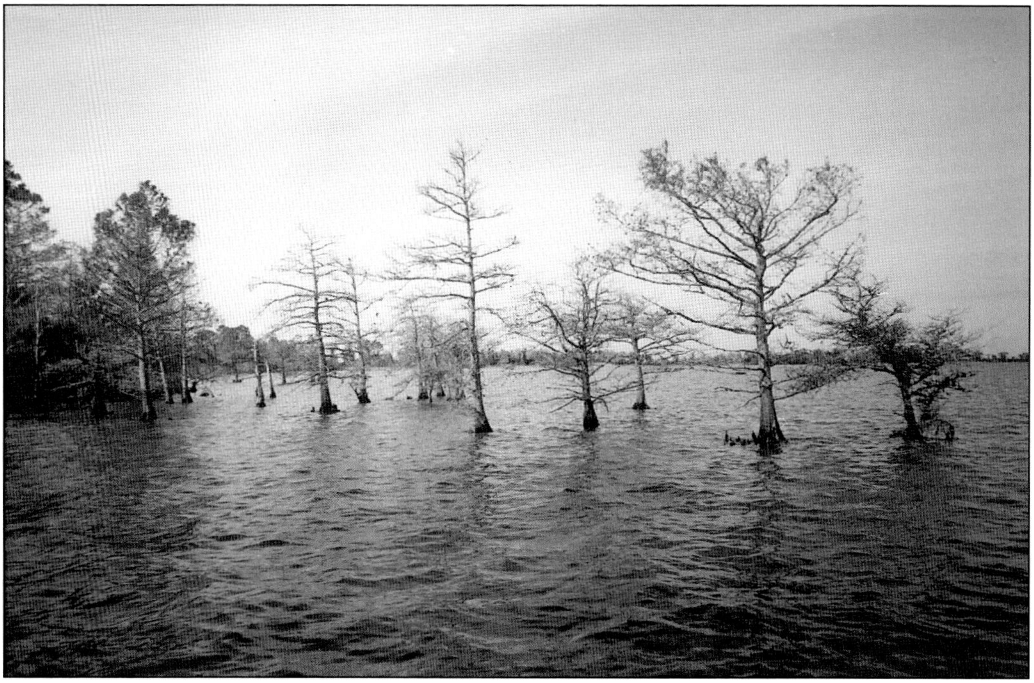

On September 7, 1909, in the *Washington Daily News*, Gilbert T. Stephenson commented on the project the State Board of Education and farmers of Hyde County were undertaking and speculated that the lake bottom would yield 150 bushels of corn per acre and the drained land would be worth $200 per acre. (Courtesy of Lewis Forrest.)

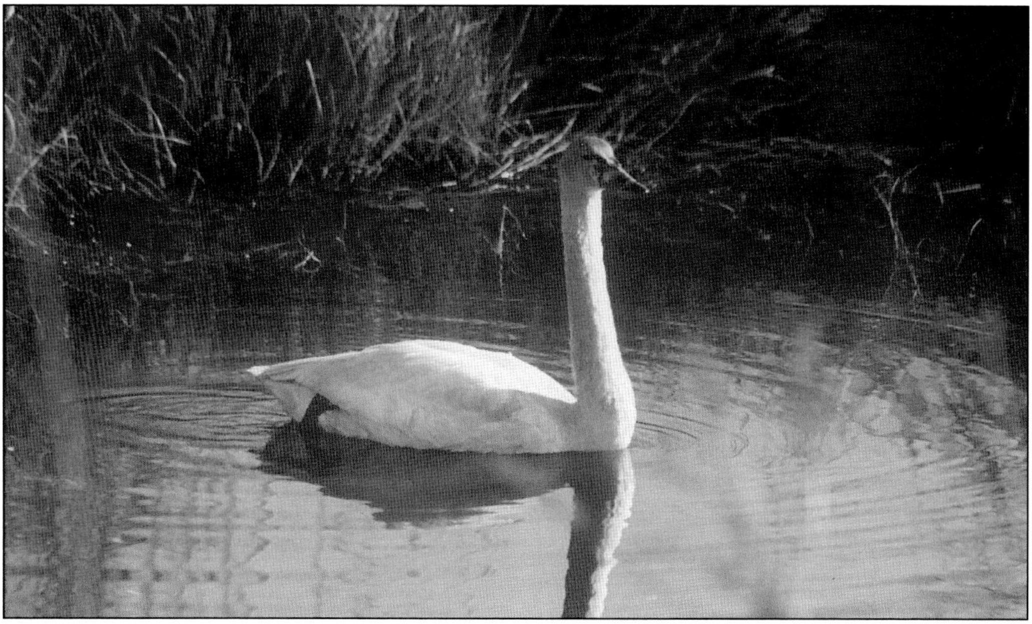

Not fully appreciating the environmental impact of draining the wetlands, Douglas N. Graves declared that Lake Mattamuskeet was "too shallow to be used for transportation, too low to be drained by gravity." He said "it just stood in the way, fulfilling no useful purpose than to supply an occasional hunter with a bag of wild fowl." (Courtesy of Lewis Forrest.)

The Southern Land Reclamation Company, with its president, Douglas Nelson Graves (pictured here), bought the lake in January 1911 for $99,660 or $2.04 per acre. The owners planned to invest an additional $10 per acre in draining and improving the property and then sell it for $100 or more per acre. They fully expected a ten-fold return on their investment. (Courtesy of Lennie Jones Christenson.)

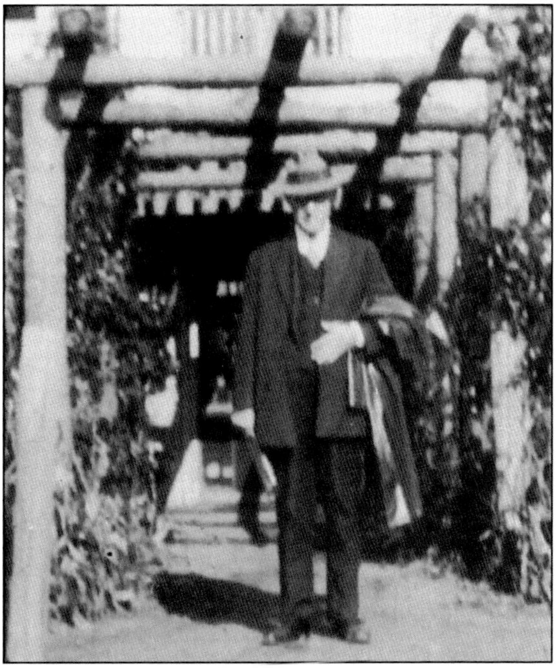

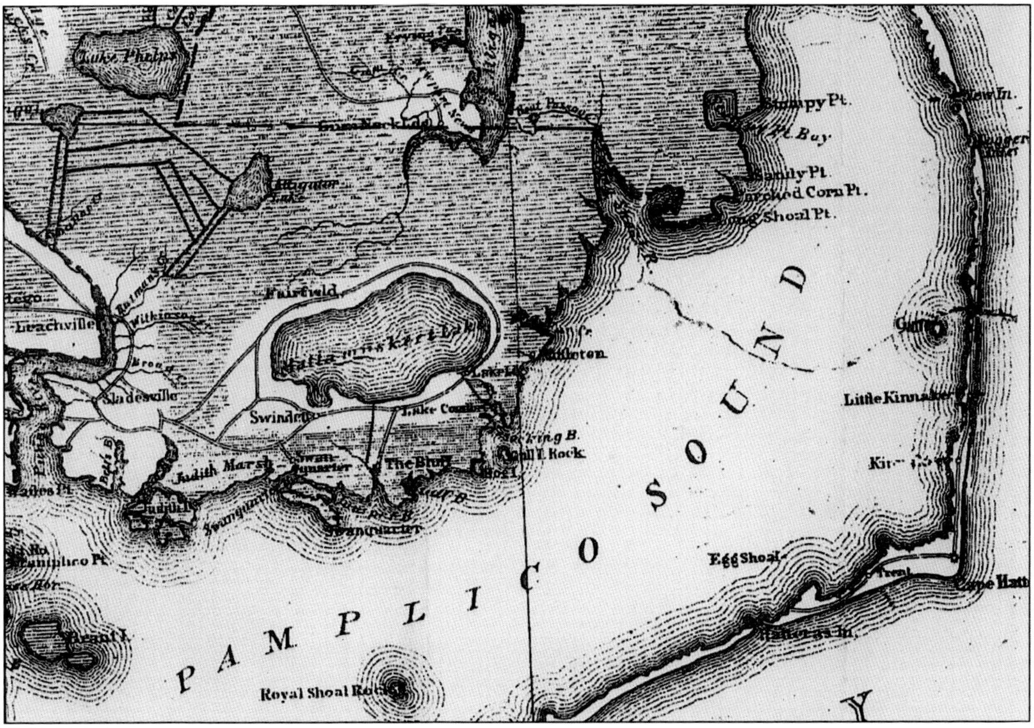

This 1865 U.S. Coast Survey map of eastern North Carolina identifies the lake as "Mattamuskeet" instead of by its ancient Native American name of Paquippe. The map shows a road around the lake and very few canals compared to the maps showing Hyde County 100 years later. This map is held at the North Carolina Division of Archives and History. (Courtesy of Lewis Forrest.)

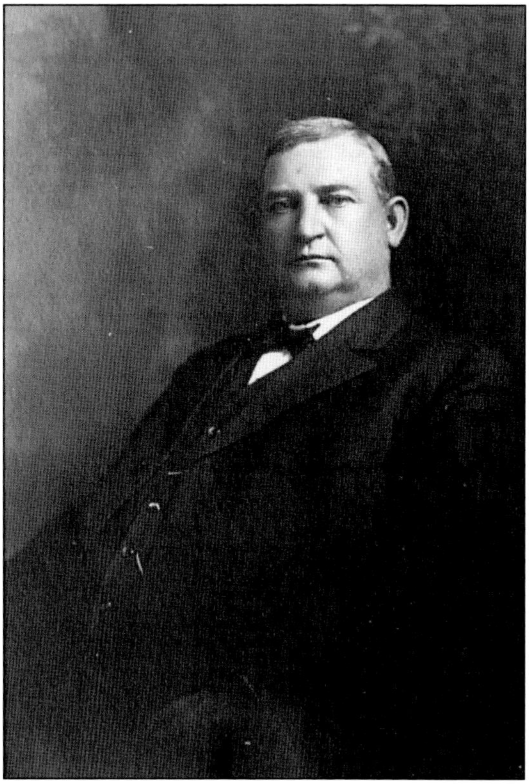

John P. Kerr and Charles A. Webb of Asheville invested in the Southern Land Reclamation Company. Julian Smith Mann (pictured here) chose not to invest in the private ownership of the lake but served as the first chairman of the Mattamuskeet Drainage District. Eighty-five years later, his grandson, Julian Mann III, was elected to be the first chairman of The Mattamuskeet Foundation. (Courtesy of Julian Mann III.)

Public Managers of the District	Private Owners of the Lake	Private Owners of Land Around the Lake
Mattamuskeet Drainage District, Managed by three Commissioner Board 1909-1934	Southern Land Reclamation Company (became New Holland Farms, Inc.) 1911-1918 North Carolina Farms Company 1918-1925 New Holland Corporation 1925-1934	About 550-575 Hyde County landowners outside of the lake bed. 1911-1934

Three groups cooperated in the Mattamuskeet Drainage District. They were the three commissioners who managed the district, including building and maintaining the drainage system; the three private corporations that successively owned the lake bed from 1911 to 1934; and the 550–575 landowners whose property was outside the lake bed but within the 100,000-acre district. (From the Mattamuskeet Records.)

Two

Floating Dipper Dredges Excavate Drainage Canals

The drainage commissioners awarded the first dredging contract to A.V. Wills & Sons of Pittsville, Illinois. The dredges used by A.V. Wills & Sons to excavate the large canals for draining Lake Mattamuskeet were built in Belhaven, North Carolina, 30 miles west of the lake, beginning in July 1913. The company constructed four floating dipper dredges of various sizes and designs, in hopes of having a suitable machine for any condition they might encounter in the wetlands of Hyde County.

The dredging machines were steam powered and fueled by coal. The boom on each dredge could rotate about 30 degrees in either direction, and the bottom of each bucket was hinged to allow the soil to drop to the adjacent bank.

Once constructed, the dredges traveled down the Pungo River into the Pamlico Sound and slowly made their way east to Hyde County. In April of 1914, the contractor began work on what would be a five-year project and would create 130 miles of large navigable canals within the district.

The dredging crews lived on the rigs or sometimes on cabin boats that followed the rigs. They had accommodations for cooking, sleeping, and other necessities, and they worked on 12-hour shifts, six days each week. Each man was allowed one day off per week, but due to the isolated location of Hyde County, it was hard for the crewman to go very far in that short time and impossible for him to return to Illinois to see his family.

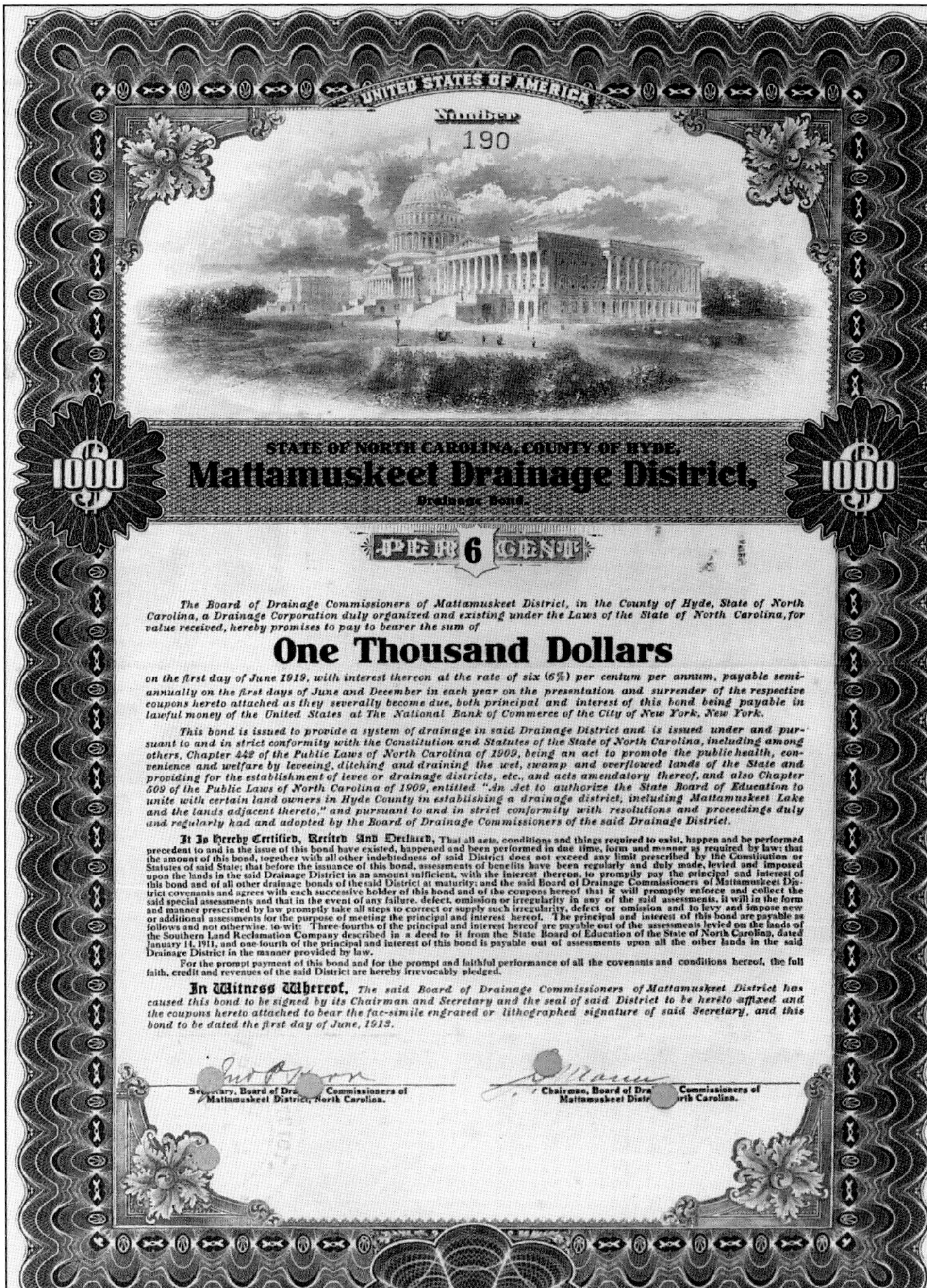
UNITED STATES OF AMERICA

Number 190

1000 | 1000

STATE OF NORTH CAROLINA, COUNTY OF HYDE.

Mattamuskeet Drainage District,

Drainage Bond.

PER 6 CENT

The Board of Drainage Commissioners of Mattamuskeet District, in the County of Hyde, State of North Carolina, a Drainage Corporation duly organized and existing under the Laws of the State of North Carolina, for value received, hereby promises to pay to bearer the sum of

One Thousand Dollars

on the first day of June 1919, with interest thereon at the rate of six (6%) per centum per annum, payable semi-annually on the first days of June and December in each year on the presentation and surrender of the respective coupons hereto attached as they severally become due, both principal and interest of this bond being payable in lawful money of the United States at The National Bank of Commerce of the City of New York, New York.

This bond is issued to provide a system of drainage in said Drainage District and is issued under and pursuant to and in strict conformity with the Constitution and Statutes of the State of North Carolina, including among others, Chapter 442 of the Public Laws of North Carolina of 1909, being an act to promote the public health, convenience and welfare by leveeing, ditching and draining the wet, swamp and overflowed lands of the State and providing for the establishment of levee or drainage districts, etc., and acts amendatory thereof, and also Chapter 509 of the Public Laws of North Carolina of 1909, entitled "An Act to authorize the State Board of Education to unite with certain land owners in Hyde County in establishing a drainage district, including Mattamuskeet Lake and the lands adjacent thereto," and pursuant to and in strict conformity with resolutions and proceedings duly and regularly had and adopted by the Board of Drainage Commissioners of the said Drainage District.

It Is Hereby Certified, Recited And Declared, That all acts, conditions and things required to exist, happen and be performed precedent to and in the issue of this bond have existed, happened and been performed in due time, form and manner as required by law: that the amount of this bond, together with all other indebtedness of said District does not exceed any limit prescribed by the Constitution or Statutes of said State; that before the issuance of this bond, assessments of benefits have been regularly and duly made, levied and imposed upon the lands in the said Drainage District in an amount sufficient, with the interest thereon, to promptly pay the principal and interest of this bond and of all other drainage bonds of the said District at maturity; and the said Board of Drainage Commissioners of Mattamuskeet District covenants and agrees with each successive holder of this bond and of the coupons hereof that it will promptly enforce and collect the said special assessments and that in the event of any failure, defect, omission or irregularity in any of the said assessments, it will in the form and manner prescribed by law promptly take all steps to correct or supply such irregularity, defect or omission and to levy and impose new or additional assessments for the purpose of meeting the principal and interest hereof. The principal and interest of this bond are payable as follows and not otherwise, to-wit: Three-fourths of the principal and interest hereof are payable out of the assessments levied on the lands of the Southern Land Reclamation Company described in a deed to it from the State Board of Education of the State of North Carolina, dated January 14, 1911, and one-fourth of the principal and interest of this bond is payable out of assessments upon all the other lands in the said Drainage District in the manner provided by law.

For the prompt payment of this bond and for the prompt and faithful performance of all the covenants and conditions hereof, the full faith, credit and revenues of the said District are hereby irrevocably pledged.

In Witness Whereof, *The said Board of Drainage Commissioners of Mattamuskeet District has caused this bond to be signed by its Chairman and Secretary and the seal of said District to be hereto affixed and the coupons hereto attached to bear the fac-simile engraved or lithographed signature of said Secretary, and this bond to be dated the first day of June, 1913.*

Se[illegible]ary, Board of Dra[illegible] Commissioners of Mattamuskeet District, North Carolina.

Chairman, Board of Dra[illegible] Commissioners of Mattamuskeet Distr[illegible]rth Carolina.

On June 1, 1913, the commissioners of Mattamuskeet Drainage District sold 500 six-percent drainage bonds in $1,000 denominations at par to the New First National Bank of Columbus, Ohio, raising $500,000. The funds were for dredging 83 miles of canals, building the world's largest pumping plant, and operating the district until they could begin collecting drainage taxes to repay the bonds and support operating costs. John P. Kerr and J.S. Mann signed each bond. (From the Mattamuskeet Records.)

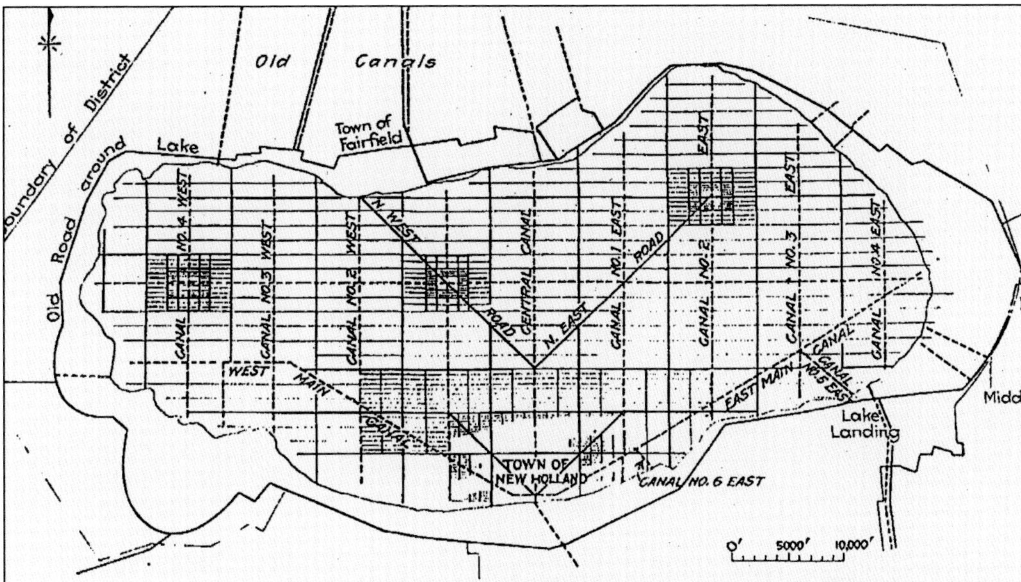

FIG. 2. GENERAL LAYOUT OF MATTAMUSKEET DRAINAGE DISTRICT

The drainage system specified a series of parallel canals, spanning the width of the lake from south to north, at intervals of 1.5 miles, flowing south into west and east main canals that led to the pumping plant. The pumps would lift the water into a single outfall canal that would extend from the pumping plant to the Pamlico Sound. (Courtesy of *Engineering News*.)

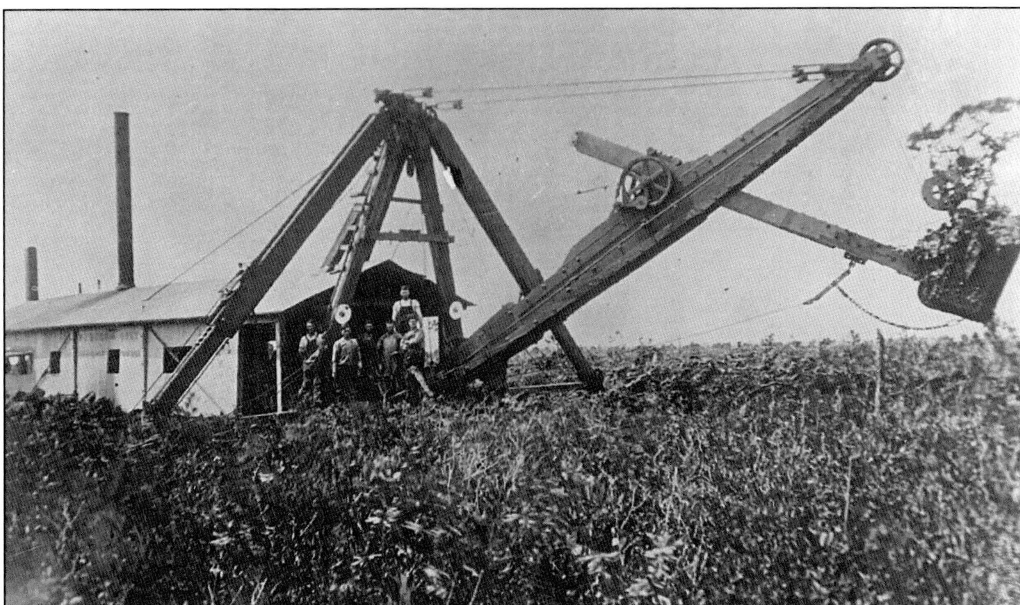

On July 16, 1913, the drainage commissioners contracted to pay A.V. Wills & Sons of Pittsville, Illinois, $266,965 for "the dredging of 83 miles of canals in Lake Mattamuskeet, excavation of 3,100,000 cubic yards of earth, building levees, and construction of a system of drainage for Lake Mattamuskeet and surrounding lands of the Mattamuskeet Drainage District." Later modifications expanded the contract. (Courtesy of Hal Swindell.)

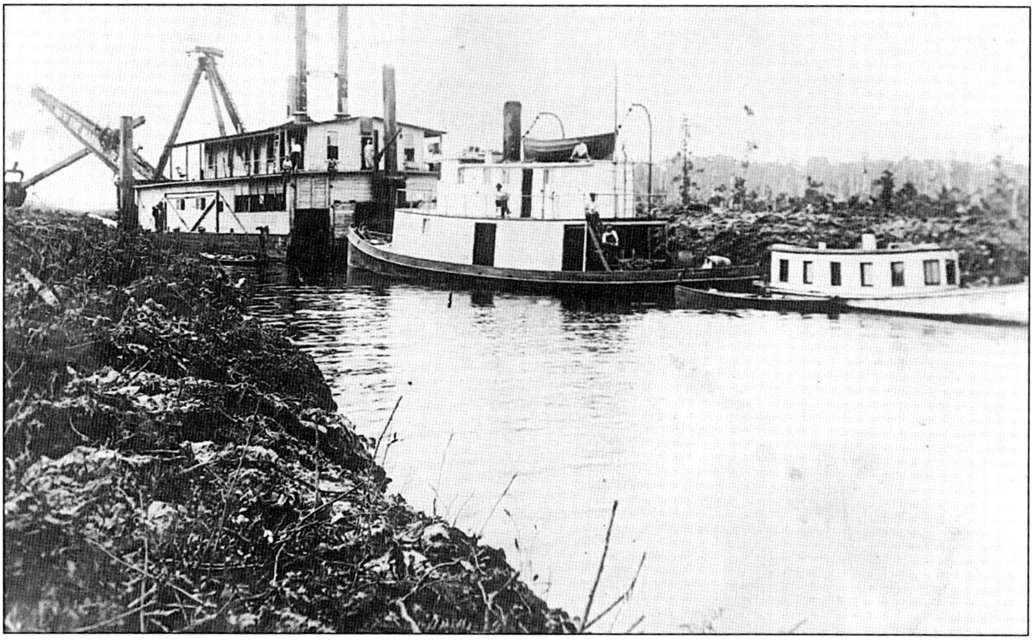

The huge floating dipper dredges were designed for round-the-clock operations, with a steam-powered generator to provide electric lights for the living quarters and headlights for dredging at night. When the dredge was digging, the crew would stabilize the dredging platform by lowering special beams to the canal bottom. (Courtesy of Leonard T. Pugh Sr.)

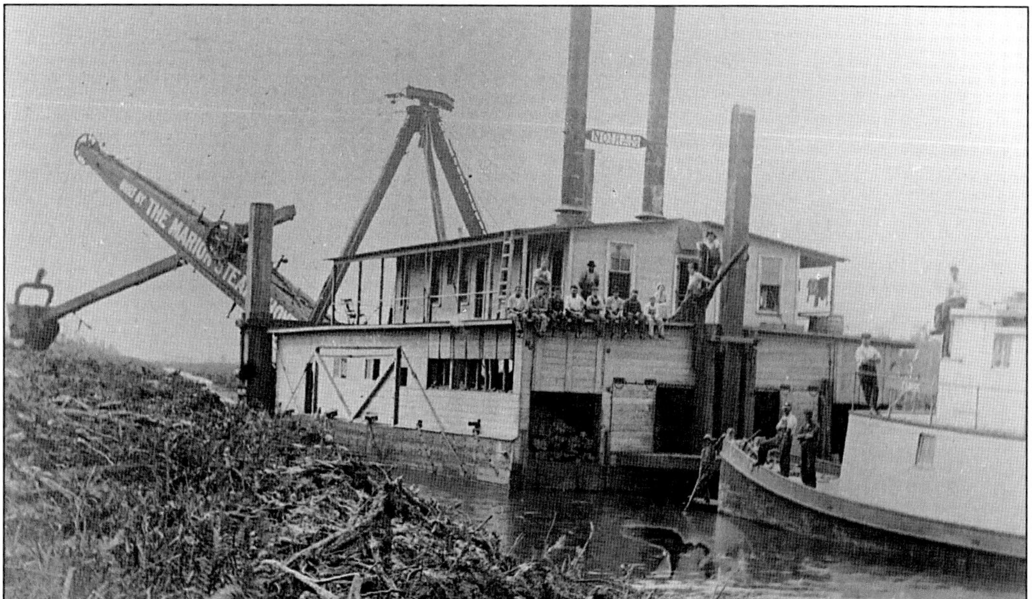

The drainage commissioners calculated that, with other commitments already made and budgeted, only $159,000 would be available from the bond proceeds to pay the dredging contract for $266,965. The Southern Land Reclamation Company gave the district $107,965 for the dredging in an effort to keep the project moving forward. (Courtesy of Virginia Pugh.)

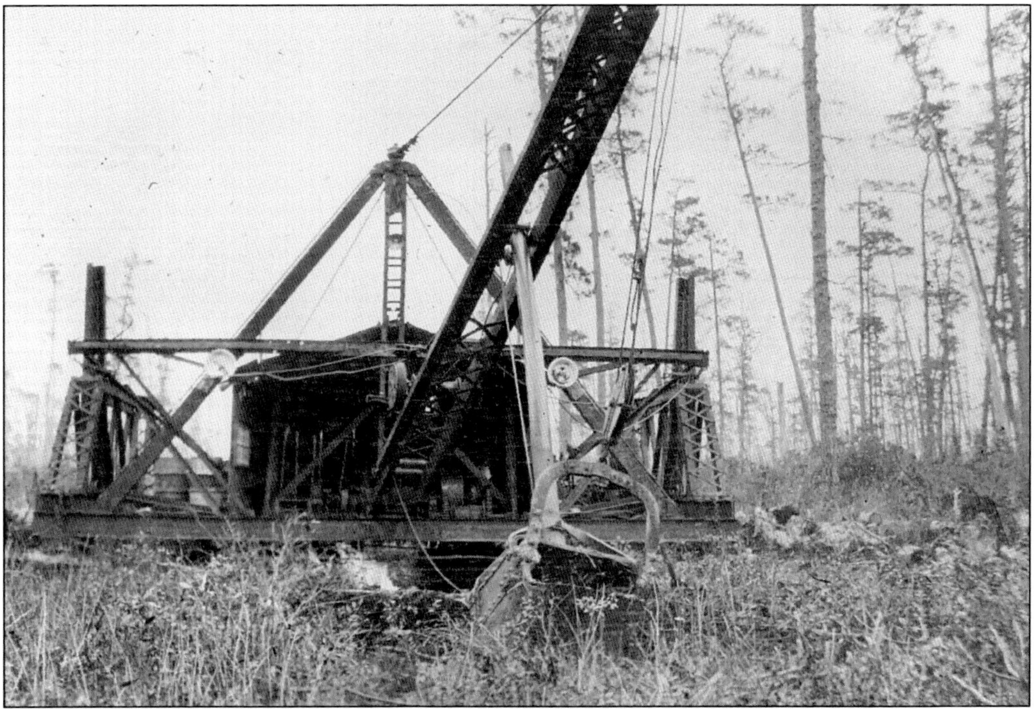

The dredging of the drainage canals began at the south end of Outfall Canal in April of 1914 and moved northward to the lake with two floating dipper dredges working on a 24-hour schedule. A floating dipper dredge would dig ahead of the canal in which it floated, digging as far as the boom and bucket would reach and depositing the soil on both banks. (Courtesy of Carolyn Ponzer Taylor.)

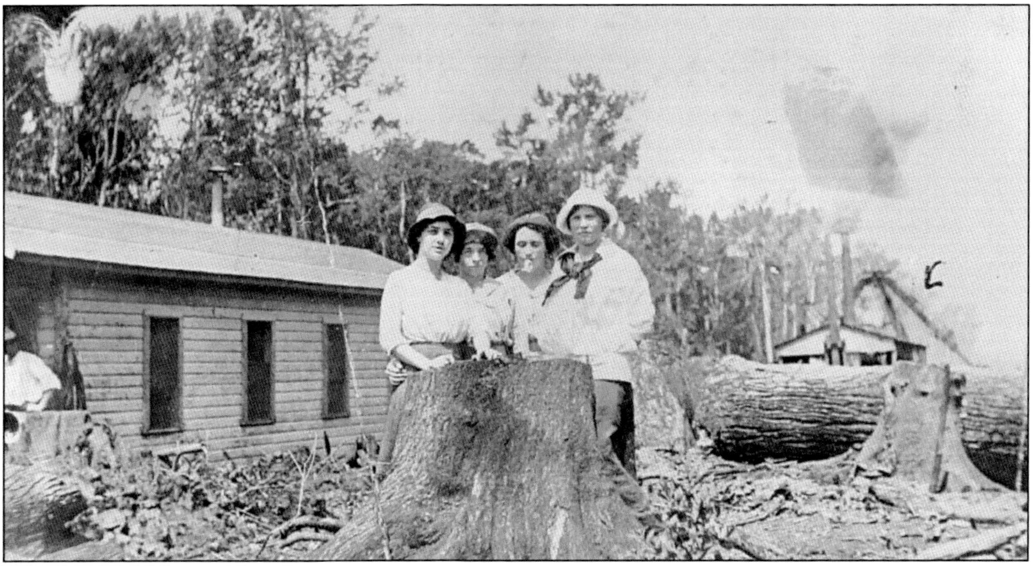

In digging Outfall Canal, the huge dredges cut through swamps, forests, and open lands on a straight line from the Pamlico Sound to the lake. The dredging contract required the workmen to leave the stumps of trees along the right-of-way 3 feet tall so the undisturbed roots would stabilize the canal banks. (Courtesy of Hal Swindell.)

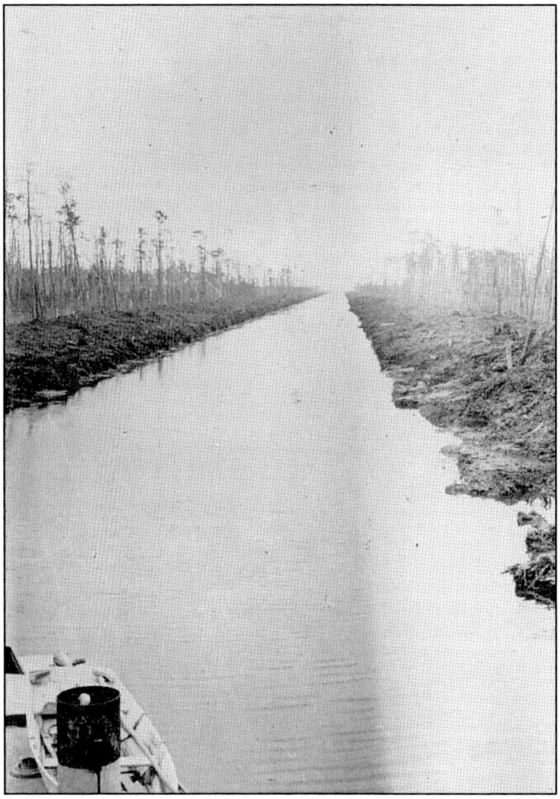

Outfall Canal (pictured here) was 7 miles long, 70 feet wide at the top, 60 feet wide at the bottom, and had an average water depth of 13 feet below sea level. It took A.V. Wills & Sons just eight months to dig this canal, and they excavated more than 900,000 cubic yards of earth. (Courtesy of Carolyn Ponzer Taylor.)

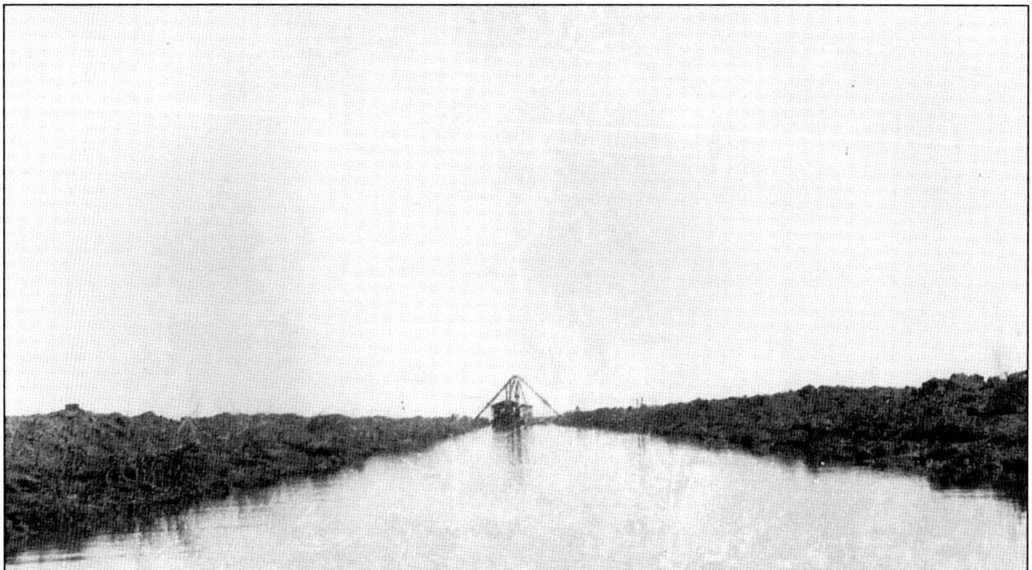

While dredging Outfall Canal (pictured here) from April through December of 1914, A.V. Wills & Sons also completed the following: Sections One and Two of the Boundary Levy; Central Canal (7 miles); Canals 4, 5, 6, and 7 East (about 25 miles); Canal 7 West (3 miles); and the entire reservoir on the north side of the pumping plant. (Courtesy of Carolyn Ponzer Taylor.)

The boom of this floating dipper dredge operated by A.V. Wills & Sons could rotate about 60 degrees right or left of center to deposit the soil from the canal onto the bank. This dredge is shoveling silt that had washed back into a canal excavated at some earlier time. The remains of this dredge are still in Lake Mattamuskeet (see page 30). (Courtesy of Lizzie Mae Credle Britton.)

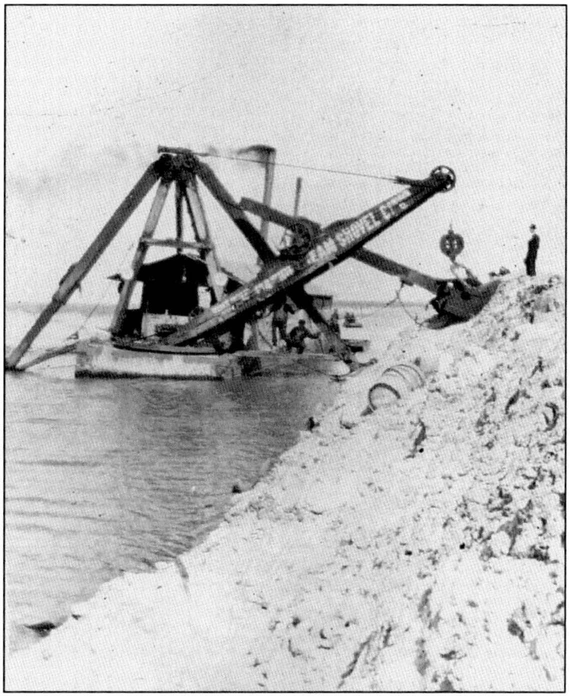

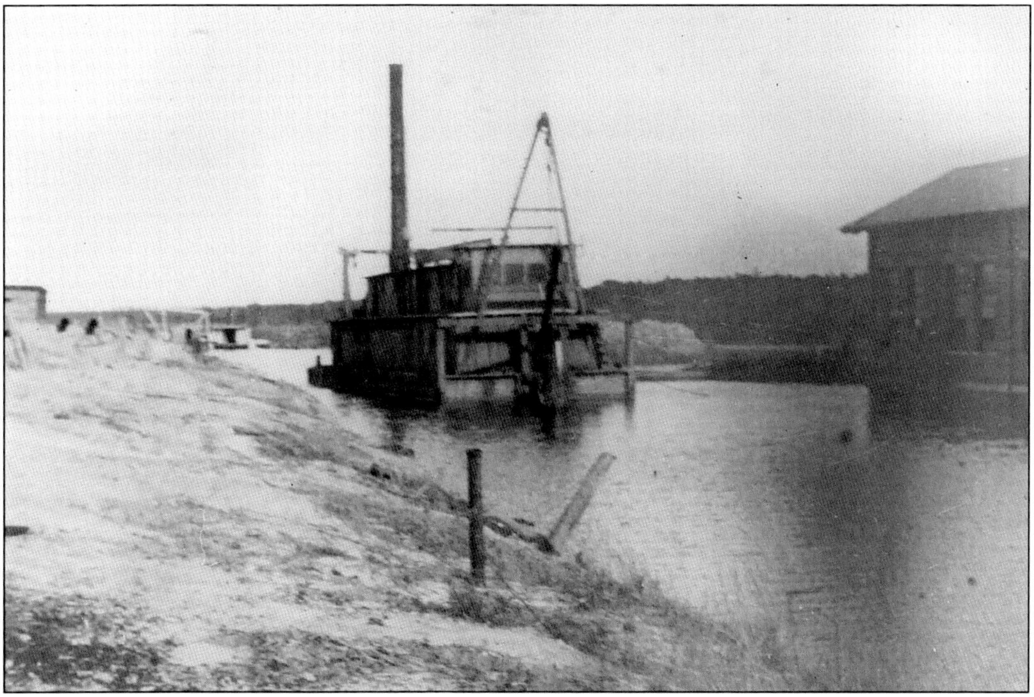

When A.V. Wills & Sons completed their contract and moved on to their next job, they had dredged 130 miles of canals in the Mattamuskeet Drainage District and had excavated over 4 million cubic yards of earth. In 1920, the drainage commissioners contracted dredging with the Foundation Company of New York, who shifted to a steam-powered suction dredge and a walking dredge. (Courtesy of Leon Ballance.)

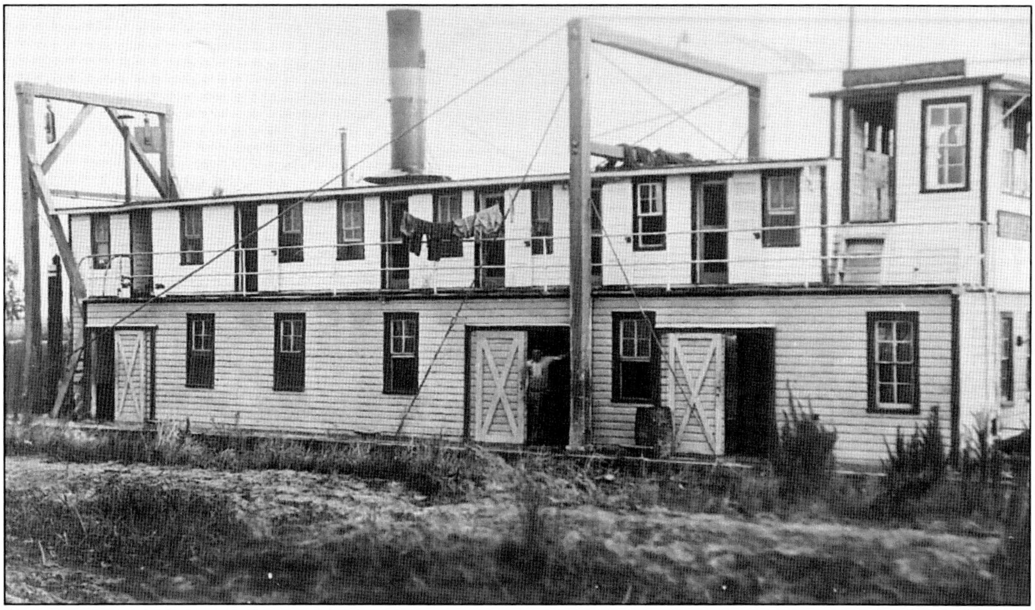

In 1925, the drainage commissioners entered into their third and final dredging contract, this time with S.J. Grove & Sons, of Minneapolis, Minnesota, who subcontracted the work to Wilson Brothers, also of Minneapolis. This floating hydraulic dredge operated by Wilson Brothers in the late 1920s provided living accommodations for the crew as well as the power plant for the dredge. (Courtesy of George R. Scott and Edna E. Harris.)

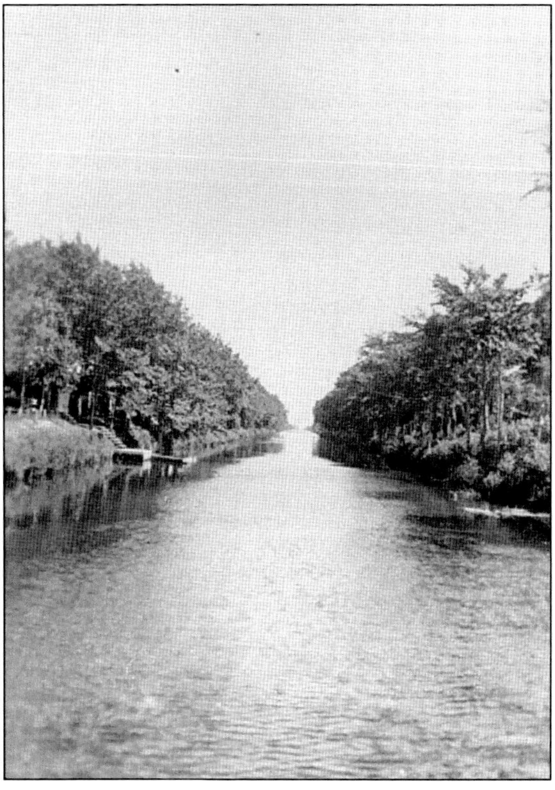

Wilson Brothers' first task upon undertaking their drainage contract in late 1925 was to dredge the silt from the mouth of Outfall Canal (pictured here) at the Pamlico Sound, permitting the dredge and coal barges to travel the 7 miles inland to the pumping plant. Note how the vegetation had grown on the canal banks over the 11 years since the canal was first completed in late 1914. (Courtesy of Patricia Auman.)

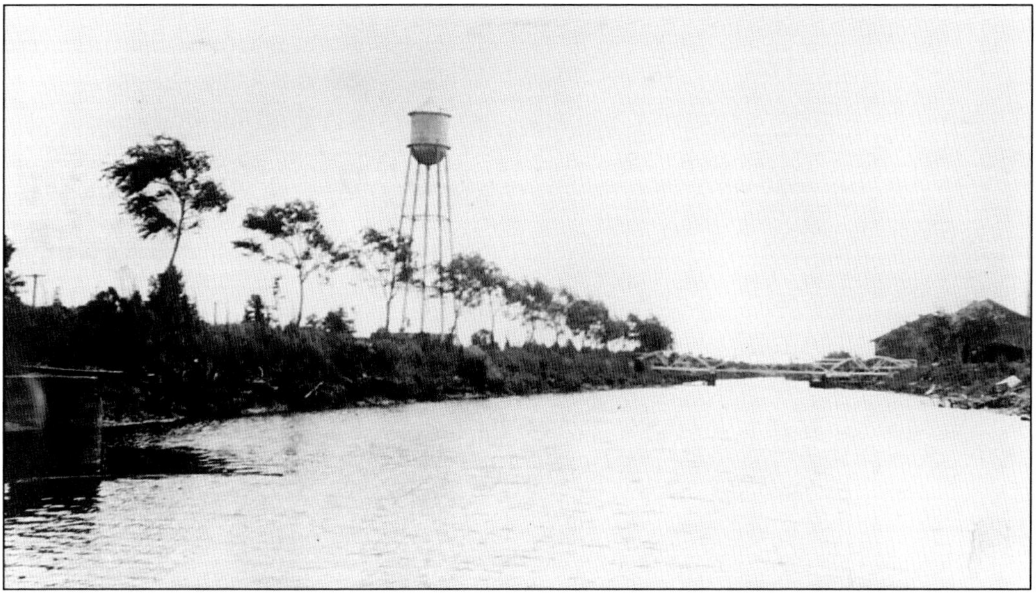

Silt carried by the water as it moved to the pumps created bars that cut down on the efficiency of the drainage efforts and hindered navigation in the canals. It was necessary for dredges to work continuously in the canals, removing the bars and other obstructions. This 1927 photo shows West Main Canal, approximately 100 feet wide and 13 feet deep. (Courtesy of George R. Scott and Edna E. Harris.)

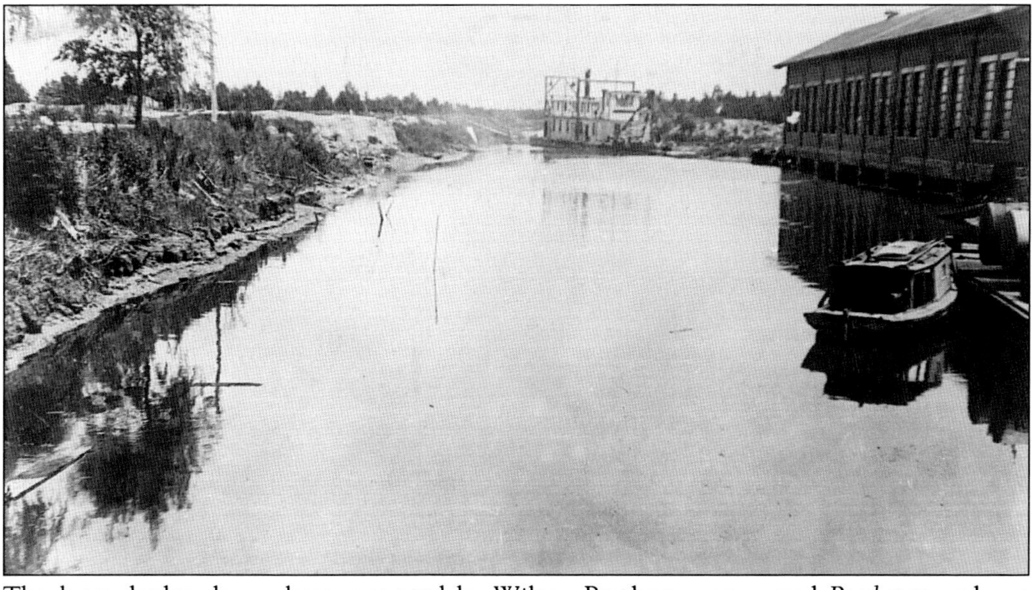

The large dredge shown here, operated by Wilson Brothers, was named *Powhatan* and was electrically operated from a steam-powered generating plant on board. By 1927, Wilson Brothers had five dredges working in the district: three floating dipper dredges, one hydraulic dredge, and one dragline dredge. (Courtesy of George R. Scott and Edna E. Harris.)

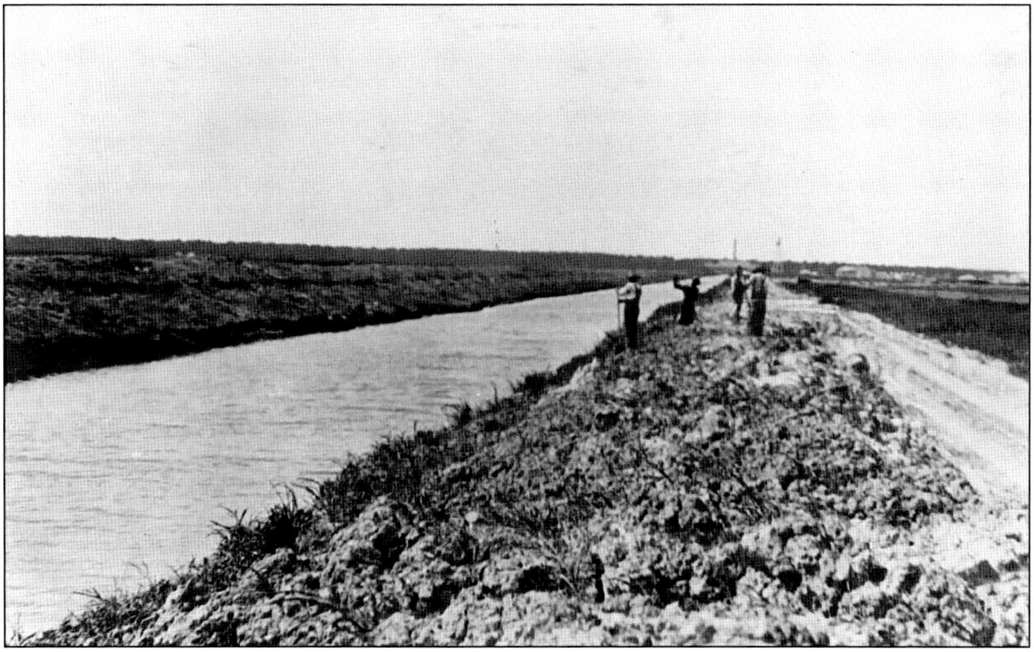

Workmen spread out the soil deposited from the dredging operation along the top banks of the canals and planted a strong native grass to discourage erosion and provide roadbeds parallel to the canals. The pumping plant and town site of the community of New Holland is visible in the distance in this July 10, 1927 photo. (Courtesy of George R. Scott and Edna E. Harris.)

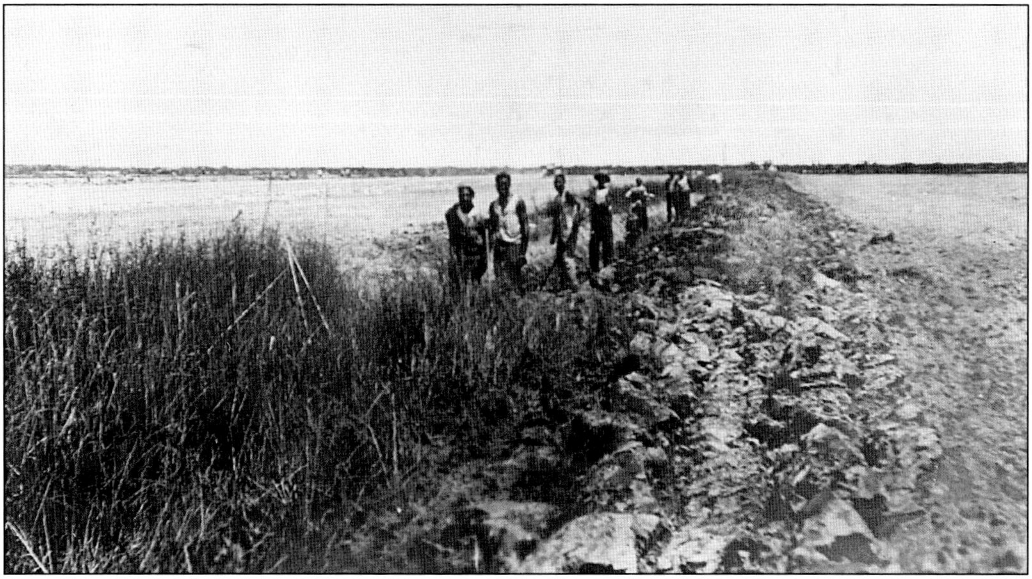

The main canals from south to north across the width of the lake were 1.5 miles apart. To drain the low spots in the lake bed, it became necessary to excavate lateral canals. Laborers dug these smaller ditches with shovels until about 1930 when New Holland Corporation bought a ditching machine that they pulled behind a Caterpillar 60. (Courtesy of George R. Scott and Edna E. Harris.)

In 1926, Earl Pugh of Hyde County worked for Wilson Brothers, the dredging contractor. Pugh operated a small gasoline-powered skiff and pulled coal barges to the dredge. His brother Leonard used a skiff to pull barges of fresh water to the dredge for the steam engines. His friend in this photo is Nora Daniel, whose mother was a cook on the dredge. (Courtesy of Virginia Pugh.)

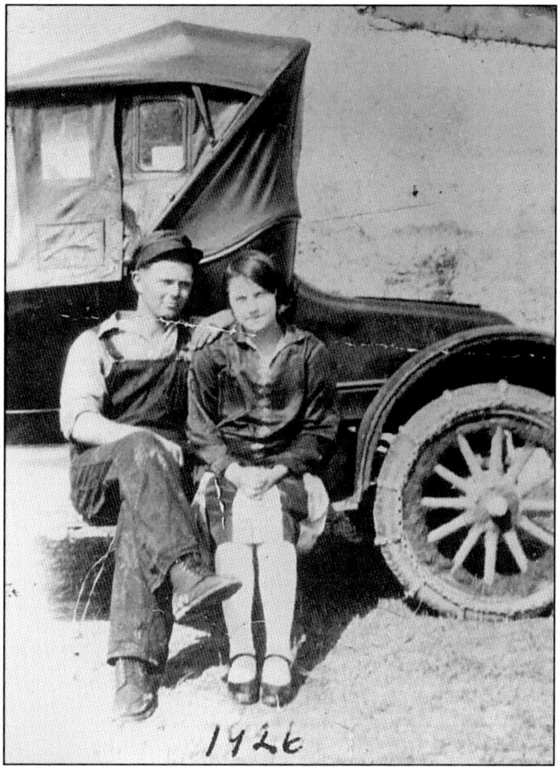

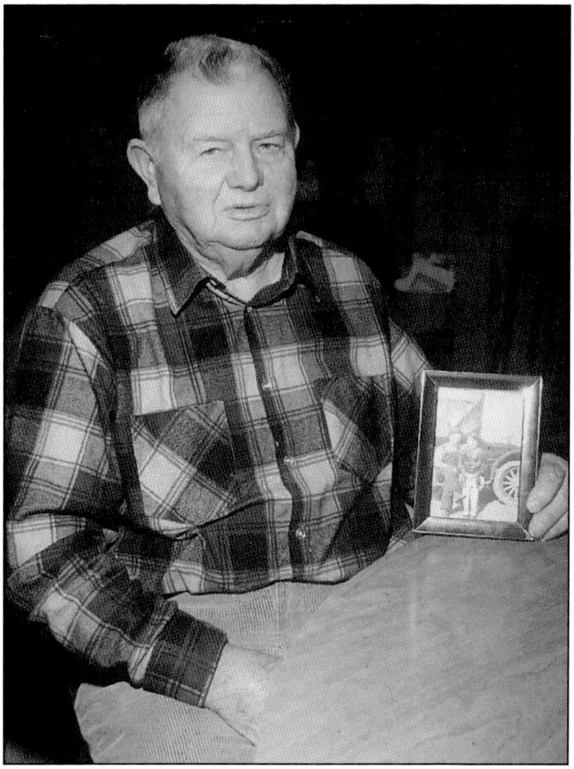

This photo was made of Earl Pugh in 1988, 62 years after he worked for Wilson Brothers supplying coal to the dredge. Earl Pugh died in 1993 at the age of 87. He is survived by his wife, Virginia, and one son, Earl Jr., who farms a large acreage in Hyde County and serves on the Hyde County Board of Education. (Courtesy of Cliff Hollis.)

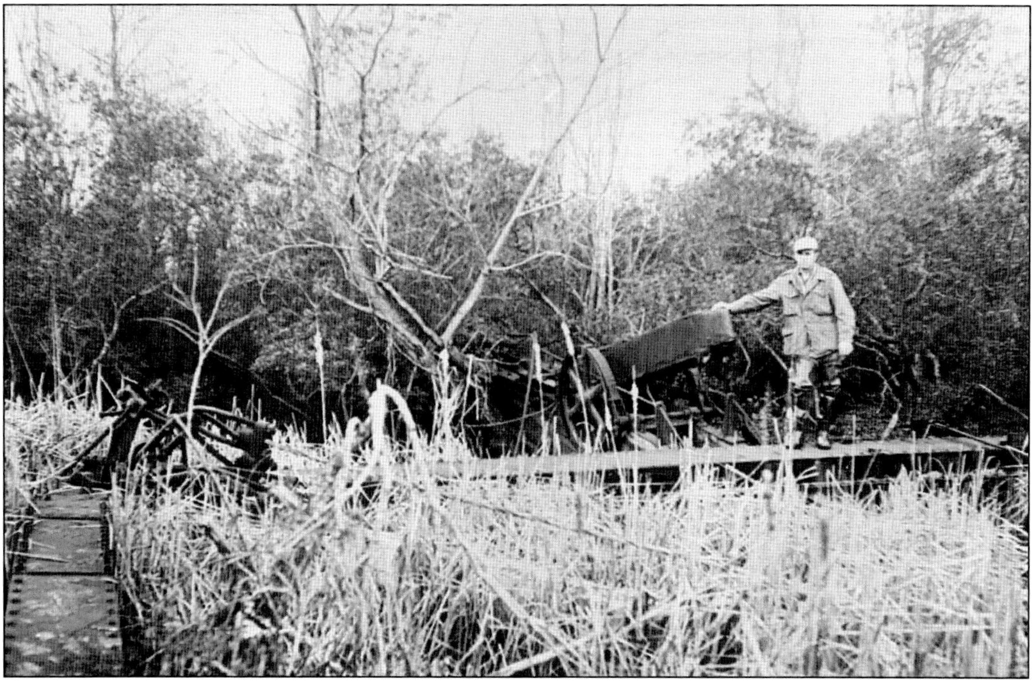

Hal Swindell worked on the Mattamuskeet National Wildlife Refuge for about 31 years. Around 1965, this photo was made of him standing on the remains of a dredge used by A.V. Wills & Sons. Built at Belhaven, North Carolina, in 1913–1914, the dredge is rusting away in a swamp on an island in the west end of Lake Mattamuskeet. (Courtesy of Hal Swindell.)

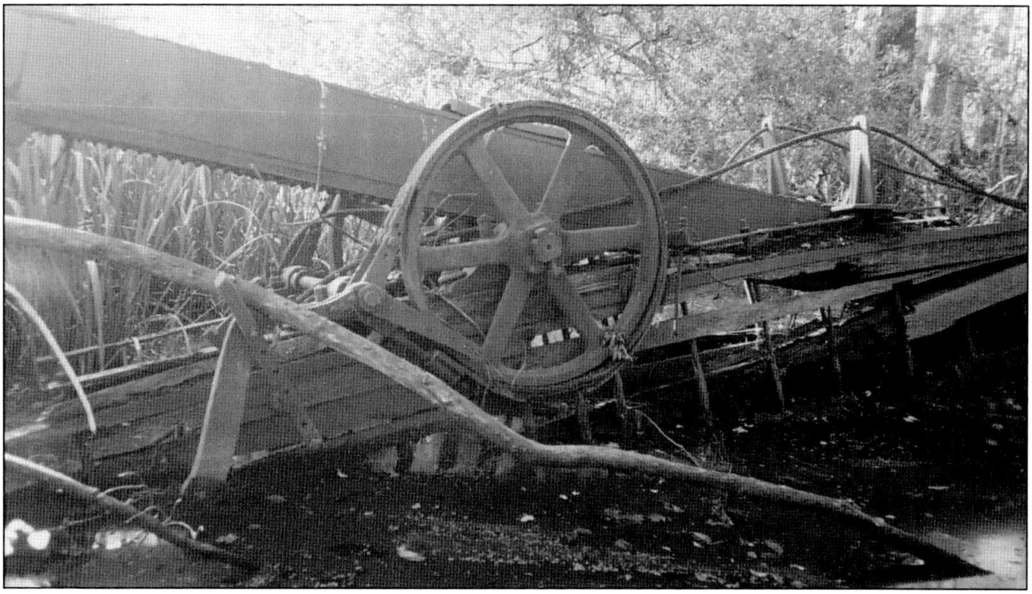

The heavy wooden and steel boom of the A.V. Wills & Sons 1914 floating dipper dredge is rotting away in a spot where it is almost inaccessible to visitors other than hunters, fishermen, or brave-hearted explorers. The Mattamuskeet Foundation hopes to recover and display these artifacts in interpreting the lake drainage history. Someday it may be accessible to all visitors of Lake Mattamuskeet. This photo was taken on October 15, 1998. (Courtesy of Lewis Forrest.)

Three

THE WORLD'S LARGEST PUMPING PLANT

The pumping plant built at Lake Mattamuskeet in 1915–1916 attracted the attention of engineers across America. Articles in *Engineering News* and *Engineering News-Record* praised the commissioners of the Mattamuskeet Drainage District for their boldness in constructing the largest pumping plant in the country to drain and reclaim what many believed to be the richest land in America.

On March 7, 1912, representatives of Morris Machine Works of Baldwinsville, New York, presented their detailed contract proposal with engineering specifications for the construction of the pumping plant. They proposed furnishing the material and the work to build a pumping station, including foundations, building, electrical generator, pumps, and other apparatus, all delivered and installed in operation on the south bank of Lake Mattamuskeet.

Morris Machine Works proposed to build a plant that would lift 1,800 cubic feet (13,465 gallons) of water per second from the intake side of the pumps into Outfall Canal on the discharge side of the plant.

The Morris proposal promised the completion of the operational plant within 12 months from the date of the execution of the contract, providing the dredging contractor had completed Outfall Canal allowing barges to transport the equipment and materials to the site. The commissioners awarded Morris the contract on July 5, 1912, but lawsuits by Hyde County residents concerned about the cost of the project delayed construction for two and a half years.

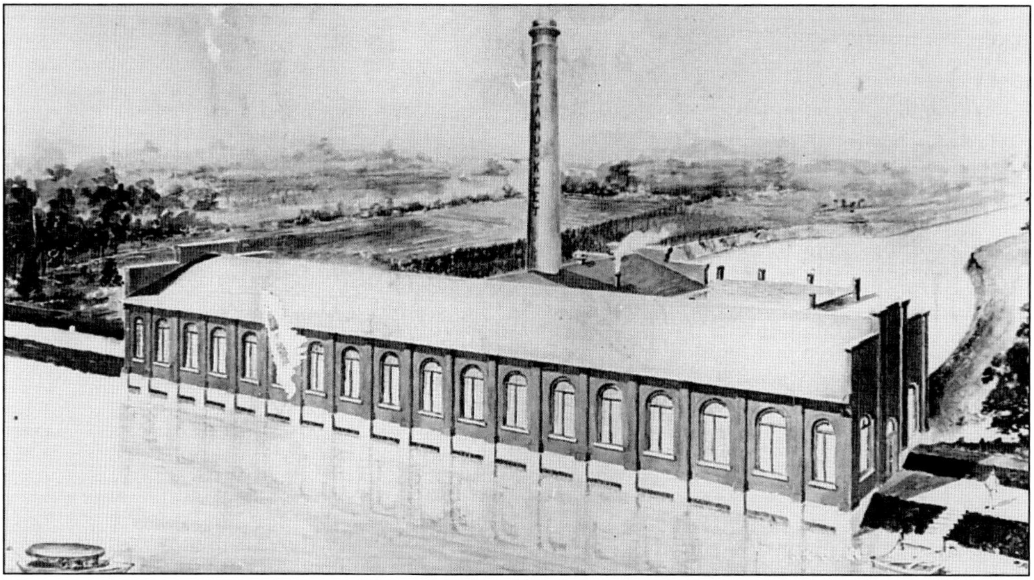

This is an architect's rendering of the pumping plant that was proposed for Lake Mattamuskeet. The word "Mattamuskeet" is on the smokestack. The actual plant turned out to be smaller and far less impressive in appearance. (Courtesy of Julian Mann III.)

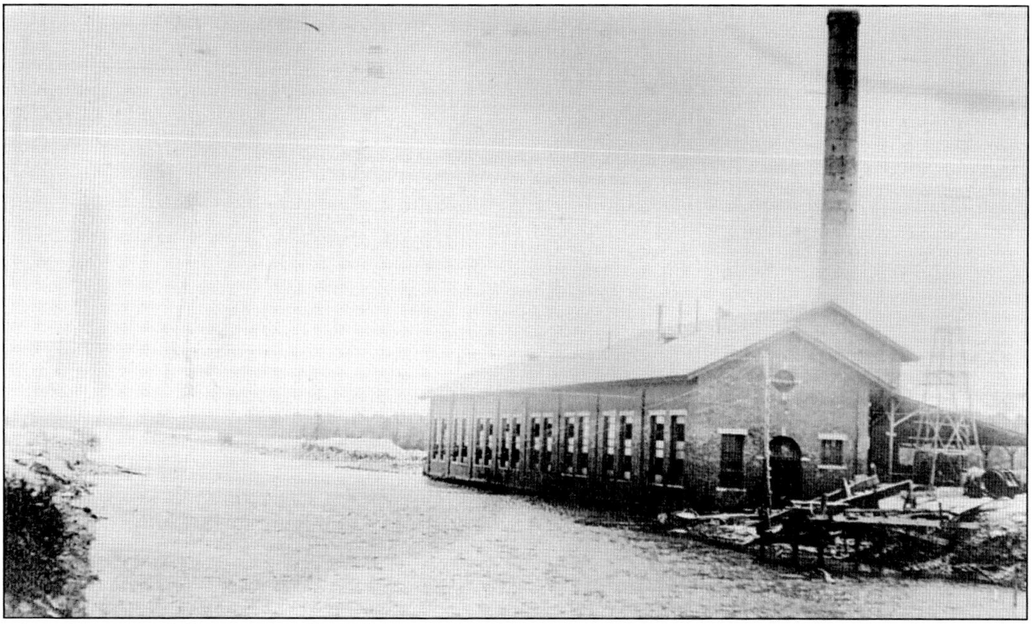

The photo is of the west end of the pumping plant built at Lake Mattamuskeet. The drainage commissioners agreed to pay Morris Machine Works $205,000 to build the pumping station, with $30,000 going for the building and $175,000 for the pumps. The Southern Land Reclamation Company contributed $55,000 towards the cost of the plant as a gift to the district above their taxes. (Courtesy of Julian Mann III.)

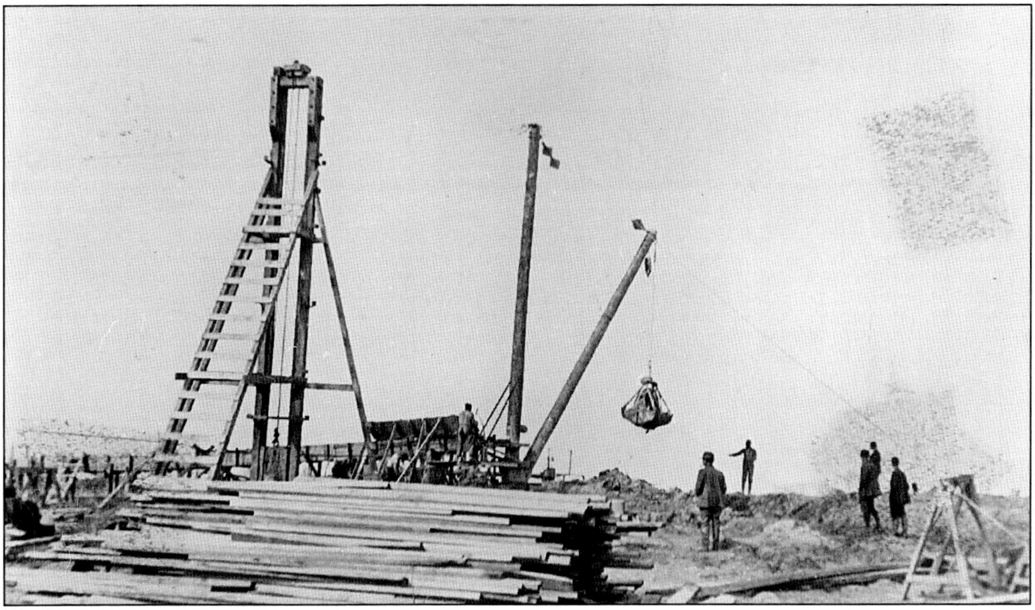

A.V. Wills & Sons completed Outfall Canal from the Pamlico Sound to the south shore of the lake by the end of 1914. This made it possible for Morris Machine Works to begin constructing the pumping plant. Workmen began preparing the foundations for the pumping plant in the spring of 1915. (Courtesy of Mattamuskeet National Wildlife Refuge, Donald E. Temple, manager.)

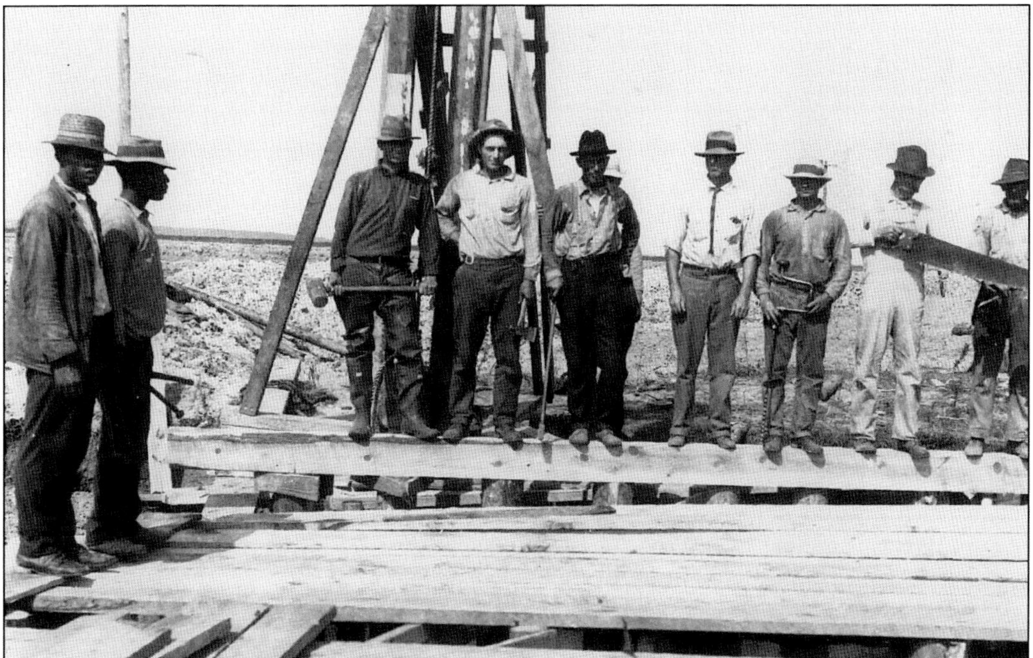

Here is another view of the crew working on the foundations of the pumping plant in the spring of 1915. (Courtesy of Mattamuskeet National Wildlife Refuge, Donald E. Temple, manager.)

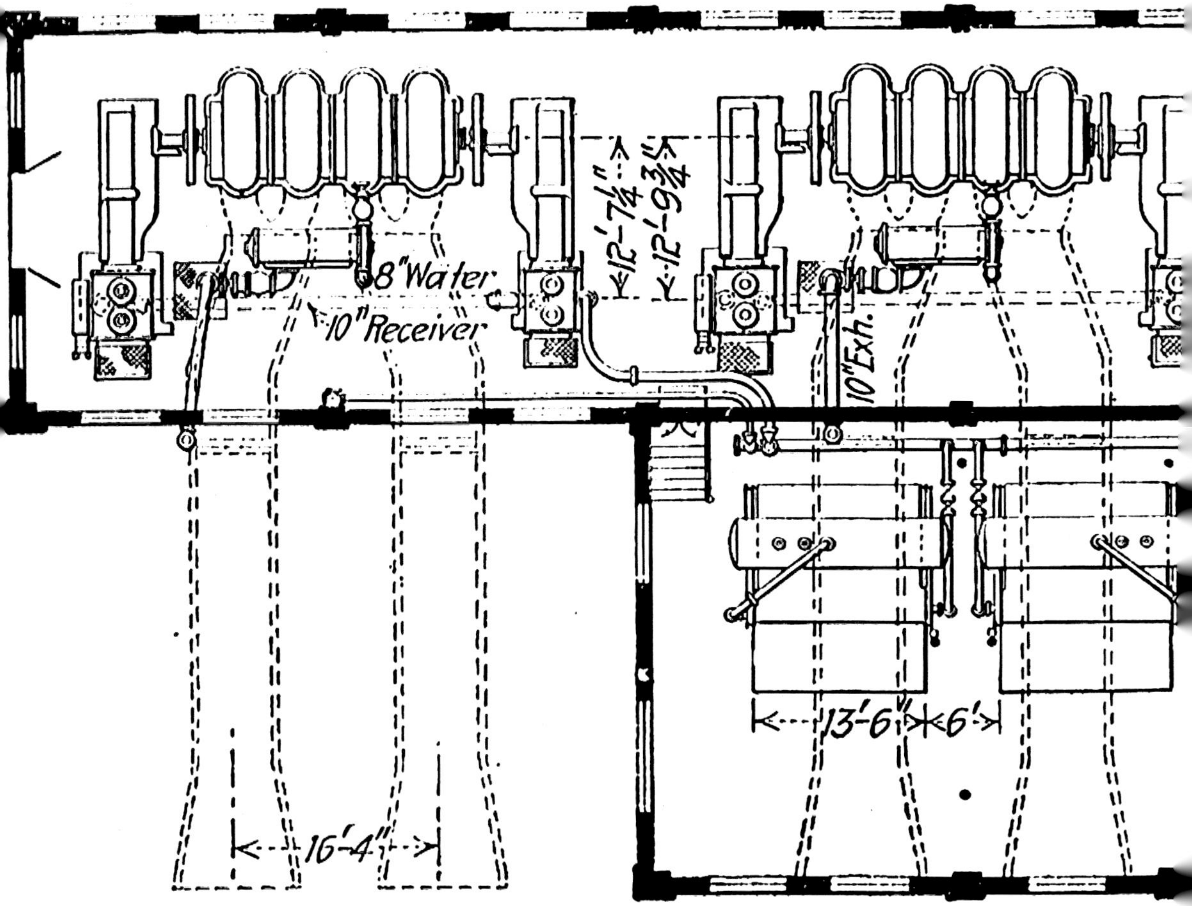

The diameter of the intake pipes for the pumps was approximately 48 inches. The discharge flumes were approximately 72 inches in diameter, flaring to about 100 inches at the point where the huge flumes discharged the water below the surface of the water into the outfall basin.

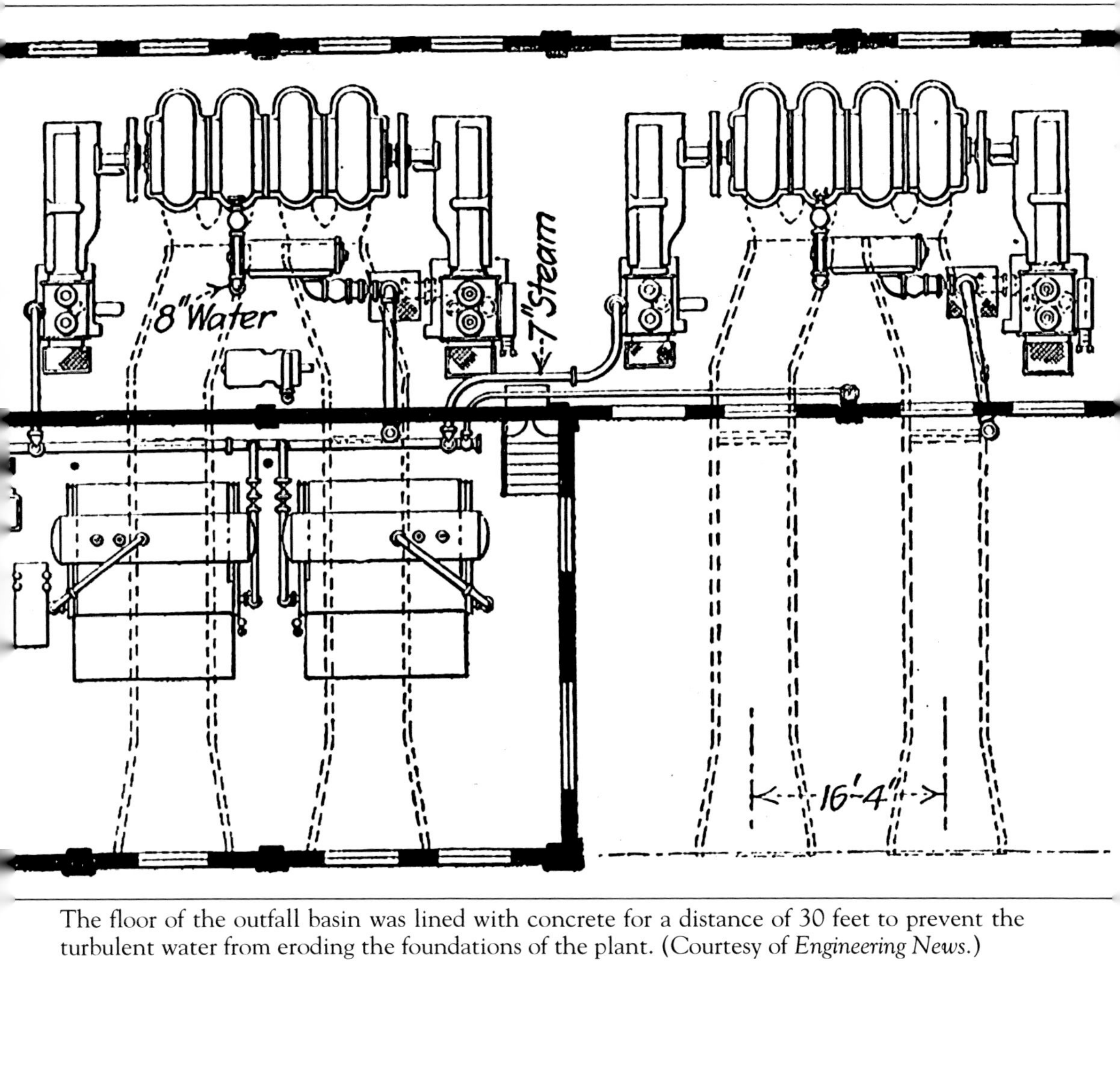

The floor of the outfall basin was lined with concrete for a distance of 30 feet to prevent the turbulent water from eroding the foundations of the plant. (Courtesy of *Engineering News*.)

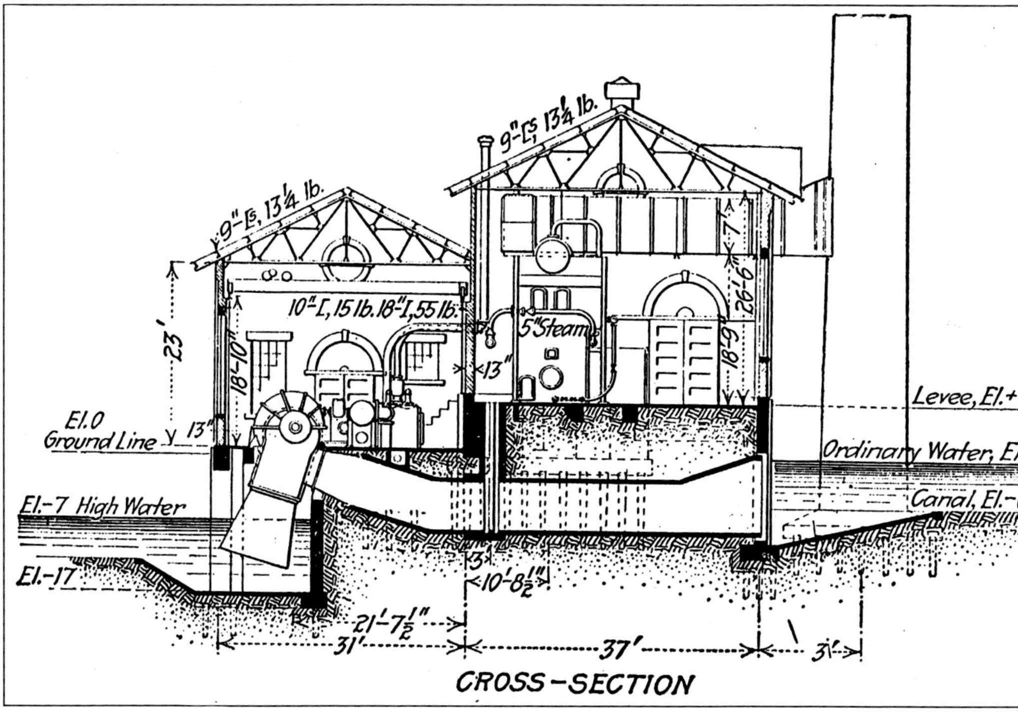

The huge pumps would suction the water from the collection basin on the north side of the building from a surface elevation of 7 feet below sea level. The water would then be lifted and thrust through the large flumes into the basin that opened into Outfall Canal at sea level. The pumps were expected to lift and thrust 13,465 gallons of water per second. (Courtesy of *Engineering News*.)

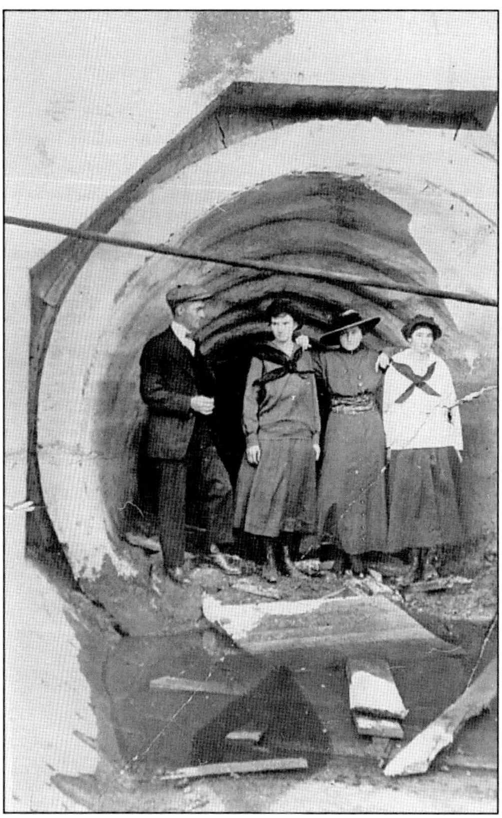

This photo was made when the pumping plant was under construction in 1915–1916. This is the discharge end of one of the eight discharge flumes under the pumping plant. The girl on the far right is Sidney Gaskill Weston at 17 years old. Ms. Weston served as the postmaster in New Holland in the late 1920s. (Courtesy of Hal Swindell.)

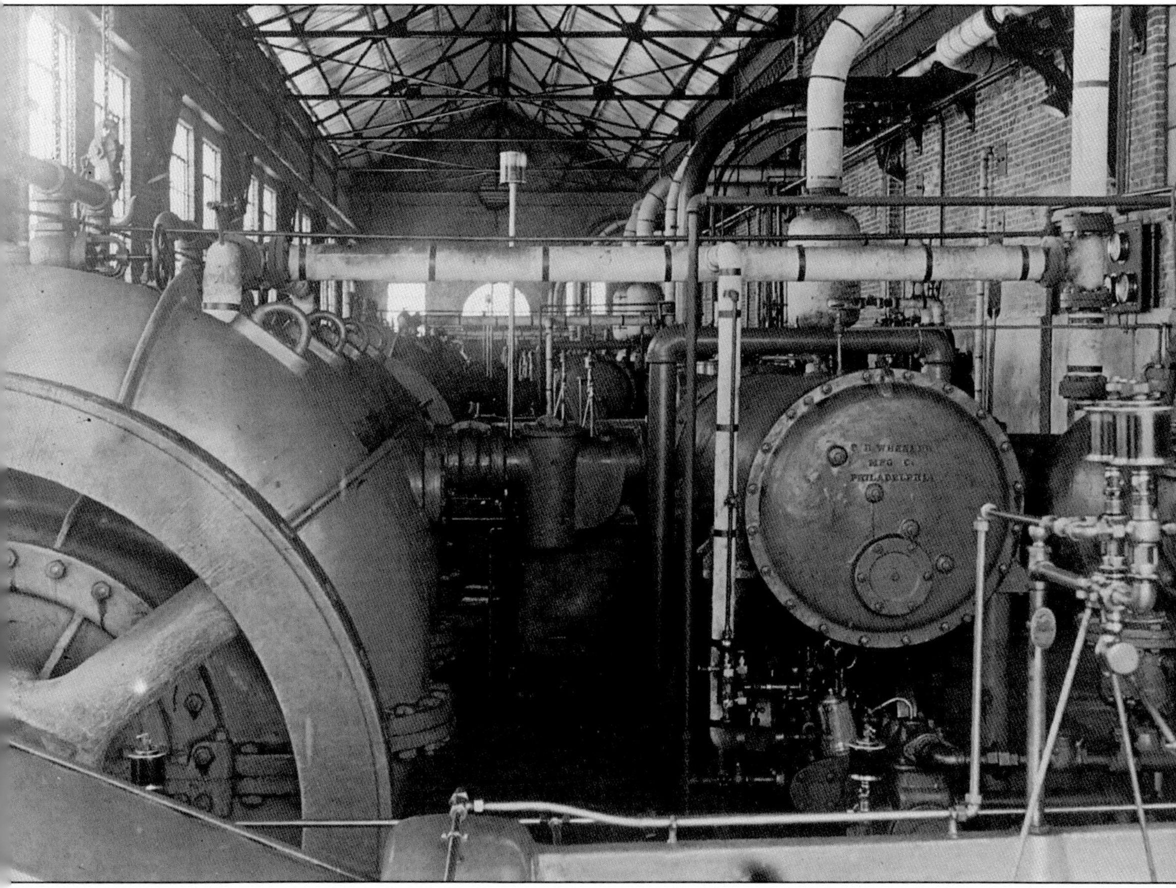

Douglas Nelson Graves described the pumping plant at Lake Mattamuskeet as having "eight sixty-inch centrifugal pumps, any one or all of which may be put into operation at once." Graves stated that "the water pumped by this plant in twenty-four hours would make a lake a mile long, a half-mile wide, and thirteen feet deep." (Courtesy of Carolyn Ponzer Taylor.)

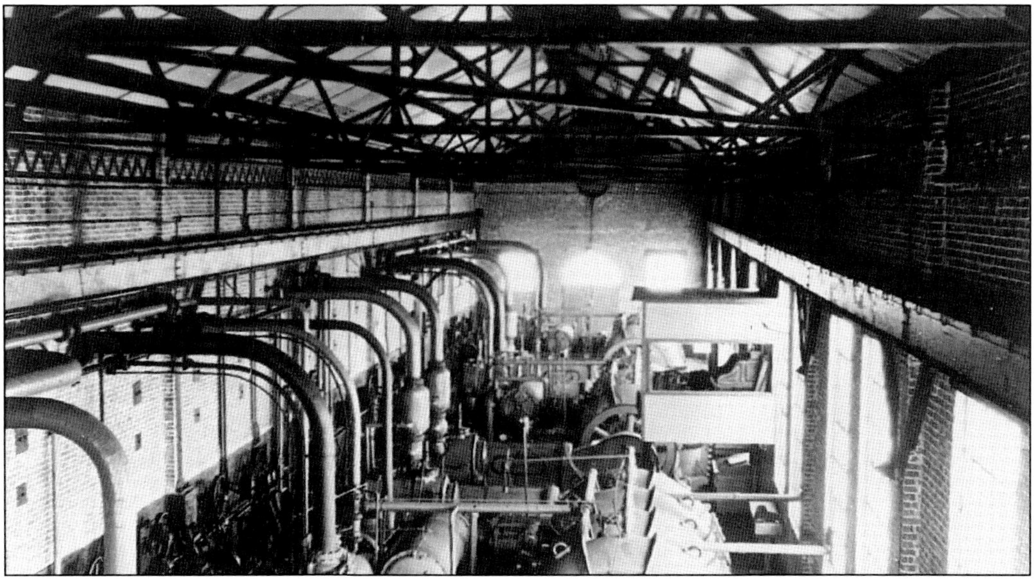

The pumping plant had four 850-horsepower, German-designed Lentz steam engines, each installed to drive two centrifugal pumps. Each pump had two 48-inch impellers, for a total of 16 impellers. Morris Machine Works claimed that Lentz steam engines were the most economical engines available in the world for this size facility. (Courtesy of George R. Scott and Edna E. Harris.)

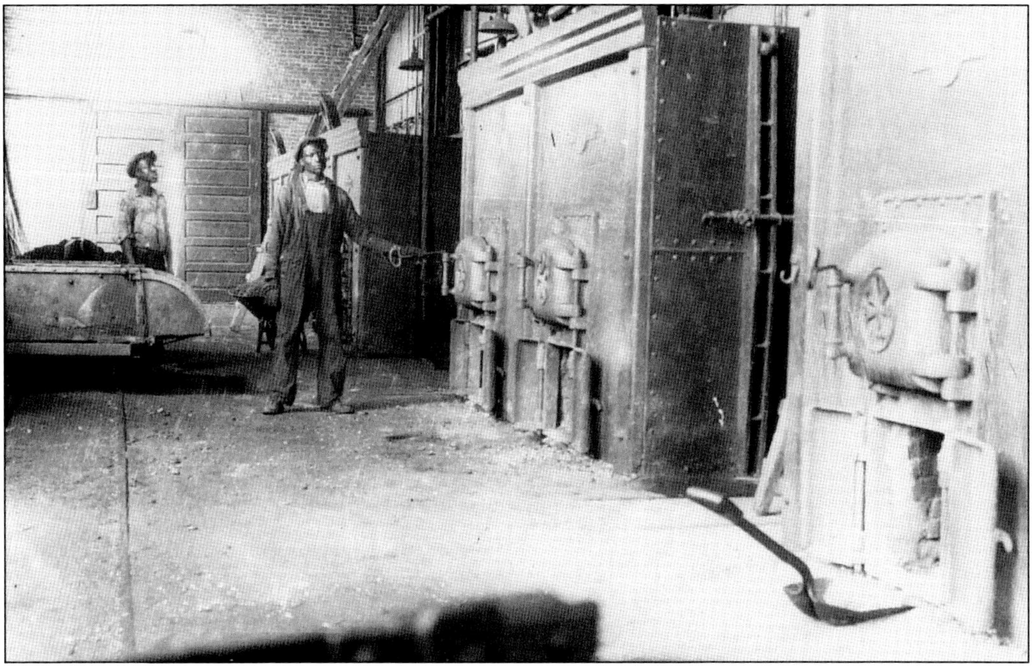

The contractors installed four vertical-type, steel-case, water-tube boilers in the south side of the building. There were 750 feet of water tubes inside the boilers. Workmen shoveled the coal into the fireboxes of the boilers, and on days when the plant was operating at full capacity, they would shovel 30-40 tons of coal into the furnaces. (Courtesy of George R. Scott and Edna E. Harris.)

On June 9, 1915, the drainage commissioners authorized Chairman Graves to prepare the wording for this bronze tablet to be placed on the wall of the pumping plant. (Courtesy of Cliff Hollis.)

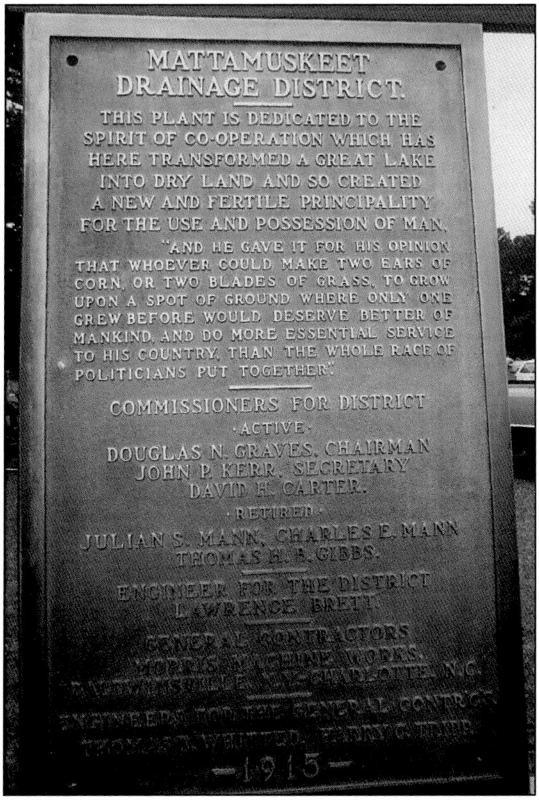

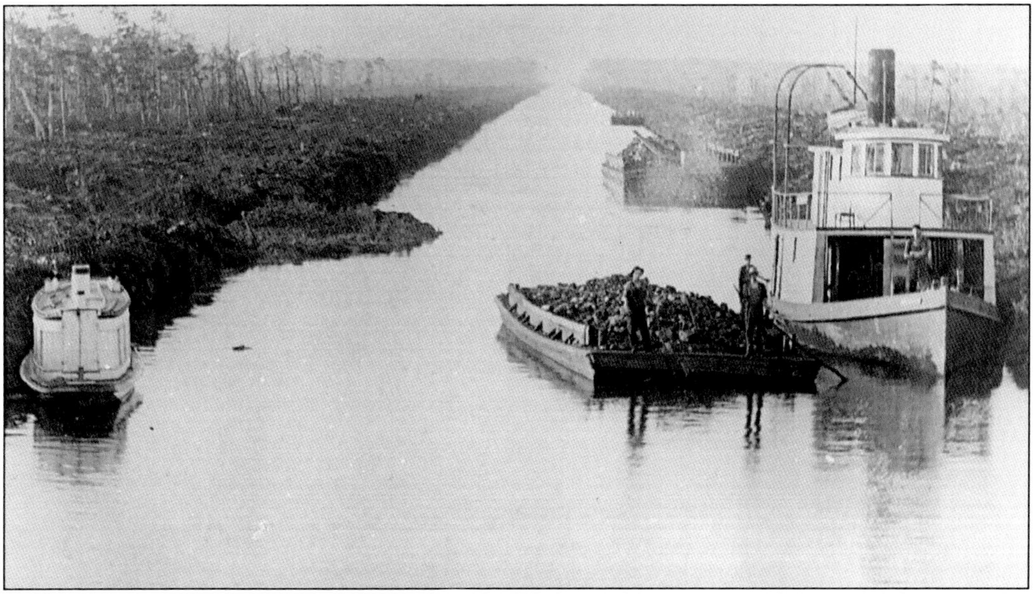

When operating at full capacity, the plant consumed 35 tons of coal every 24 hours and 150 tons of coal per week. In the early days, coal arrived by train at Belhaven where a contractor transferred it to barges and then towed the barges to New Holland, a distance by water of more than 35 miles. (Courtesy of Ercell Gibbs.)

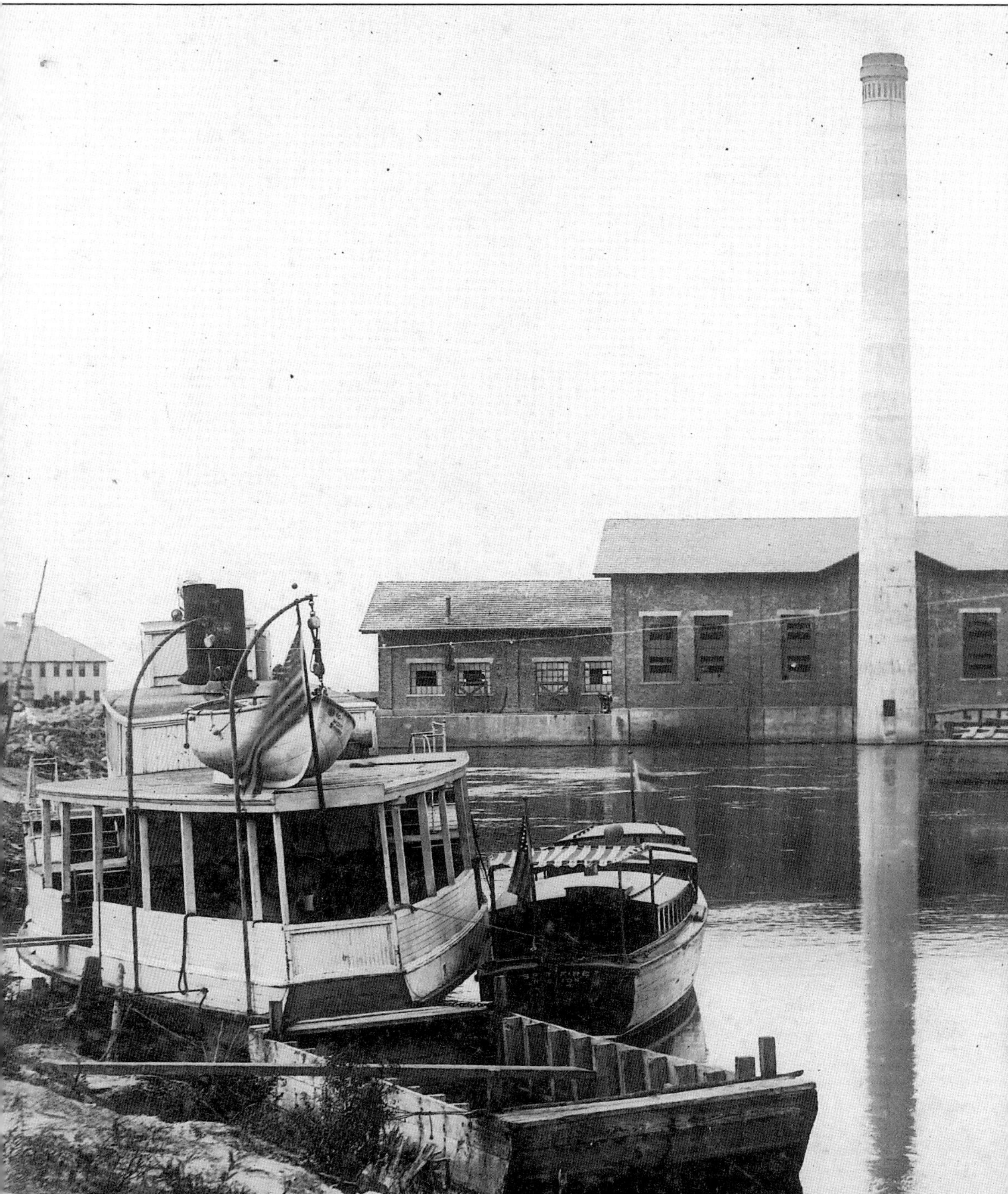

Morris Machine Works put the pumping plant at Lake Mattamuskeet into operation on May 19, 1916. Thomas B. Whitted, the manager of Morris' Charlotte office, had designed the pumping plant, assisted by Harry C. Tripp, T.C. Heyward, and the engineering department of the Morris company. Morris subcontracted the design and fabrication of the boilers and steam engines to

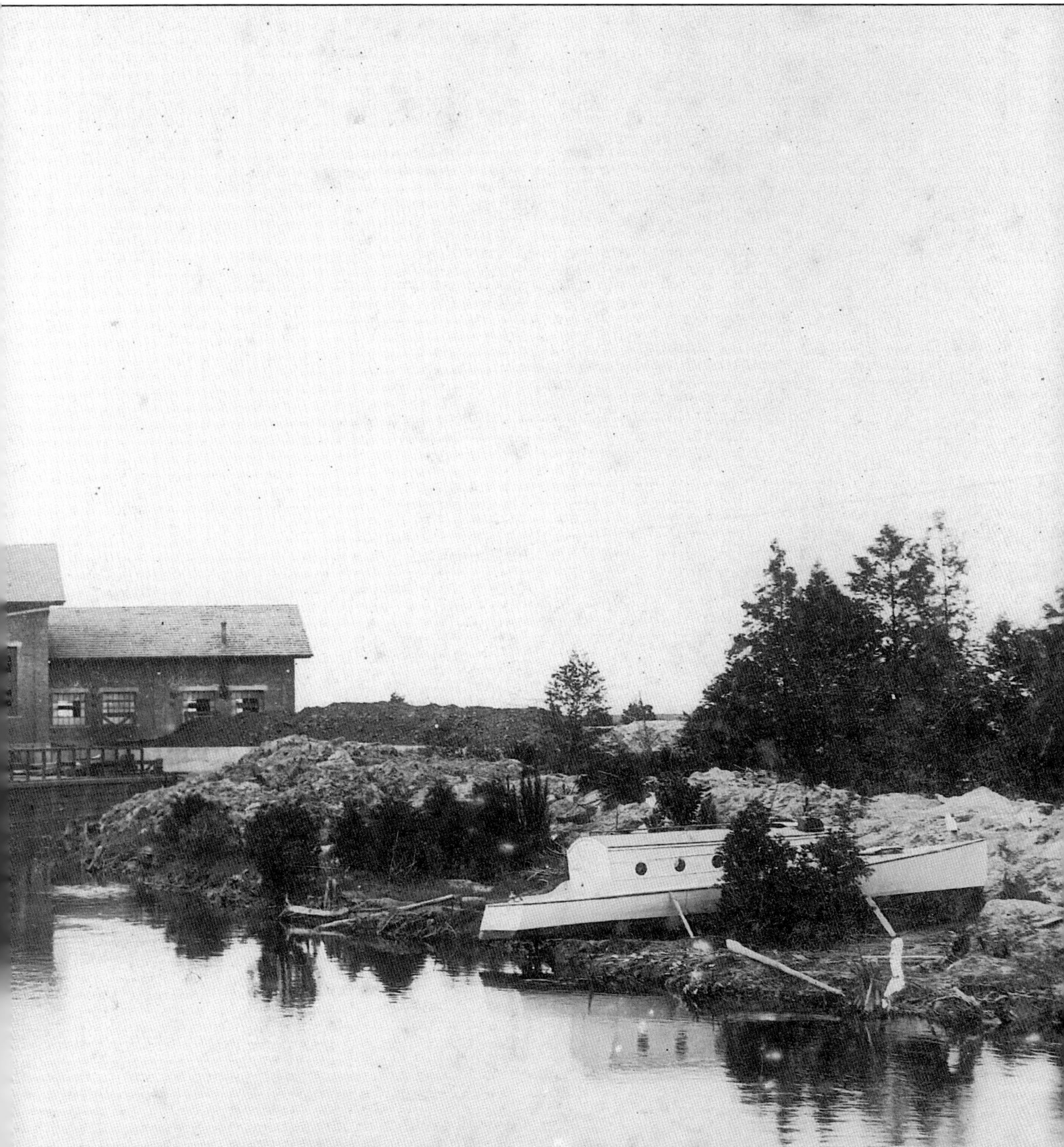

Erie City Iron Works of Erie, Pennsylvania. Harry C. Tripp served as the resident engineer at New Holland during the construction of the plant and installation of the pumps. (Courtesy of Elizabeth Butt.)

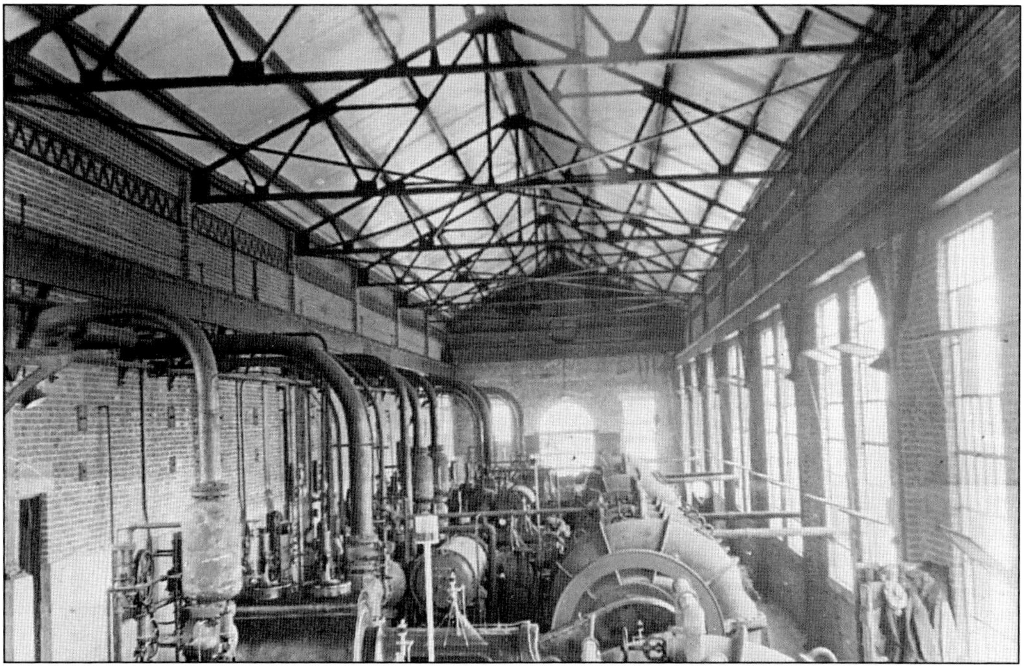

By September 1917, the pumps had run for 16 months at a very high cost and the lake was still not completely drained. A consulting engineer determined the impellers could only achieve 67 percent of the contract specifications. The contractors agreed to cast and install more efficient impellers. The drainage commissioners shut down the plant and waited for the new impellers. (Courtesy of George R. Scott and Edna E. Harris.)

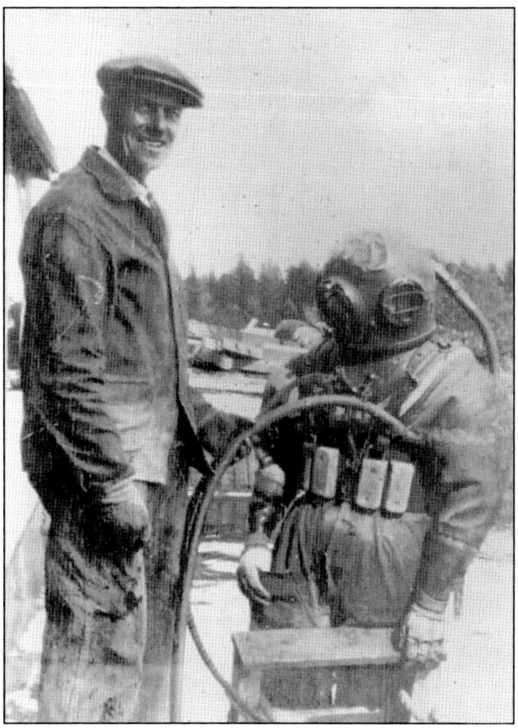

In February 1929, 13 years after the pumps began operating, a large crack broke through the apron on the south side of the plant, allowing water from Outfall Canal to back up into the lake bed. The drainage commissioners contracted with the New York Submarine Contracting Company for a diver named E.J. Tuck to investigate the damage and assist engineers in repairing the breach. (Courtesy of Patricia Auman.)

Four

The Community of New Holland

On November 25, 1915, the Southern Land Reclamation Company became New Holland Farms, Inc. through a corporate name change. This introduced a "Dutch theme" to the private development of Lake Mattamuskeet.

Between 1839 and 1853, the government of Holland drained 44,280-acre Haarlem Lake and reclaimed its bed for productive use. The Haarlem Lake drainage was accomplished with canals, dikes, and three steam-generated pumping plants. In 1908, it was reported that 16,000 Hollanders permanently lived and farmed in the former bed of Haarlem Lake. It is not clear just how the Haarlem Lake project became the model for Lake Mattamuskeet, but the similarity in the design of the canals and pumps in the two drainage districts is evident.

Graves and New Holland Farms, Inc. laid out a plan to subdivide the 48,830-acre reclaimed lake bed into 120-acre or smaller farms, residential lots, town sites, and commercial tracts. Harlan Page Kelsey of Salem, Massachusetts, one of America's foremost landscape architects, drew the plans for the project. Graves planned a community with a high standard of living and anticipated there would eventually be 20,000 permanent residents in the reclaimed bed of Lake Mattamuskeet.

On March 11, 1918, New Holland Farms, Inc. sold the lake property to a group of Ohio investors who incorporated as North Carolina Farms Company. The new owners paid $600,000 for the land and all improvements, and D.N. Graves was not involved in the drainage project from 1918 to 1925.

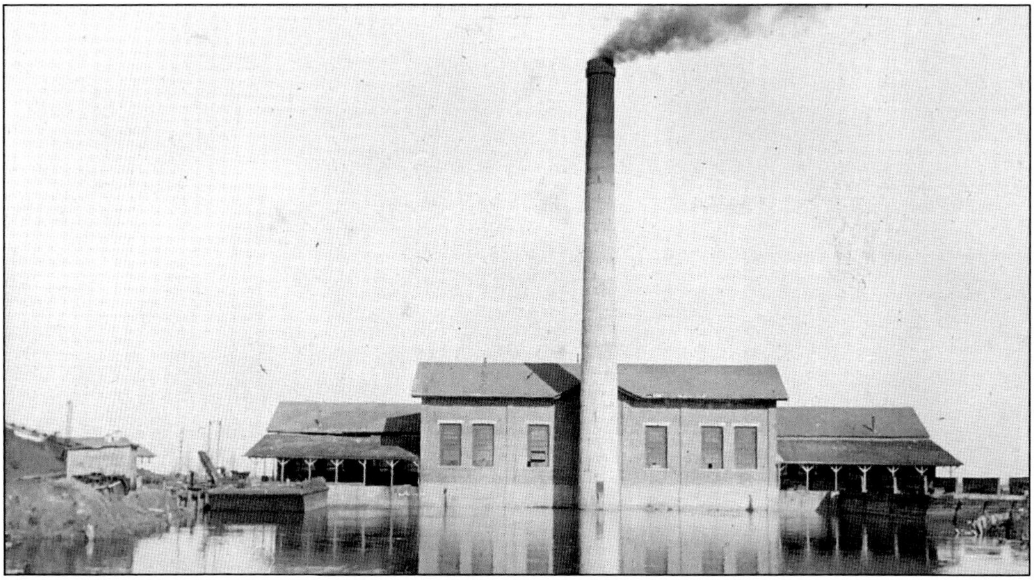

The Morris engineers designed the largest capacity pumping plant in the world. The specifications called for it to pump over 800,000 gallons of water per minute, but it eventually was capable of pumping 1,200,000 gallons per minute. The smokestack for the coal-fired steam boilers was 125 feet tall and was built to withstand winds of 100 miles per hour. (Courtesy of Carolyn Ponzer Taylor.)

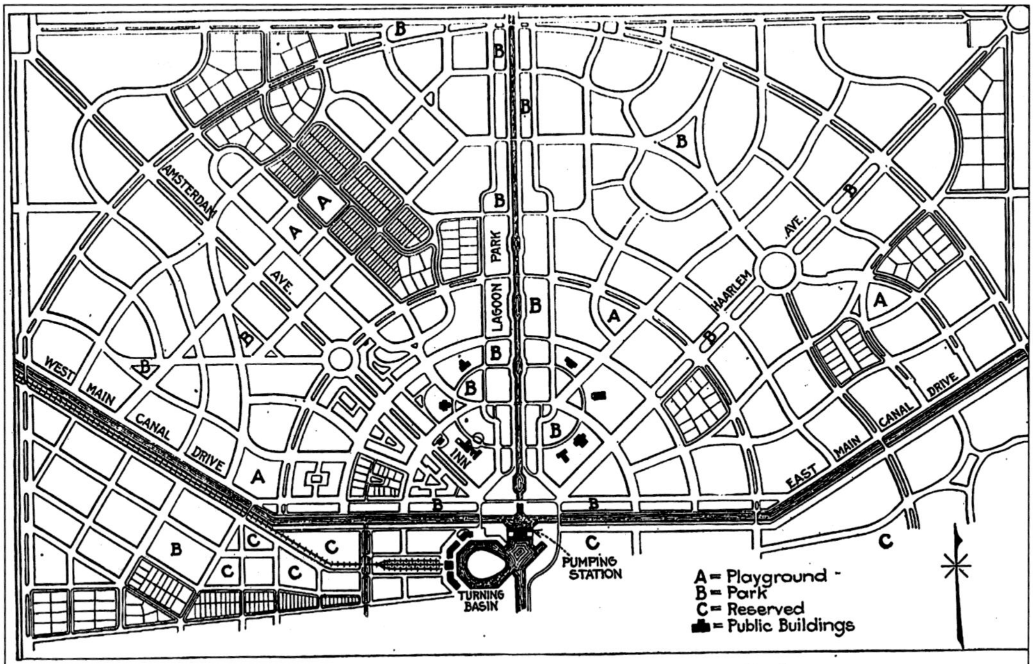

FIG. 3. PLAN OF TOWN OF NEW HOLLAND, N. C.

During 1915–1916, Harlan Page Kelsey, one of America's foremost landscape architects, designed an 800-acre town site called "New Holland," laid off in a semi-circle with streets spreading out like rays of the sun from the pumping plant. (Courtesy of *Engineering News*.)

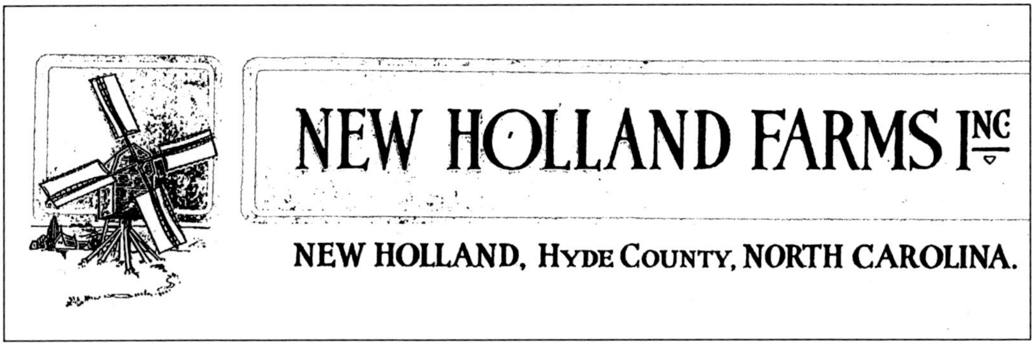

Inspired by successful Dutch drainage projects, the owners of New Holland Farms, Inc. set about to develop a carefully designed community around a Dutch theme. Contrary to the legends that surround the New Holland project, none of the owners, designers, investors, or developers of New Holland or the Mattamuskeet Drainage District were of Dutch descent. (From the Mattamuskeet Records.)

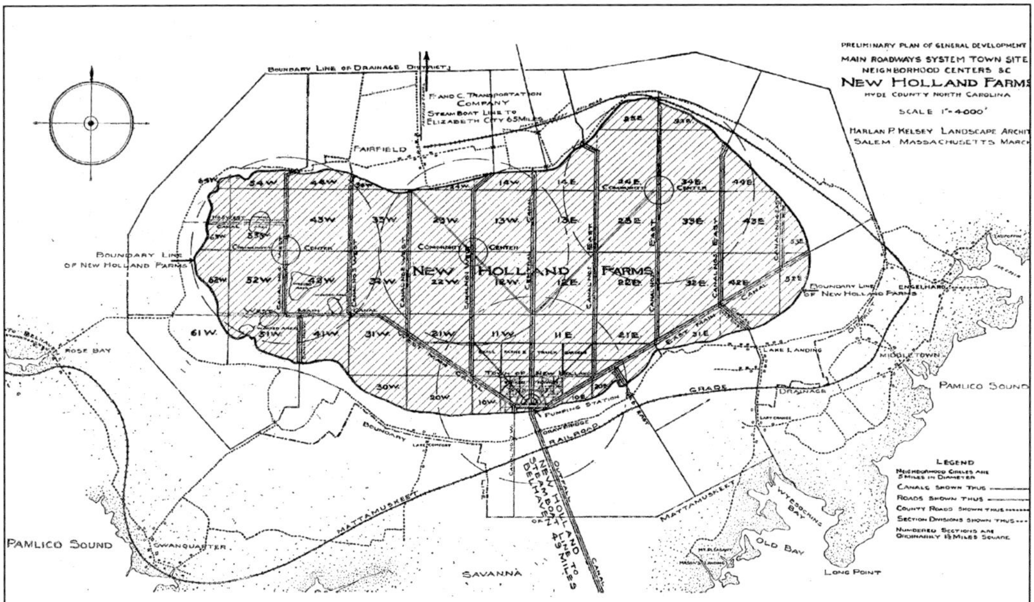

Harlan P. Kelsey subdivided the lake bed into farms ranging from 5 to 120 acres, residential and commercial tracts, and four town sites. New Holland Farms began promoting land sales in 1916. By March of 1917, the company had sold one store lot, 40 residential lots, and 21 farm tracts in the lake bed, totaling 1,050 acres. The towns other than New Holland were simply referred to as "Community Centers 1, 2, and 3" and were never developed due to changes in ownership and objectives for the property. (Courtesy of Ercell Gibbs.)

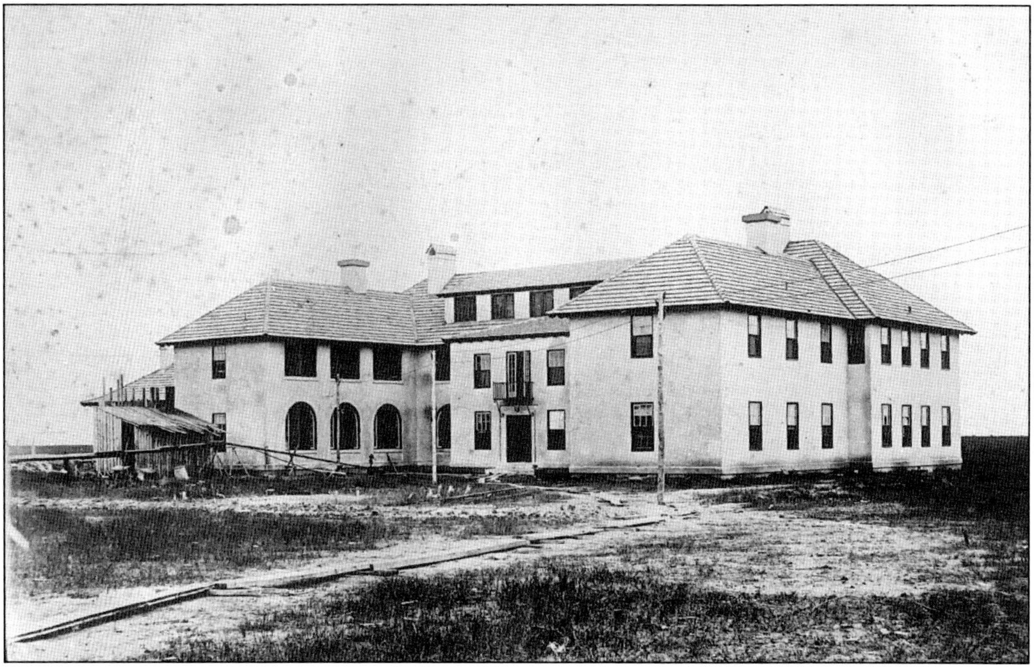

About 1915, New Holland Farms, Inc. completed the construction of a small hotel, which they called the New Holland Inn, about 200 yards northwest of the pumping plant. A front view of the New Holland Inn can be found on page 4. (Courtesy of Elizabeth Butt.)

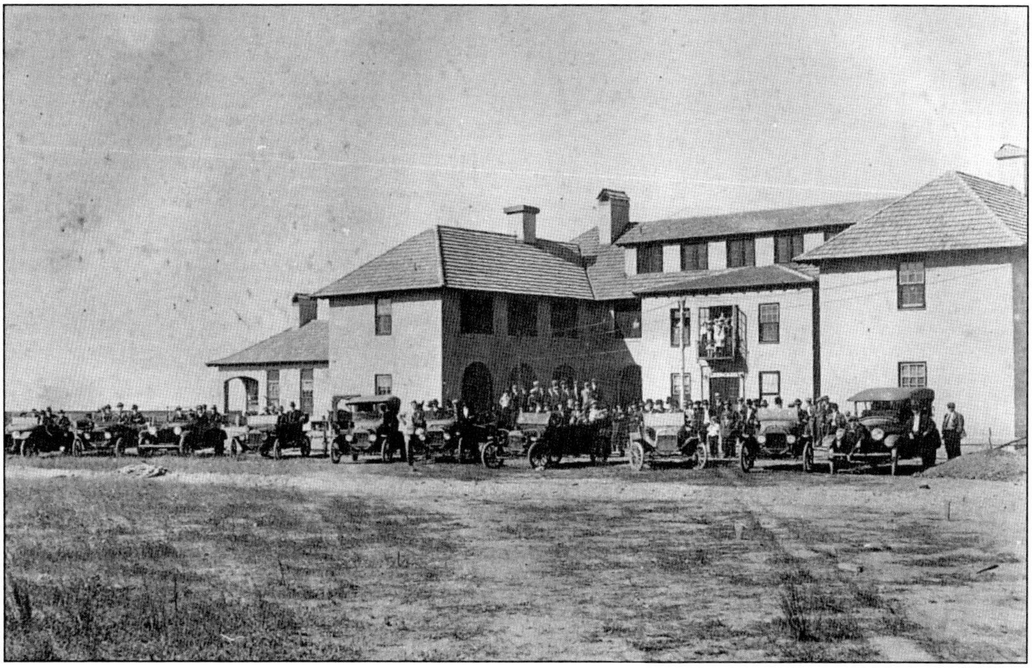

There were two dances each week at the New Holland Inn, with music provided by a self-player piano. Church services on Sunday afternoons were conducted by Mr. E.R. Stewart, the Baptist minister from Fairfield. The New Holland Inn hosted high school proms in the spring, weddings as needed, and hunters throughout each fall and winter. (Courtesy of Virginia Pugh.)

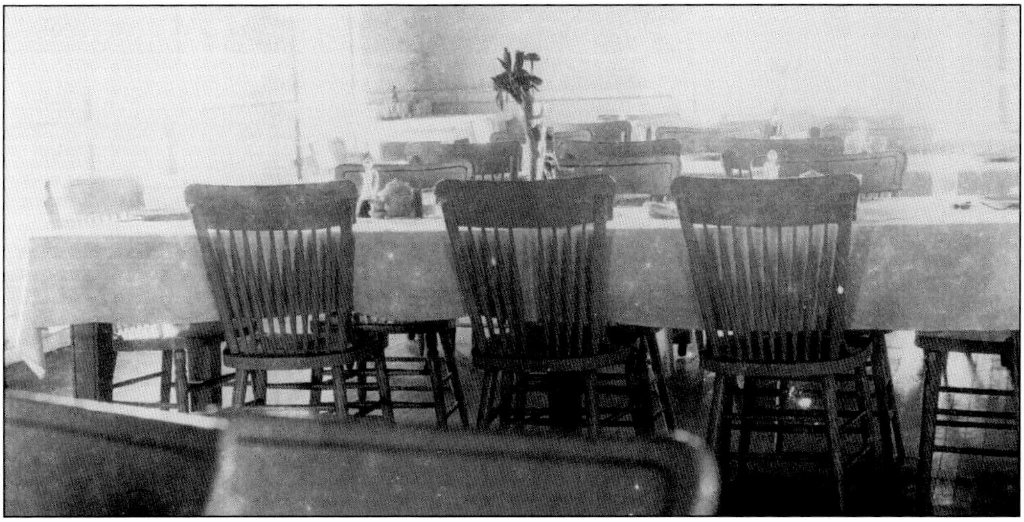

The New Holland Inn had a first-class dining room with 6 tables and 48 chairs. Waitresses served three-course meals on heated china with silver-plated serviceware. The company's windmill logo was on the china and silverware. Guests praised the hotel for serving meals equal to those served in the finest hotels of New York, Boston, and Chicago. (Courtesy of Mattamuskeet National Wildlife Refuge, Donald E. Temple, manager.)

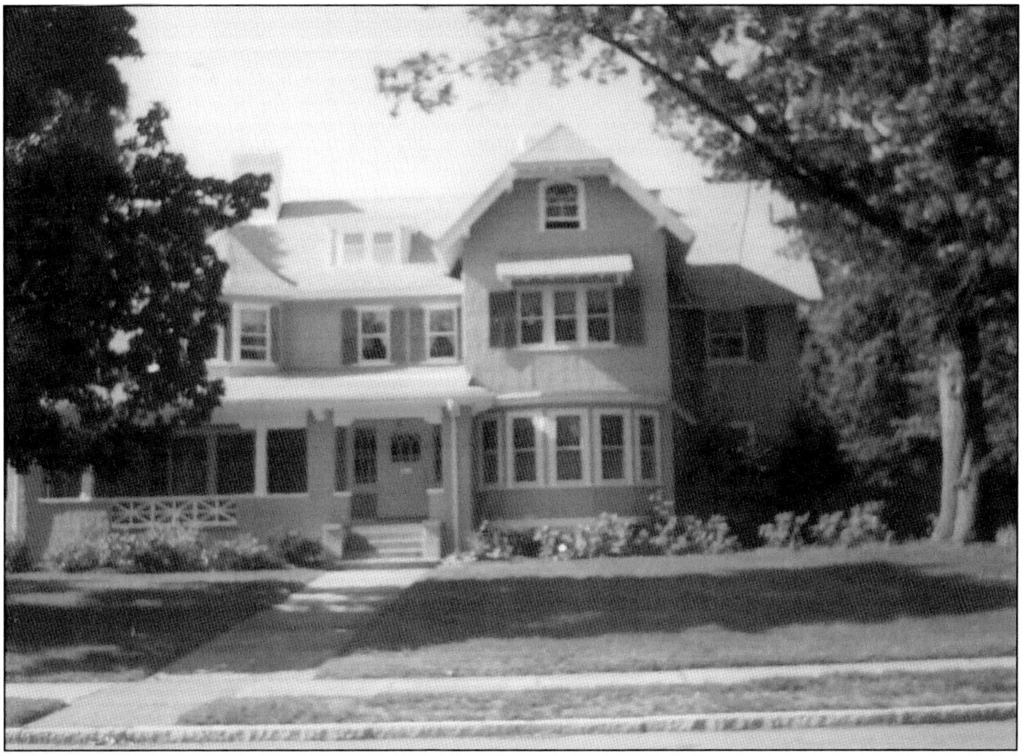

During his two periods of involvement at Lake Mattamuskeet (1911–1918 and 1925–1929), Douglas Nelson Graves maintained his residence at 31 Everett Avenue, Winchester, Massachusetts (pictured here), and commuted back and forth to Hyde County, staying a few weeks each time. (Courtesy of Lewis Forrest.)

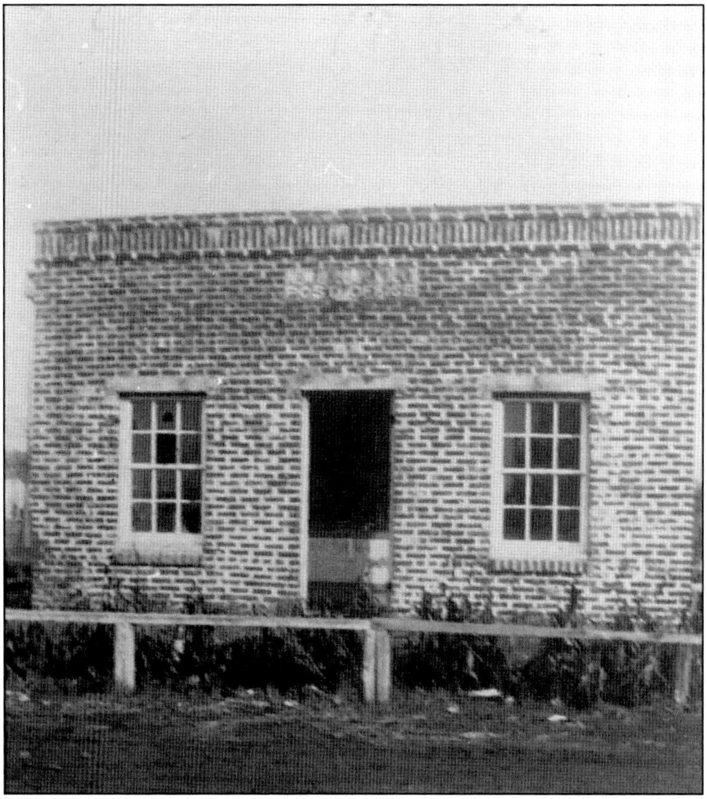

On July 19, 1916, New Holland got its own post office. Harold Smith was the first postmaster. Smith was born in Oslo, Norway. He and his wife, Martha Elixson Smith, were also the first managers of the New Holland Inn. In the late 1920s, Sidney Gaskill Weston was the New Holland postmaster. (Courtesy of Lennie Jones Christenson.)

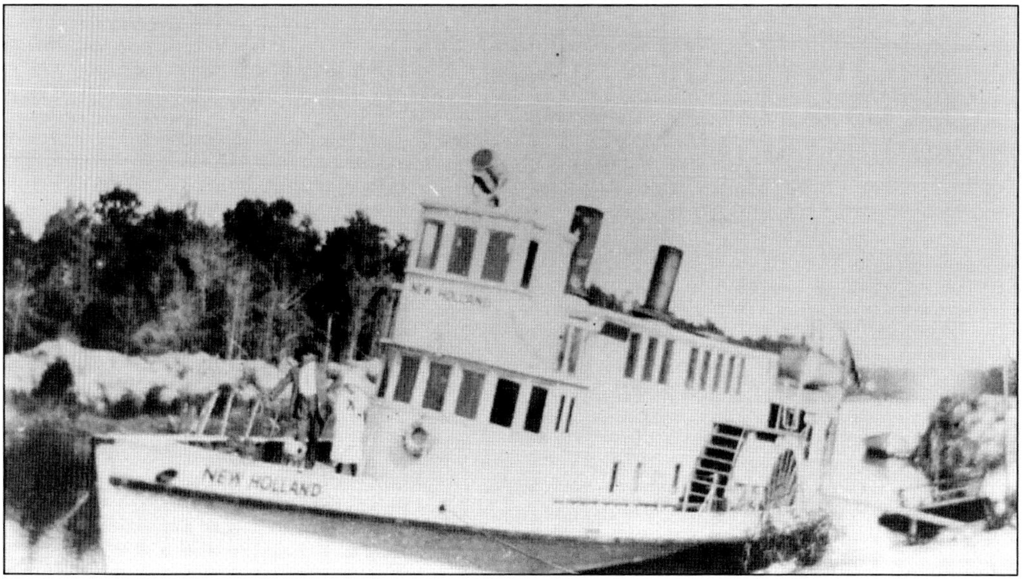

In the early years of the drainage project, Outfall Canal provided the main access to the lake bed, and New Holland Farms operated a paddle wheeler called the *New Holland*. In 1916, D.N. Graves wrote, "At Belhaven you make immediate connection with our own steamer *New Holland*, and after a short sail on Pamlico Sound are landed right at our town of New Holland." (Courtesy of Leon Ballance.)

In promoting land sales in 1916, D.N. Graves, pictured here, stated, "We have fifty thousand acres of virgin soil right in the very midst of a successful farming community . . . . land without a tree or a stone, which has never been touched with a plow, and yet has been gathering up fertility for your benefit, and waiting for your coming through a thousand years." (Courtesy of Lennie Jones Christenson.)

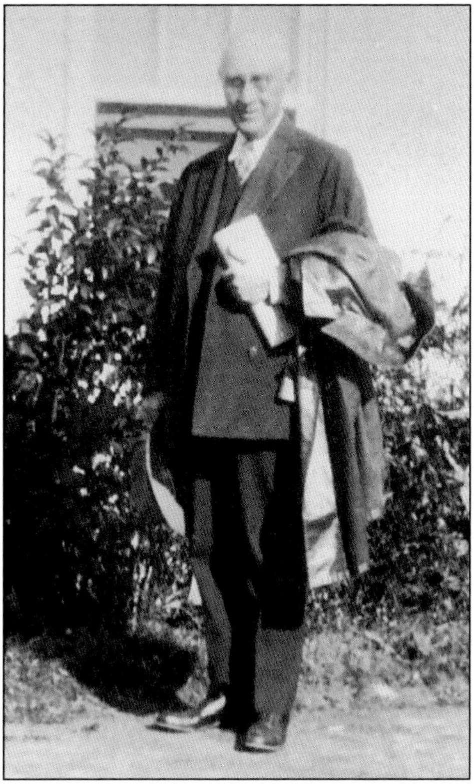

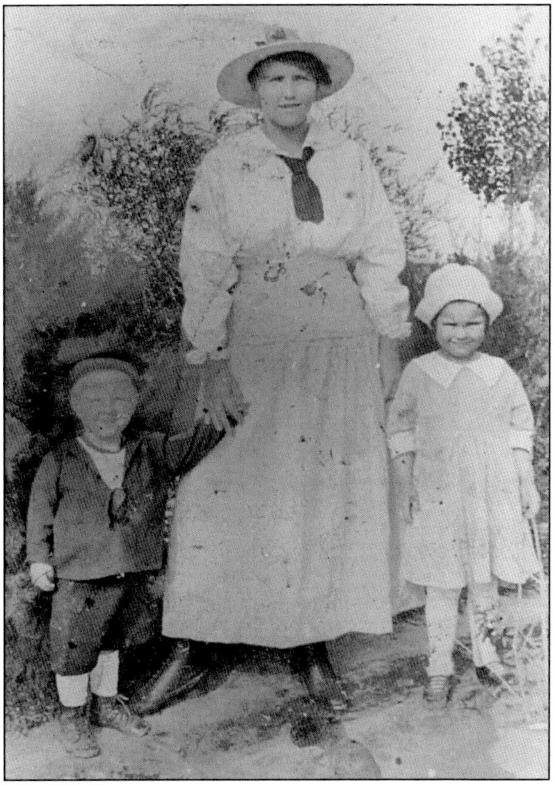

This photo from early 1917 is Alberta Froom and her children. Alberta's husband was employed in some capacity by New Holland Farms, Inc. and was Dutch. In 1929, Douglas N. Graves stated that the little Froom girl was the first child born in the lake bed. If he was referring to the girl in this photo, she was probably born about 1911 or 1912. (Courtesy of Lessie Cutrell.)

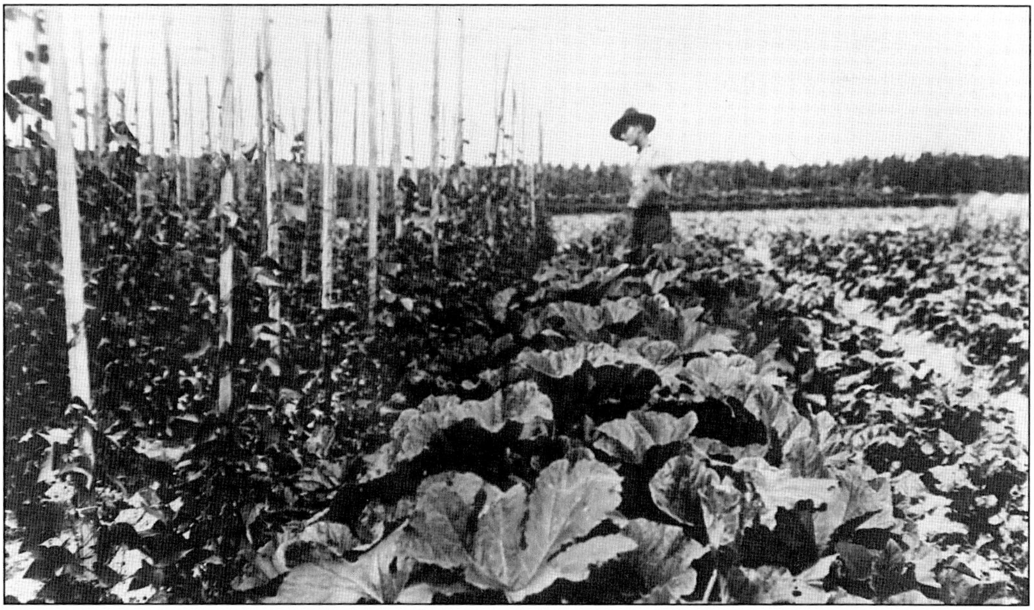

About 1928, Douglas N. Graves employed four Dutch men as gardeners at New Holland—Oldert Jensen, Andrew Stoop, Case Monster, and Paul Van Gyzen. They were each paid $15 per week and were provided with a small house for their family. They stayed at New Holland less than one year. (Courtesy of George R. Scott and Edna E. Harris.)

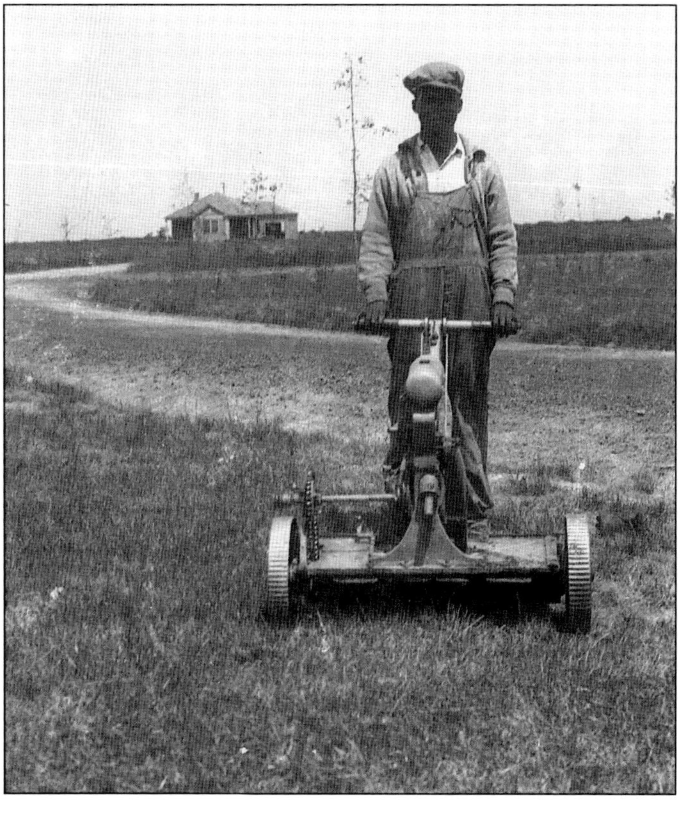

Long before grass-mowing was a major American pastime, the residents of New Holland planted grass and owned one of the first gasoline-powered lawnmowers in eastern North Carolina, c. 1928. (Courtesy of the Mattamuskeet National Wildlife Refuge, Donald E. Temple, manager.)

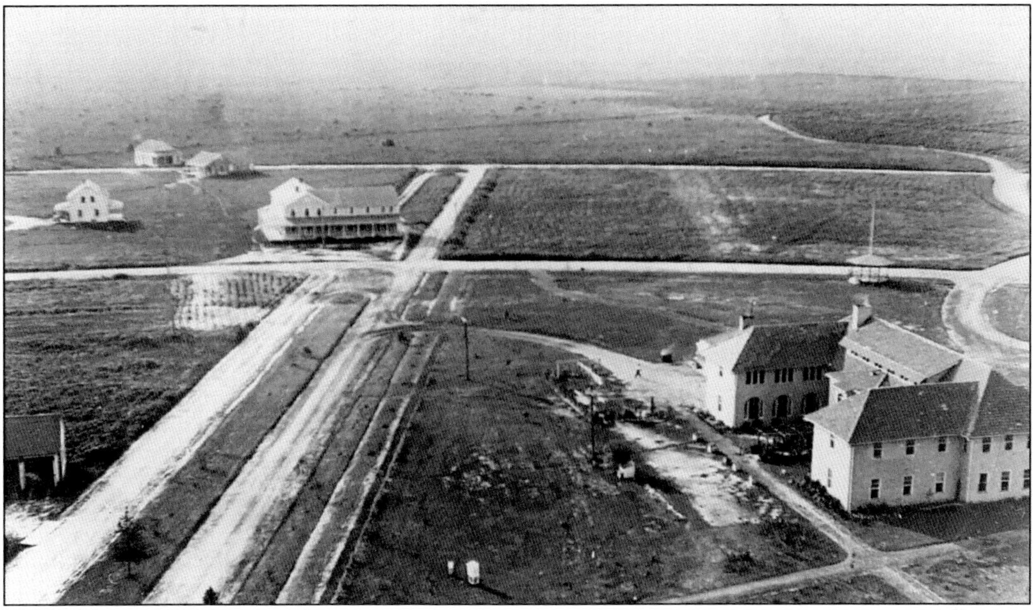

Douglas Graves's company advertised that it had set aside $100,000 from the sales of lots and farms as a permanent endowment fund for "promoting the welfare of the district, for arousing interest in agricultural developments, for maintaining the parks and playgrounds, for beautifying the locality, providing lectures and other entertainment, and for hiring a social secretary." This appeared in *Engineering News* on March 1, 1917. (Courtesy of Lennie Jones Christenson.)

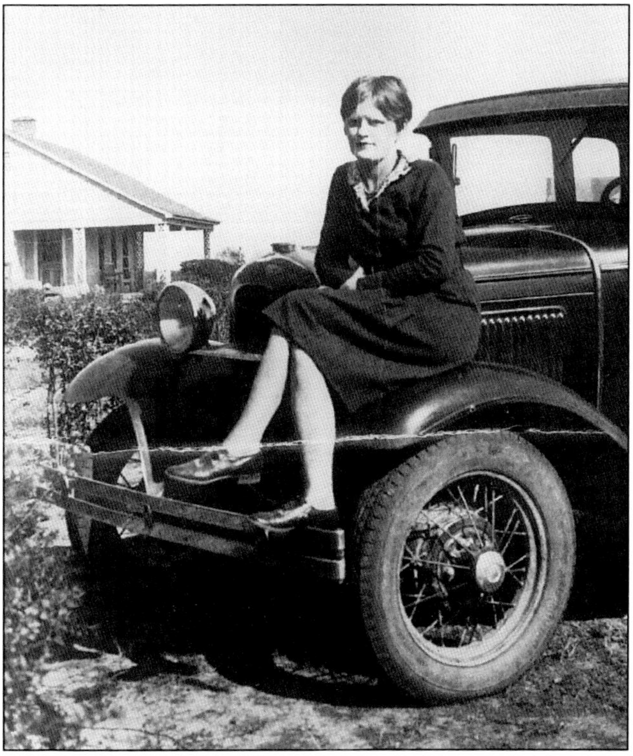

Gladys Allen, a waitress at the New Holland Inn from 1928 to 1933, adorns the fender of a Model A Ford. Bea Simmons of Washington, North Carolina, donated a 1930 Model A Ford like this one to The Mattamuskeet Foundation in 1998. The foundation uses the old car to promote interest in the history of Lake Mattamuskeet. (Courtesy of Gladys Allen Williams.)

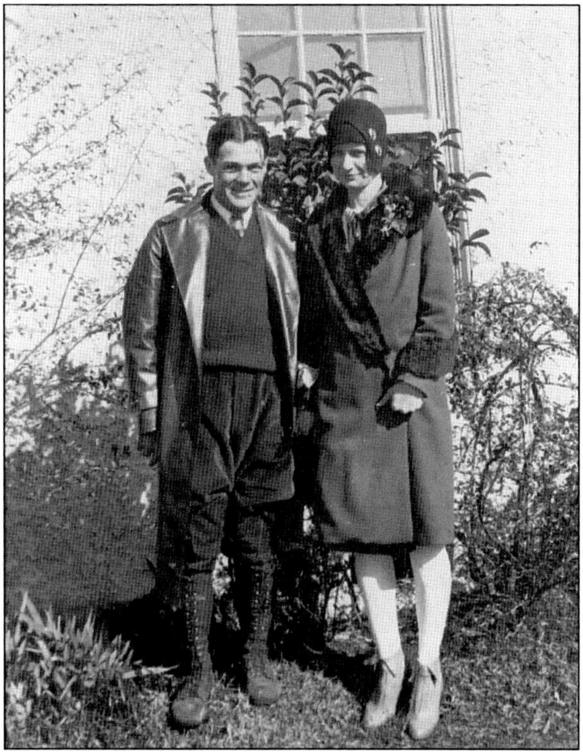

Leland Carawan and Edna Cutrell pose behind the New Holland Inn, c. 1927. Carawan was an electrician and mechanic who had unusual mechanical abilities and was also in charge of the New Holland fire department. This attractive couple was married in 1929 and managed the New Holland Inn from the middle of 1931 until it closed in 1933. (Courtesy of Patricia Auman.)

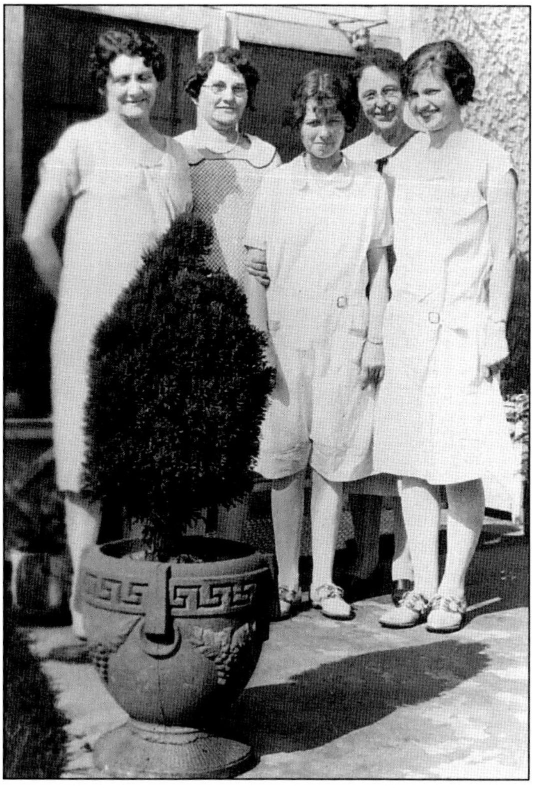

Staff and friends are pictured in front of the New Holland Inn about 1927. From left to right are unidentified; Mrs. Charles S. Jones, wife of the chief engineer at the pumping plant; Billy Jones, waitress; Martha Patten, manager of the New Holland Inn; and Edna Cutrell, waitress. (Courtesy of Lennie Jones Christenson.)

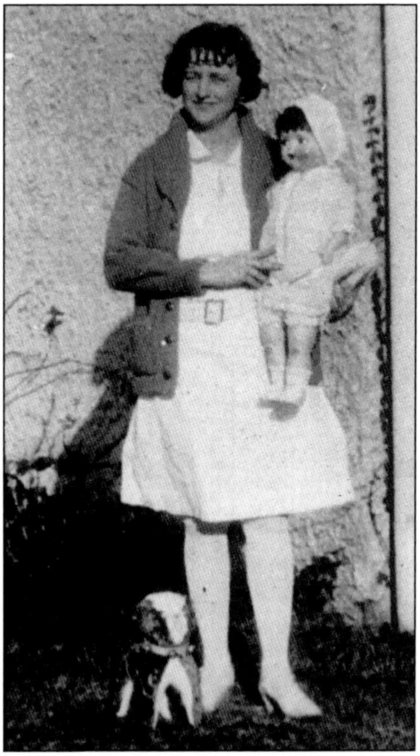

Annual Junior-Senior Banquet Friday Night

One of the outstanding social events of the school year was the annual Junior-Senior Banquet given at the New Holland Hotel Friday night, when the Junior Class of the Swan Quarter High School entertained complimentary to the Senior Class, members of the faculty, and a number of special guests.

The hotel was appropriately arranged and decorated for the occasion. Flowers, potted plants, and ferns added to party appointments which were carried out in the Junior-Senior class colors.

Several entertaining and amusing toasts and speeches were given by members of each class, and the faculty

Special music, rendered by Mr. and Mrs. Hallet Deans of Belhaven, was enjoyed during the four course dinner and throughout the entertainment.

Left: Lennie Jones Christenson grew up in nearby Tyrell County and went to work at the New Holland Inn as a waitress in 1927. She lived and worked at New Holland for about one year. Christenson was born in 1903 and in 1999, celebrated her 96th birthday in good health. (Courtesy of Lennie Jones Christenson.) *Right:* In the spring of 1927, the above newspaper story appeared in the *Washington Daily News*, reporting the 1927 Swan Quarter High School Junior-Senior prom that was held at the New Holland Inn. (Courtesy of Lona Bonner Carawan.)

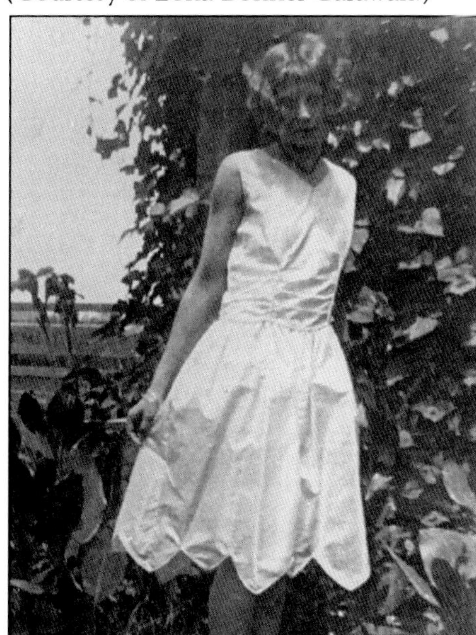

Lizzie Mae Credle models her prom dress for her 1929 high school prom at the New Holland Inn. A few years earlier, young Lizzie Mae had her tonsils removed with a group of school children at the New Holland Inn and recalls enjoying the ice cream after the surgery. (Courtesy of Lizzie Mae Credle Britton.)

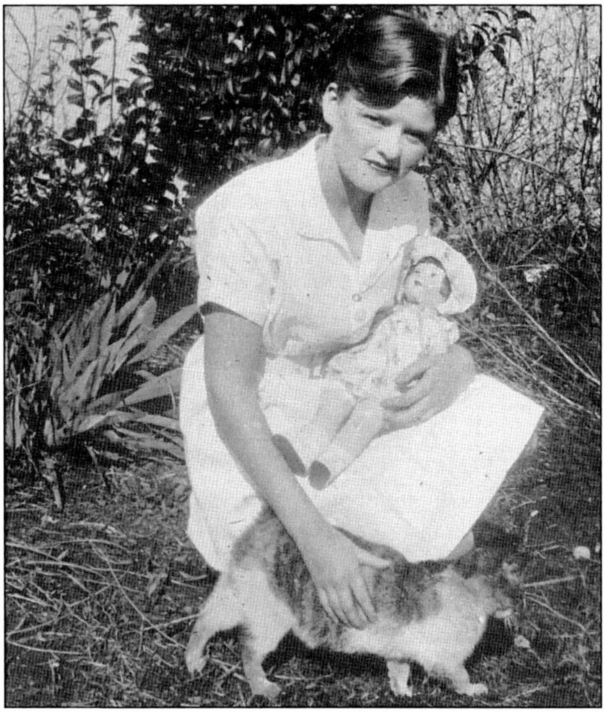

Gladys Allen began working at the New Holland Inn as a waitress in 1928. In 1930, she married Carl David Miller, a farm foreman who moved to New Holland from Hardin, Montana, when the Campbell Farming Company was contracted to run the farm in the lake bed. The wedding took place in the lobby of the New Holland Inn. (Courtesy of Patricia Auman, daughter of Gladys Allen.)

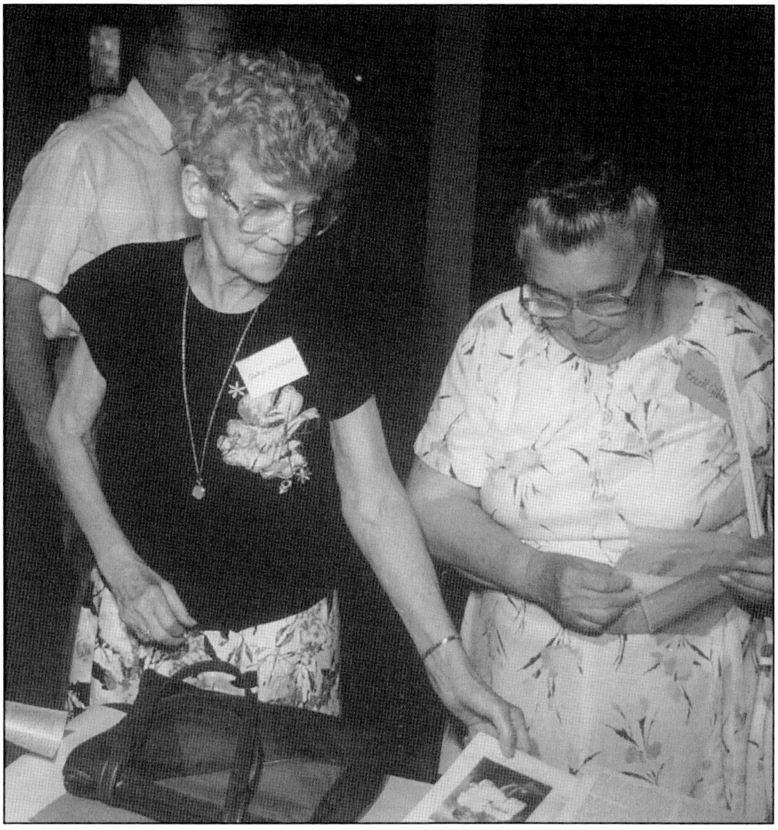

Gladys Allen (Miller) Williams (left) returned to New Holland in June of 1989 to attend a reunion for former employees of the companies involved in the drainage of Lake Mattamuskeet and enrollees of the two CCC Company 424 Camps that were in Hyde County from 1935 to 1942. On the right is Ercell Gibbs, a devoted local historian, of Hyde County. (Courtesy of Cliff Hollis.)

Five

North Carolina Farms Company Expands New Holland

North Carolina Farms Company, an Ohio corporation, acquired Lake Mattamuskeet from New Holland Farms, Inc. on March 11, 1918. North Carolina Farms Company was a subsidiary of the Columbus-based R.L. Dollings Company.

The new owners delayed beginning work on their Hyde County property until near the end of 1919 while they sold stock in the company to raise the necessary capital. In December 1919, the owners started a new Ohio corporation under the same name but with different stockholders. At the beginning of 1920, the drainage commissioners began pumping out the lake for the second time, and the new North Carolina Farms Company began further developments on the lake property.

North Carolina Farms Company built a railroad from a point in Washington County called Wenona to the pumping plant at New Holland. They built a dozen private homes for company employees, a boarding house, an automotive garage, a barber shop, a planing mill, a community water tower, a depot, a wharf at the pumping plant, several farm buildings, and other structures.

North Carolina Farms Company owned the lake property for seven years, but its accomplishments were limited to the first five. After investing about $3-4 million at the lake, the R.L. Dollings Company of Columbus, Ohio, declared bankruptcy, which included seven of its subsidiary companies. On September 1, 1923, the bankruptcy court placed North Carolina Farms Company in the hands of court-appointed receivers. Unable to collect drainage taxes and continue operations, the Mattamuskeet Drainage District was also turned over to receivers.

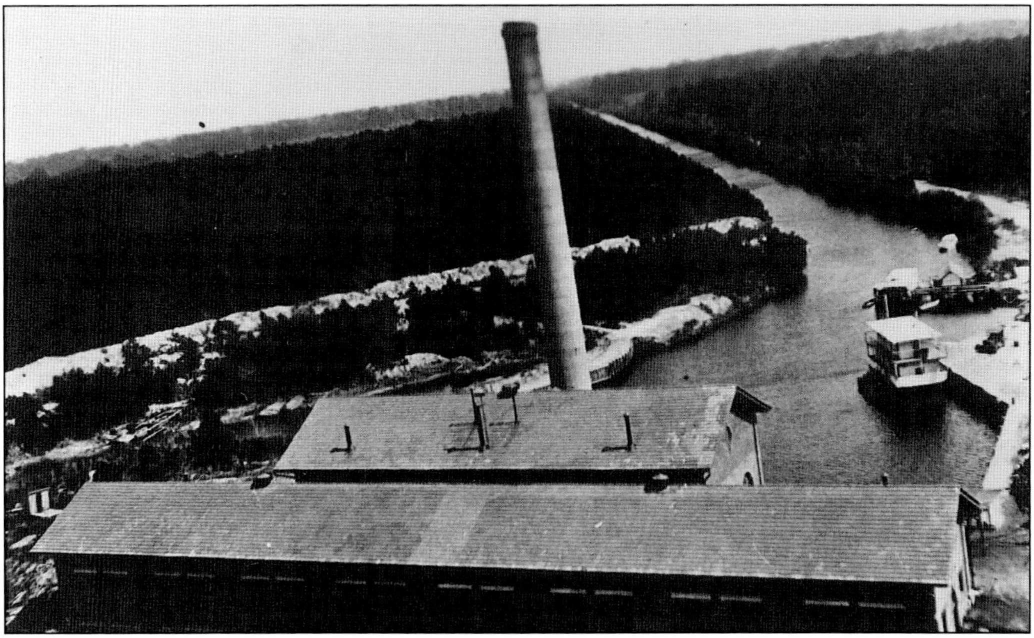

Throughout 1919, the drainage commissioners concentrated on getting the pumping plant operating again. It had been shut down for nearly two years after running almost continuously for 16 months. The plant required major repairs, and the canals had to be re-dredged to remove silt. This view of the pumping plant and Outfall Canal is looking south from the town water tank. (Courtesy of George R. Scott and Edna E. Harris.)

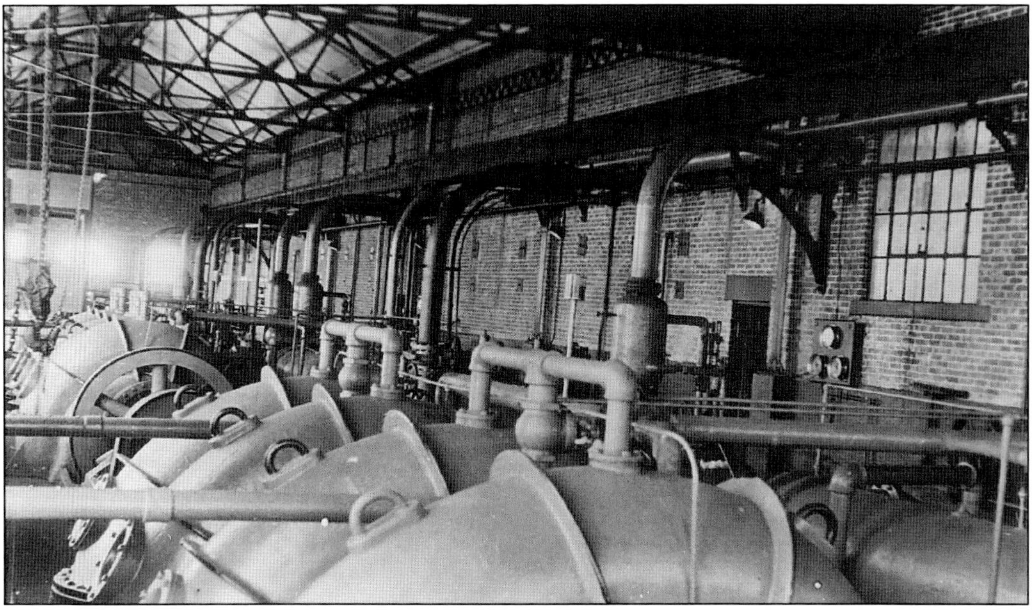

In their rush to get the pumping plant back into operation in 1919–1920, the drainage commissioners postponed installation of the new impellers designed to increase the efficiency of the pumps. This led to the same high fuel costs experienced in the first attempt to drain the lake and led to law suits over an increase in the drainage tax rate. (Courtesy of George R. Scott and Edna E. Harris.)

North Carolina Farms Company hired Karl Lewis Ponzer as its chief engineer on the entire lake development project. Ponzer advised the drainage commissioners on pumping and dredging issues and began addressing the engineering needs of the new owners of the lake. From the start, Ponzer enjoyed hunting and fishing in Hyde County. (Courtesy of Carolyn Ponzer Taylor.)

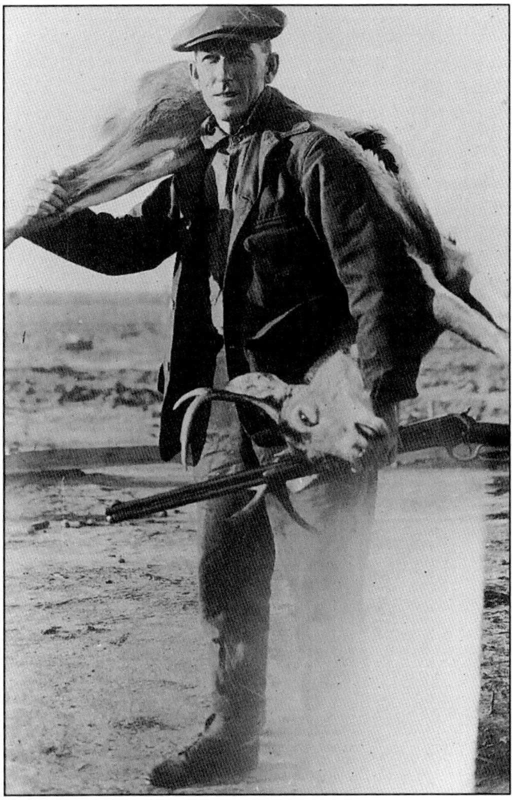

The lake bed owners needed a railroad to ensure the success of the New Holland project. There were no paved roads into Hyde County until 1927 and none to New Holland until much later. Dirt roads in Hyde County were often impassable during rainy periods. Travel by water was slow and was also affected by bad weather. (Courtesy of Carolyn Ponzer Taylor.)

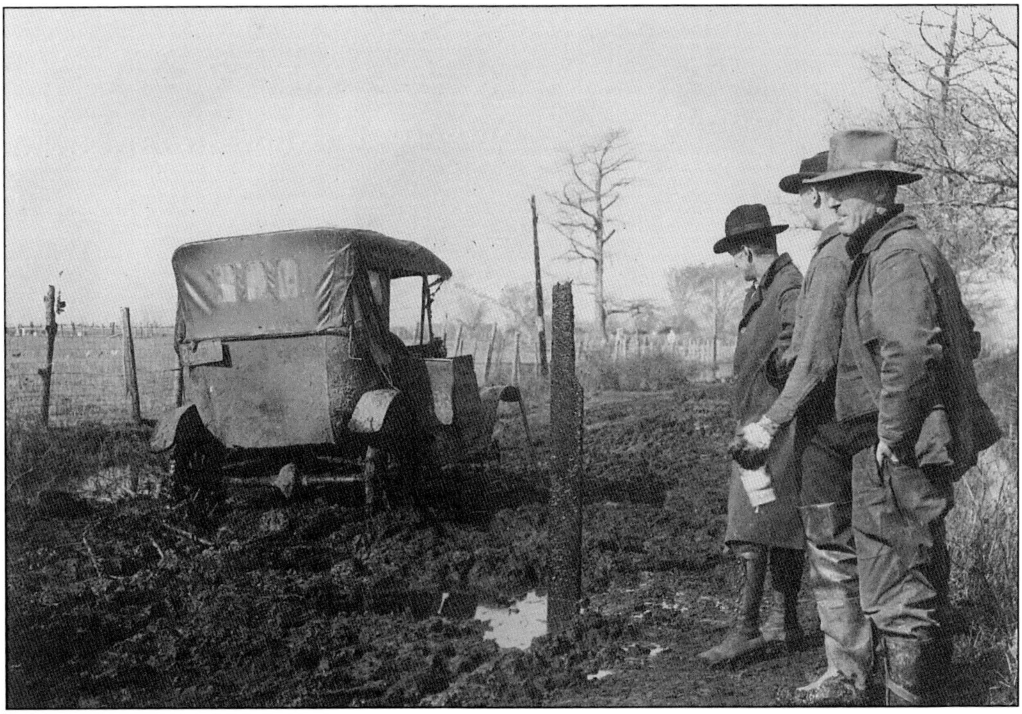

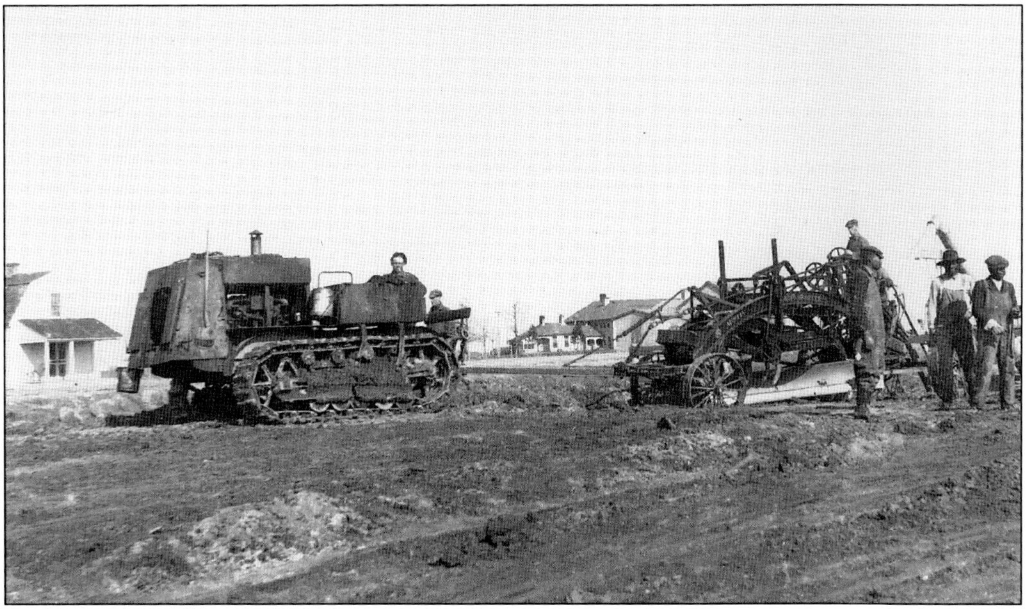

North Carolina Farms Company laid out and graded additional streets in New Holland during 1920–1923. The house on the left with the Dutch gambrel roof is one of the few buildings from this period that remains in Hyde County today. (Courtesy of Mattamuskeet National Wildlife Refuge, Donald E. Temple, manager.)

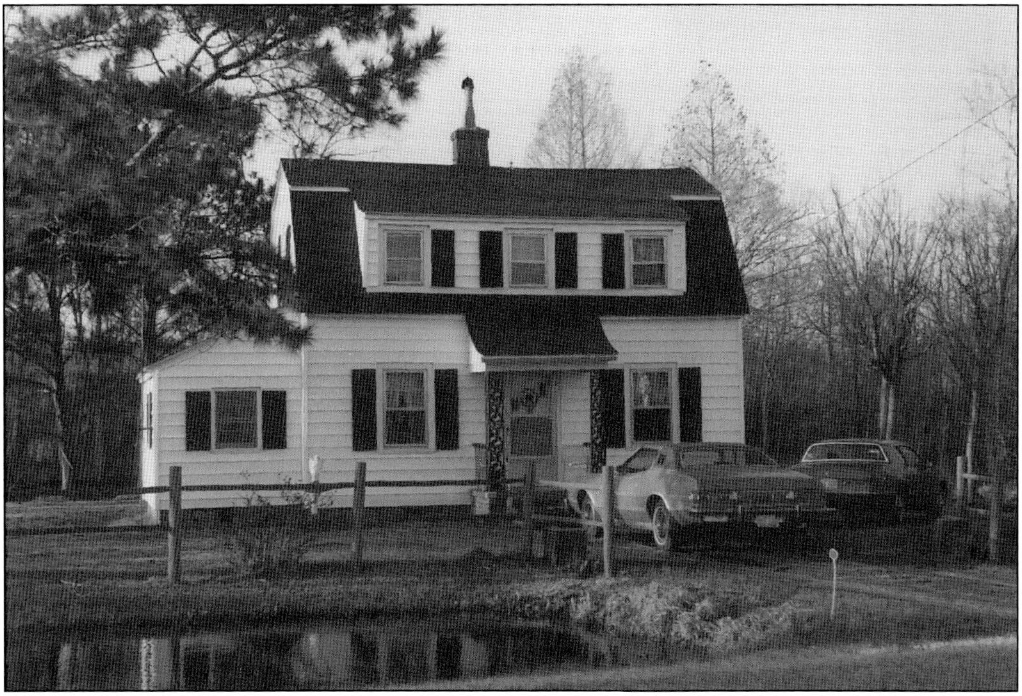

This house is now located on the north side of Highway 264 just east of the New Holland bridge that crosses Outfall Canal. It is one of a few houses from old New Holland that still survives today, and it was the only one in New Holland that had a Dutch gambrel roof. (Courtesy of Lewis Forrest.)

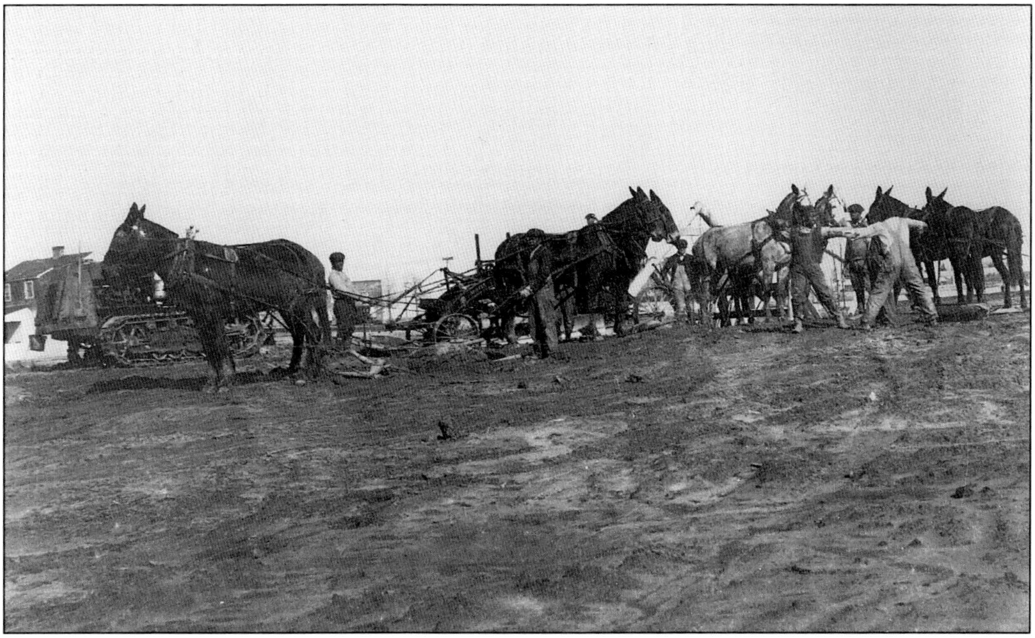

Here is another scene of the street construction in New Holland, around 1920–1923, on the south side of West Main Canal. The pumping plant, post office, depot, automotive garage, and planing mill were located on the south side of the canal. (Courtesy of Mattamuskeet National Wildlife Refuge, Donald E. Temple, manager.)

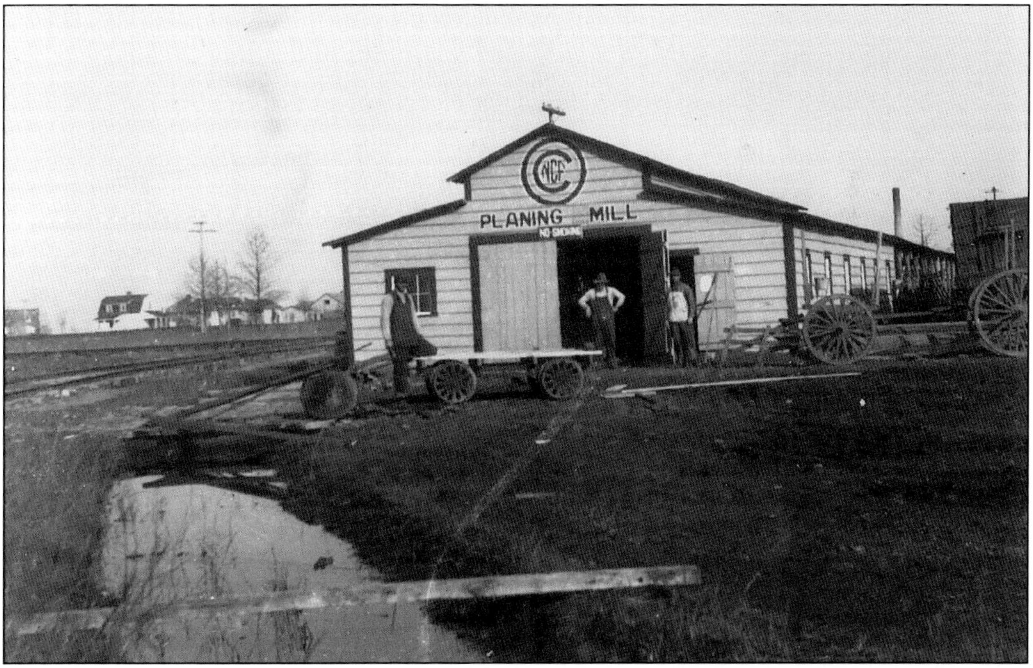

North Carolina Farms Company built a planing mill in New Holland around 1922, just west of the pumping plant. The smokestack of the pumping plant is in the background beyond the planing mill, and a boxcar is on a side track on the south side of the building. (Courtesy of Mattamuskeet National Wildlife Refuge, Donald E. Temple, manager.)

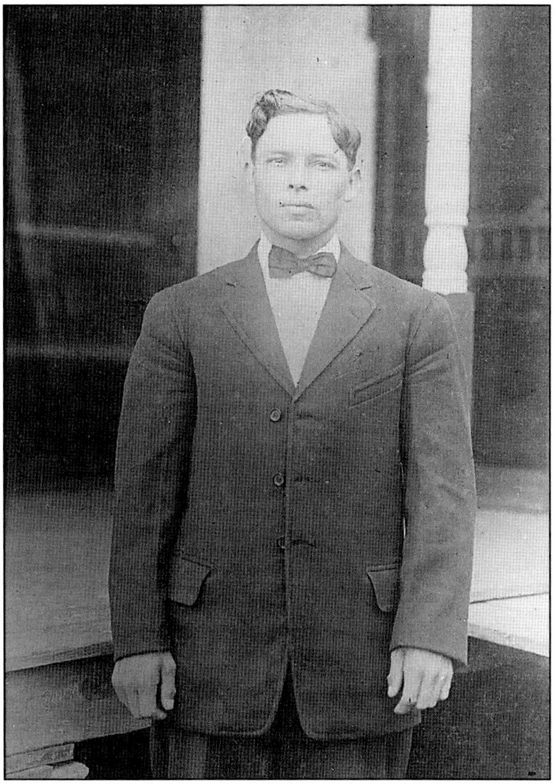

During the early 1920s, Ronald Otto Payne from Hyde County worked for North Carolina Farms Company as a bookkeeper and manager of the company store. He and his wife lived in the New Holland community. On April 24, 1921, Lida Everette Payne gave birth to the first baby born in New Holland after North Carolina Farms Company bought the lake. (Courtesy of Lizzie Mae Credle Britton.)

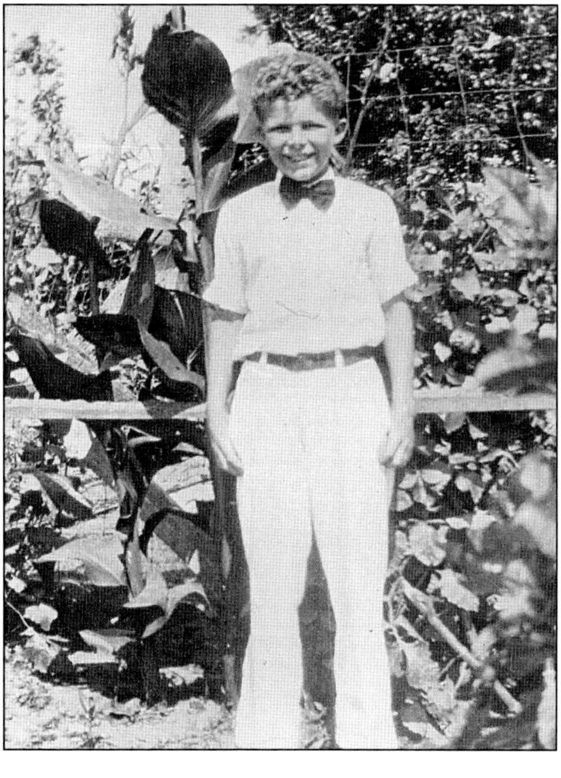

Oral history says that North Carolina Farms Company offered to pay Ronald and Lida Payne to name their baby boy "New Holland" Payne. An April 1921 accounting entry in New Holland Farms Company books mentions a $25 check written to "Baby Payne." Tragically, Holland was killed at the age of 21 in a diving accident while swimming with friends at Elizabeth City. (Courtesy of Lizzie Mae Credle Britton.)

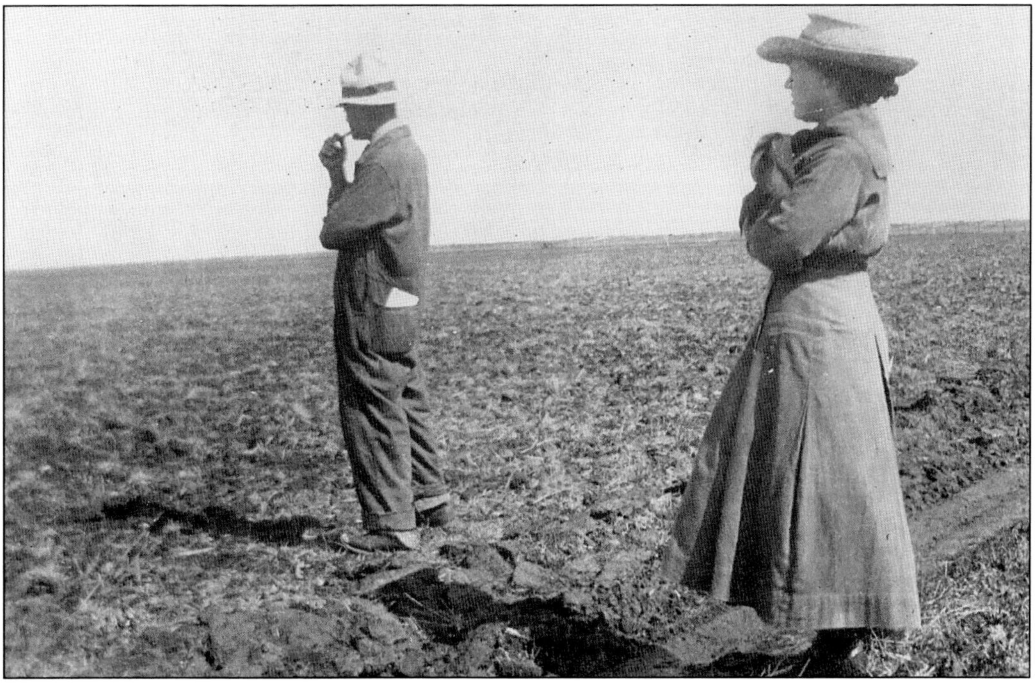

Karl and Grace Ponzer look at the dry lake bed. In 1916, D.N. Graves wrote, "You don't have to clear off a tree or stump, a bush or stone. You can set a plow in your land the day after you buy it and begin farming. It is largely a deep, rich, sandy loam, of the right texture to cultivate easily and drain readily." (Courtesy of Carolyn Ponzer Taylor.)

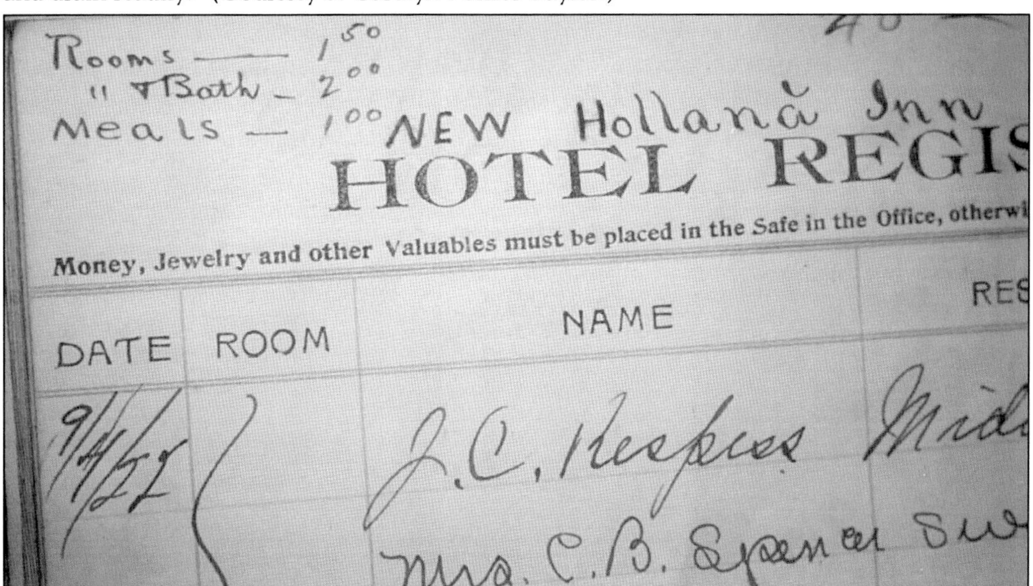

North Carolina Farms Company continued to operate the New Holland Inn. In 1922, a person could stay in the New Holland Inn with room and board for $40 per month. Daily room rates ran $1.50 for a room, $2 for a room with private bath, and $1 per day for meals. (Register courtesy of the North Carolina Division of Archives and History; photo courtesy of Cliff Hollis.)

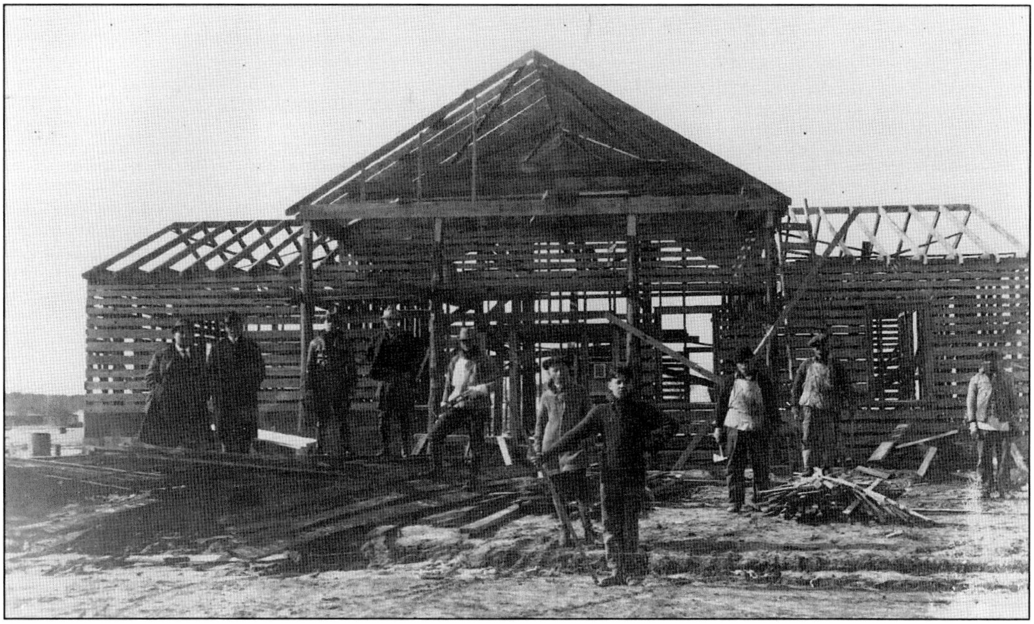

Local carpenters and laborers worked for the companies that owned the lake bed, building houses, digging ditches, operating farm equipment, and doing whatever else needed to be done. Here, a group of local carpenters poses with some of North Carolina Farms Company people in front of the framed skeleton of the new administration building in 1922. (Courtesy of Mattamuskeet National Wildlife Refuge, Donald E. Temple, manager.)

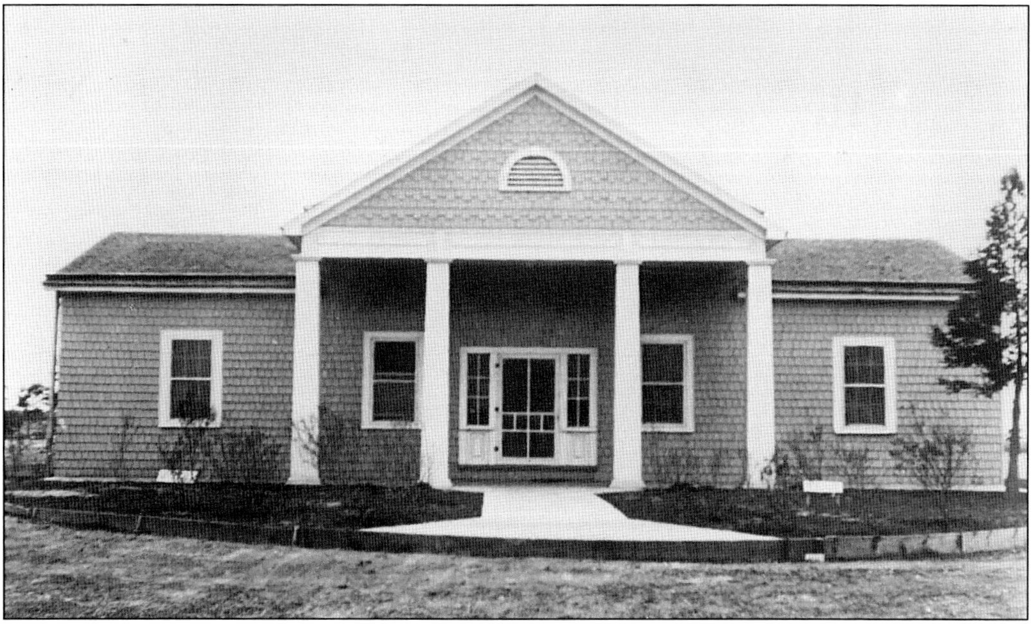

This attractive administrative building was constructed by North Carolina Farms Company in 1922. They budgeted $5,000 for the building, and it served as their main office at New Holland as well as the office of their successor, the New Holland Corporation. CCC enrollees demolished the building in June of 1937 (see page 97). (Courtesy of George R. Scott and Edna E. Harris.)

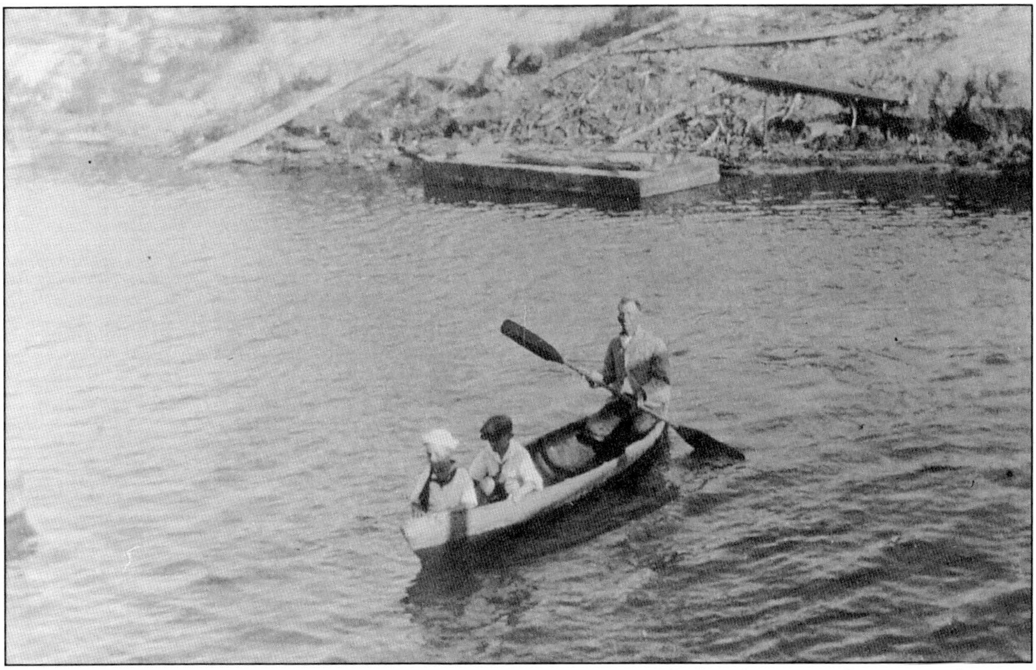

Surviving photos that depict the Ponzer family's life in New Holland suggest that every day was an exciting learning experience for young Karl Jr. and John Ponzer. Both Mr. and Mrs. Ponzer were 32 years old when they moved to New Holland in 1918, and their sons were seven and five, respectively. The Ponzers remained at New Holland until 1924. (Courtesy of Carolyn Ponzer Taylor.)

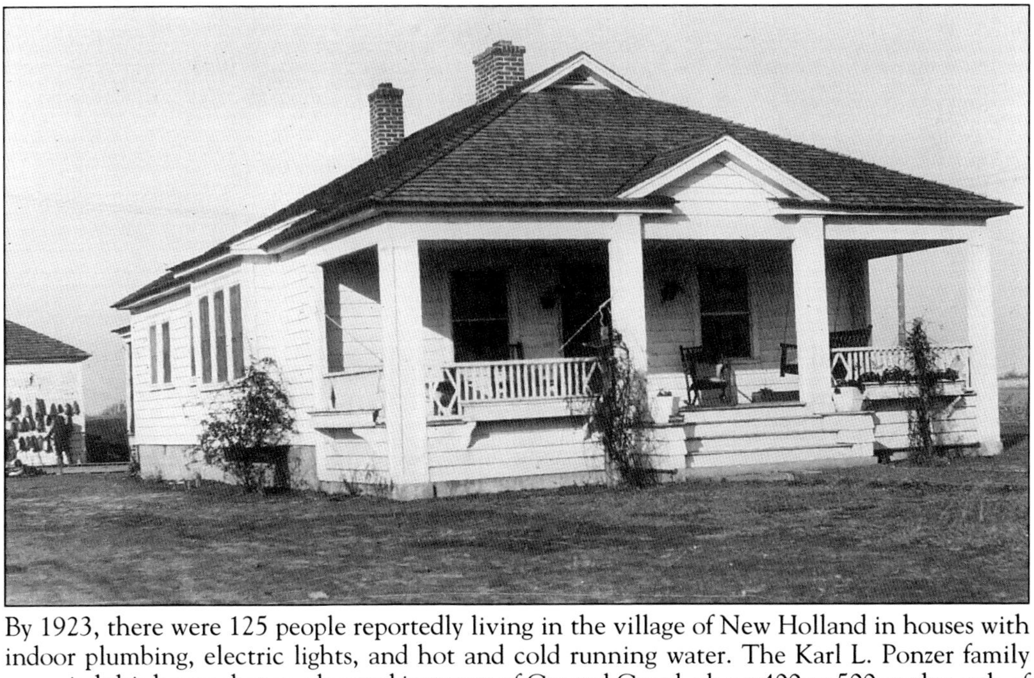

By 1923, there were 125 people reportedly living in the village of New Holland in houses with indoor plumbing, electric lights, and hot and cold running water. The Karl L. Ponzer family occupied this house that was located just west of Central Canal, about 400 to 500 yards north of the pumping plant. (Courtesy of Carolyn Ponzer Taylor.)

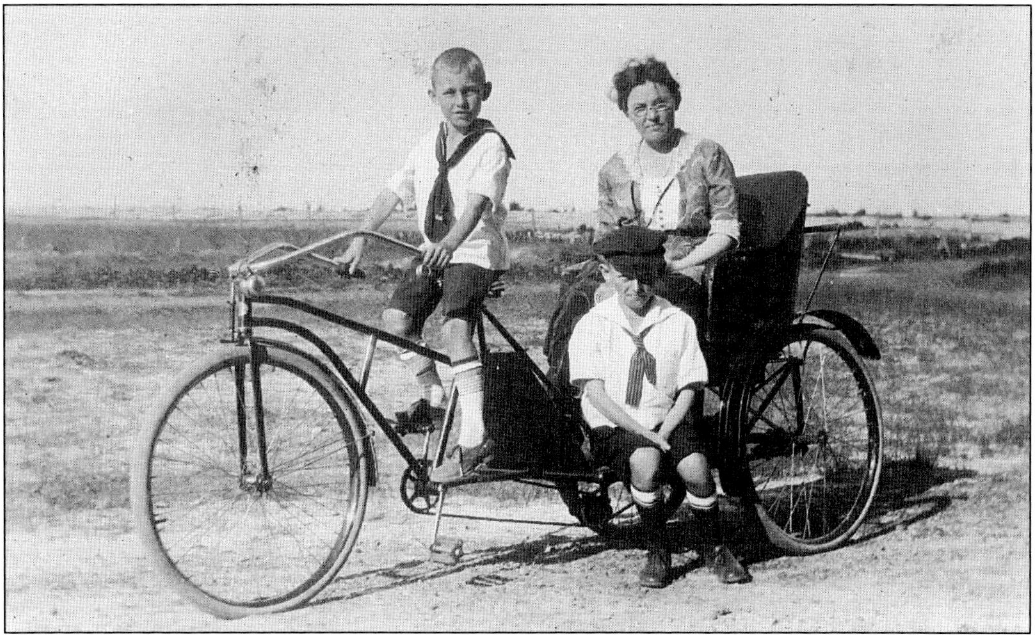

Grace Short Ponzer, the wife of Karl L. Ponzer, and their two sons, Karl Lewis Jr. (left) and John Lewis ride on an interesting bicycle sulky. The boys attended nearby Weston School, a two-room frame structure where oral history says their mother was the principal and taught the older students *c.* 1920–1922. (Courtesy of Carolyn Ponzer Taylor.)

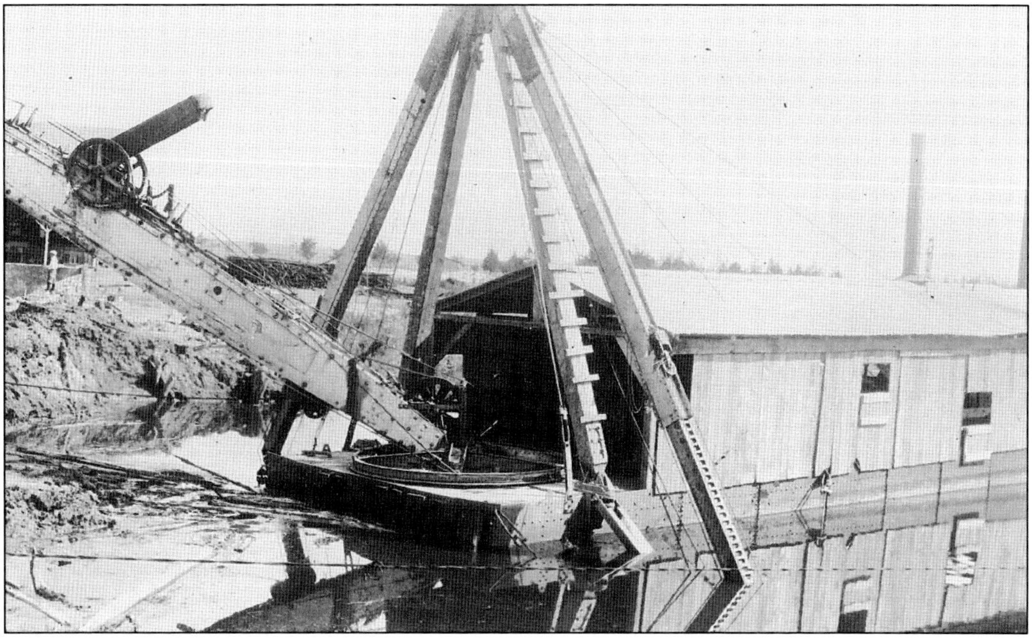

North Carolina Farms Company declared bankruptcy in September of 1923. The drainage commissioners shut down the pumping plant and ordered a "bypass" opened around the plant to allow gravity drainage of all water above sea level. This prevented most of the New Holland town site from flooding and allowed residents to continue living in the village. (Courtesy of Carolyn Ponzer Taylor.)

Six

New Holland, Higginsport, and Mt. Vernon Railroad

New Holland Farms, Inc. had planned a railroad from the pumping plant to connect with the Norfolk Southern Railroad Company, but they sold out in 1918 before building the railroad line. Between 1919 and 1921, the second private owners of the lake property, the Ohio-based North Carolina Farms Company, built and equipped a 35-mile private railroad from Wenona in Washington County to the pumping plant at New Holland at a cost of $977,353.

North Carolina Farms Company contracted the Foundation Company of New York to build the line. Engineers began surveying the line before pumping resumed in 1920 following a shut down due to inefficiencies in the pumping plant design and a World War I coal embargo. The railroad bed ran through the west end of the lake, with 9 miles directly in the lake bottom.

In September 1923, North Carolina Farms Company went into bankruptcy, marking the end of public passenger service on the railroad. August Heckscher bought the bankrupt assets of North Carolina Farms Company in May 1925. He limited the use of the railroad to hauling freight for the commercial farming operation his company developed in the lake bed, plus transporting an occasional business associate or hunter to New Holland.

All railroad service in and out of Hyde County permanently ceased when the lake drainage project ended in late 1932. A year later, a company from Birmingham, Alabama, salvaged the tracks and rolling stock. This was the only public railroad to ever serve Hyde County.

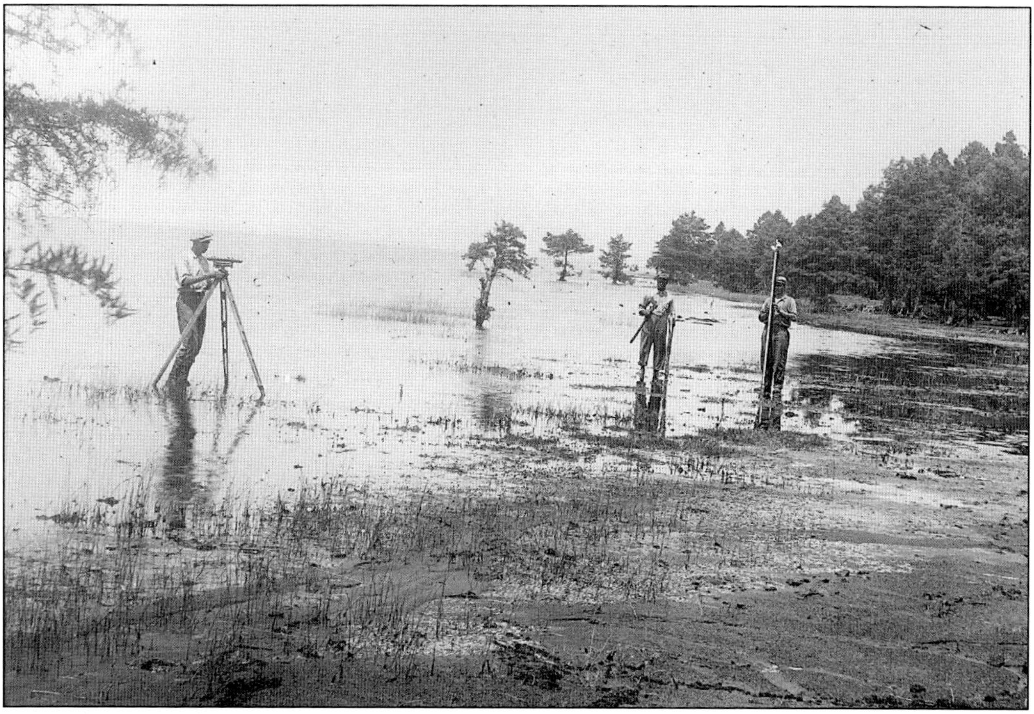

Around 1920, Karl L. Ponzer and his crew surveyed a railroad line from New Holland to Wenona in Washington County. Ponzer gained the favor of the people of Hyde County by laying out the 35-mile railroad line with minimal encroachment on valuable farmland. In 1923, the people of the Shallop Creek community in western Hyde County changed their community's name to "Ponzer." (Courtesy of Carolyn Ponzer Taylor.)

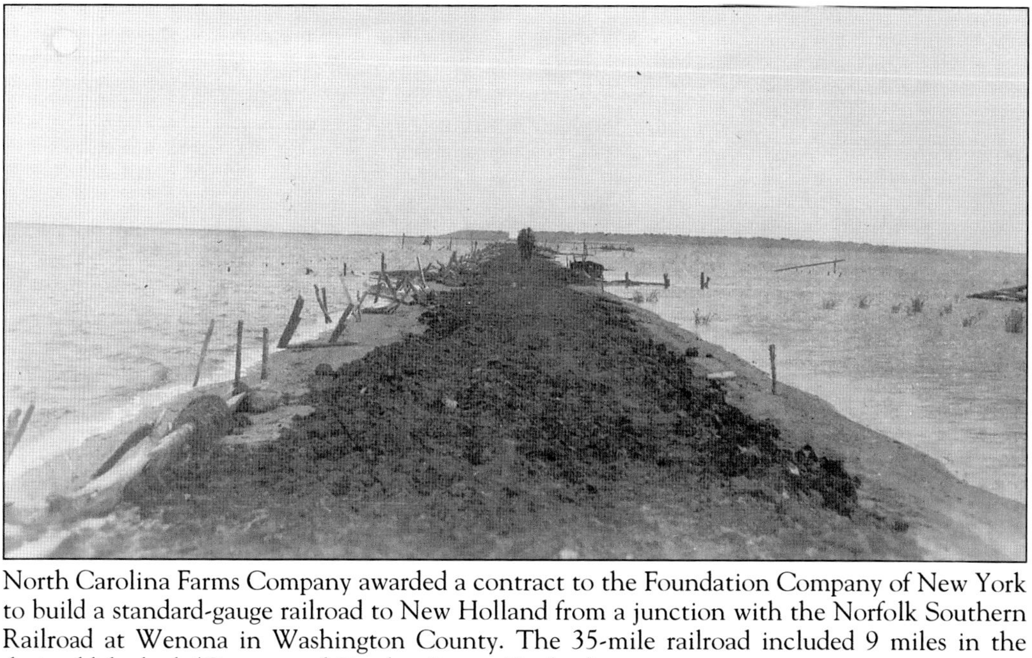

North Carolina Farms Company awarded a contract to the Foundation Company of New York to build a standard-gauge railroad to New Holland from a junction with the Norfolk Southern Railroad at Wenona in Washington County. The 35-mile railroad included 9 miles in the drained lake bed. (Courtesy of Carolyn Ponzer Taylor.)

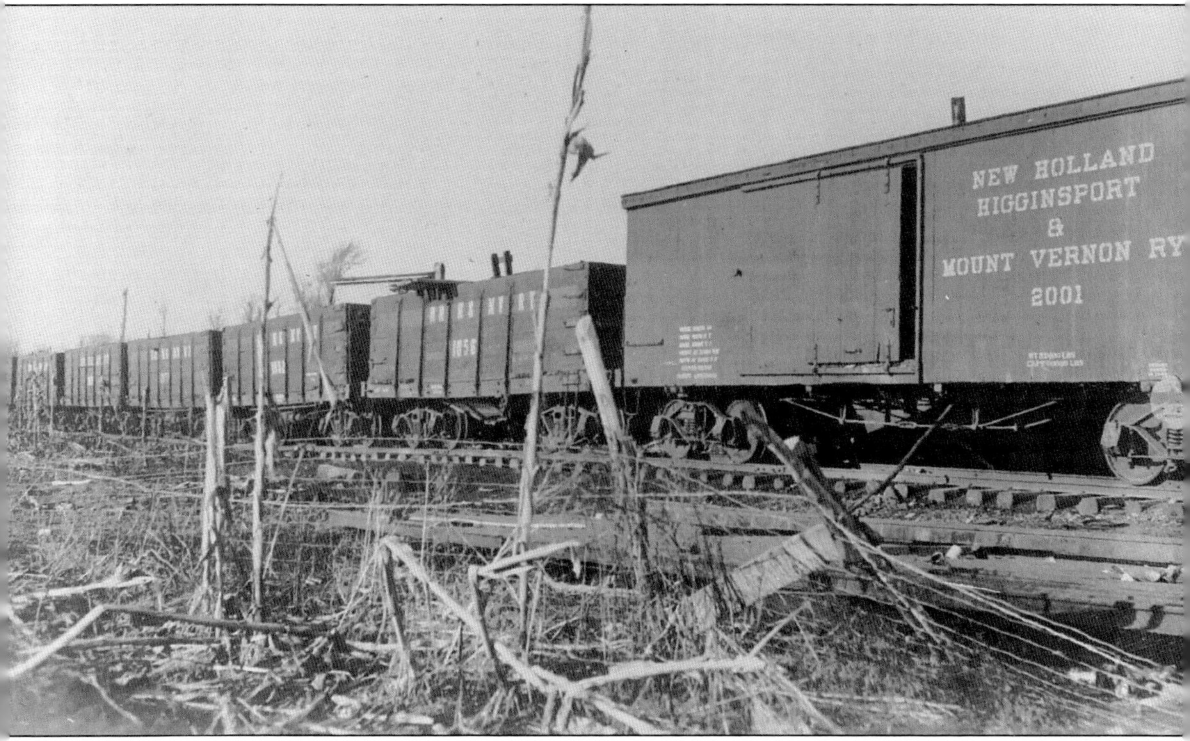

At a Farmers' Institute meeting in Swan Quarter, North Carolina, on September 30, 1908, J.O. Wright, the chief drainage engineer of the U.S. Department of Agriculture, made the following statement: "The area of the county is 247,680 acres. If it were all drained and cultivated as it can be and it produced corn at 40 bushels to the acre, it would yield 9,907,200 bushels. If this were loaded on box cars at 400 bushels per car, it would require 24,768 cars to haul the product away. Allowing 23 cars to a train and running three trains a day, it would require one year's time to remove the crop. Selling this corn at 60 cents a bushel, it would bring a revenue to the county of $5,944,320." (Courtesy of Carolyn Ponzer Taylor.)

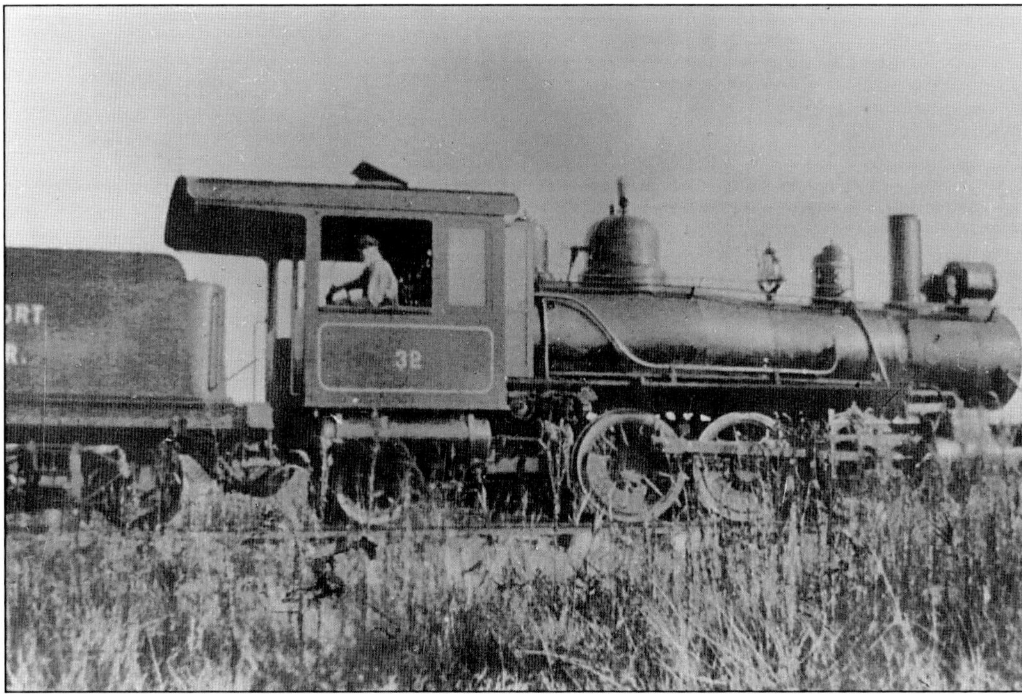

On April 20, 1921, North Carolina Farms Company bought a used Baldwin 2-6-2 Prairie type coal-powered locomotive, #41292, road #32, class 1020 1/2 D 21, built in 1914. They bought the engine from Roper Lumber Company for $8,500. (Courtesy of Sybble Smithwick.)

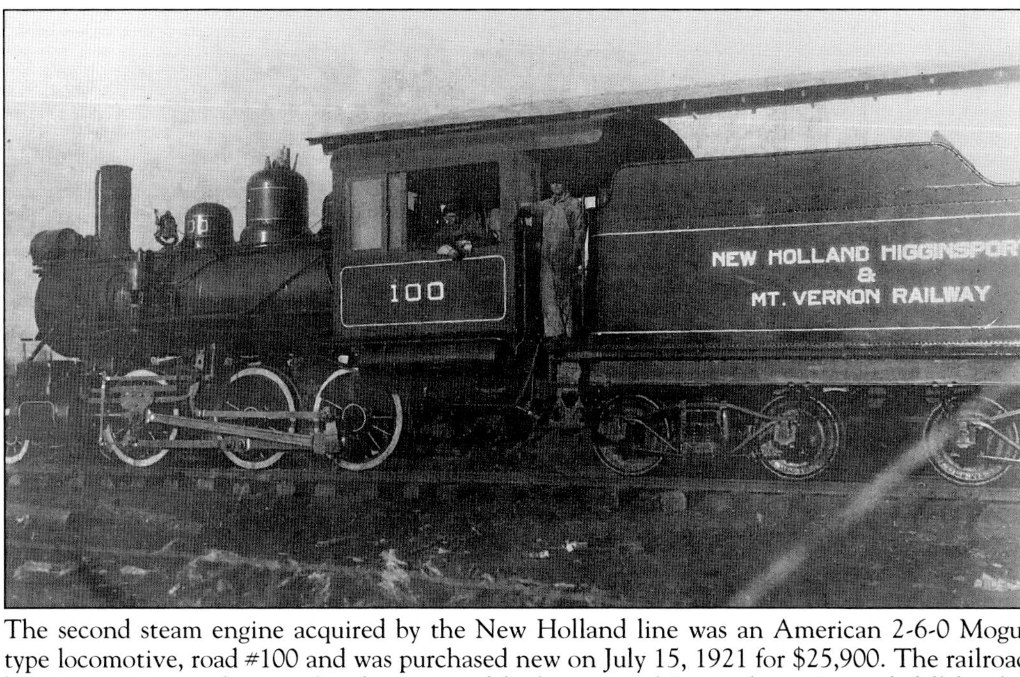

The second steam engine acquired by the New Holland line was an American 2-6-0 Mogul type locomotive, road #100 and was purchased new on July 15, 1921 for $25,900. The railroad began operating on the completed portions of the line around September 1921, with full freight, passenger, and mail service by the beginning of 1922. (Courtesy of Carolyn Ponzer Taylor.)

Rufus W. Smithwick from Shallop Creek Community (later called Ponzer Community) was a locomotive engineer on the New Holland Railroad. This photo is of Smithwick (center) and two unidentified friends on engine #100. (Courtesy of Sybble Smithwick.)

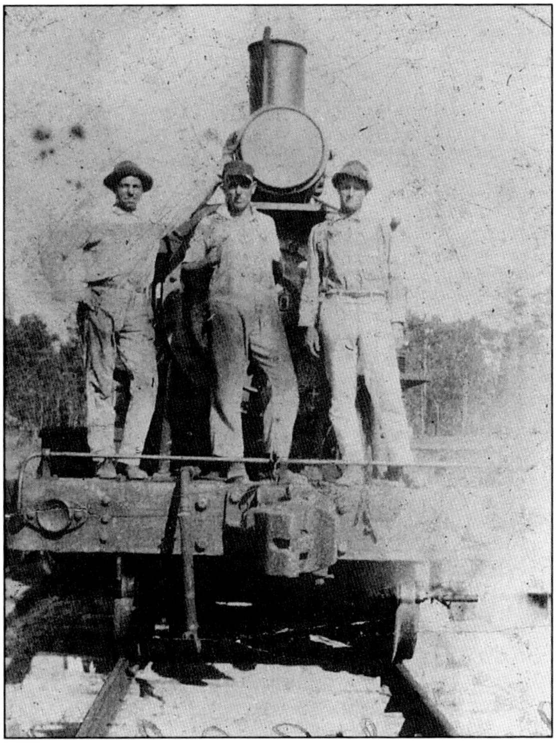

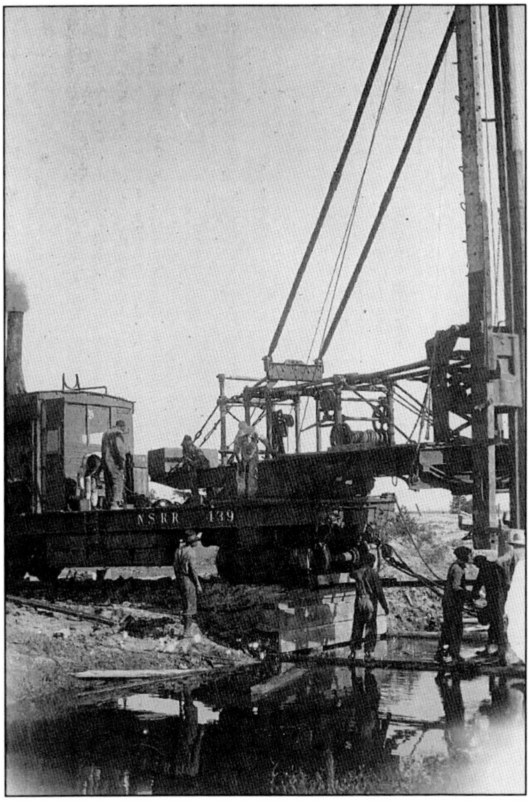

It was necessary to drive pilings and build trestles across each canal in the west half of Lake Mattamuskeet, as well as across existing creeks and canals from the west end of the lake to the terminus at Wenona. A trestle was added across the Intracoastal Waterway after the U.S. Army Corps of Engineers excavated the huge canal through Hyde County in 1926 and 1927. (Courtesy of Carolyn Ponzer Taylor.)

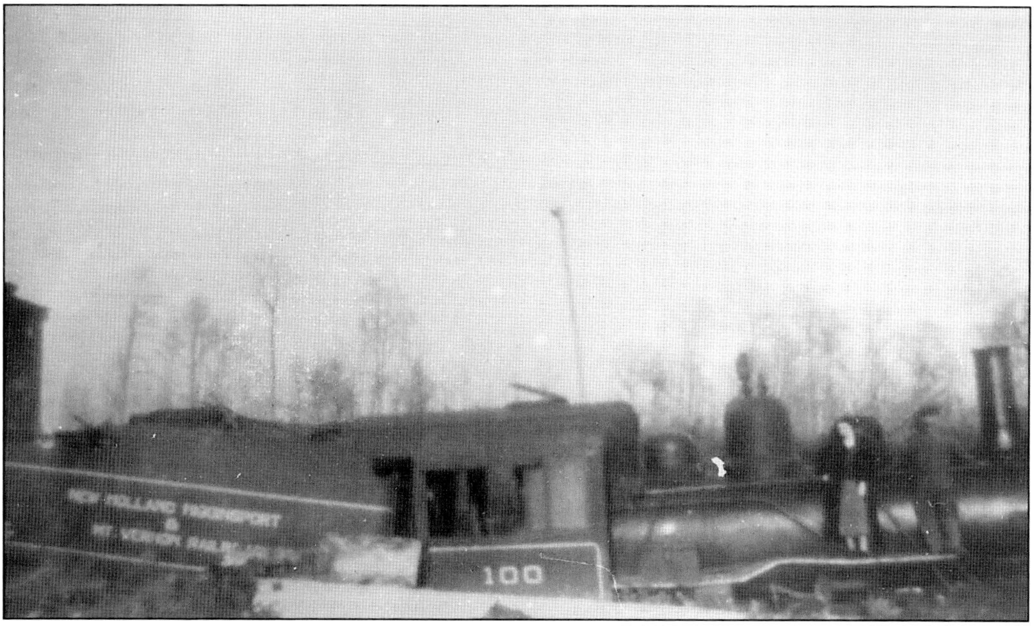

Sometime in 1922 or 1923, engine #100 jumped the tracks and went into the marsh south of Wenona in the vicinity of "C Canal," near the western end of the New Holland, Higginsport and Mt. Vernon Railroad line. (Courtesy of Geoffrey and Gerald Furbee.)

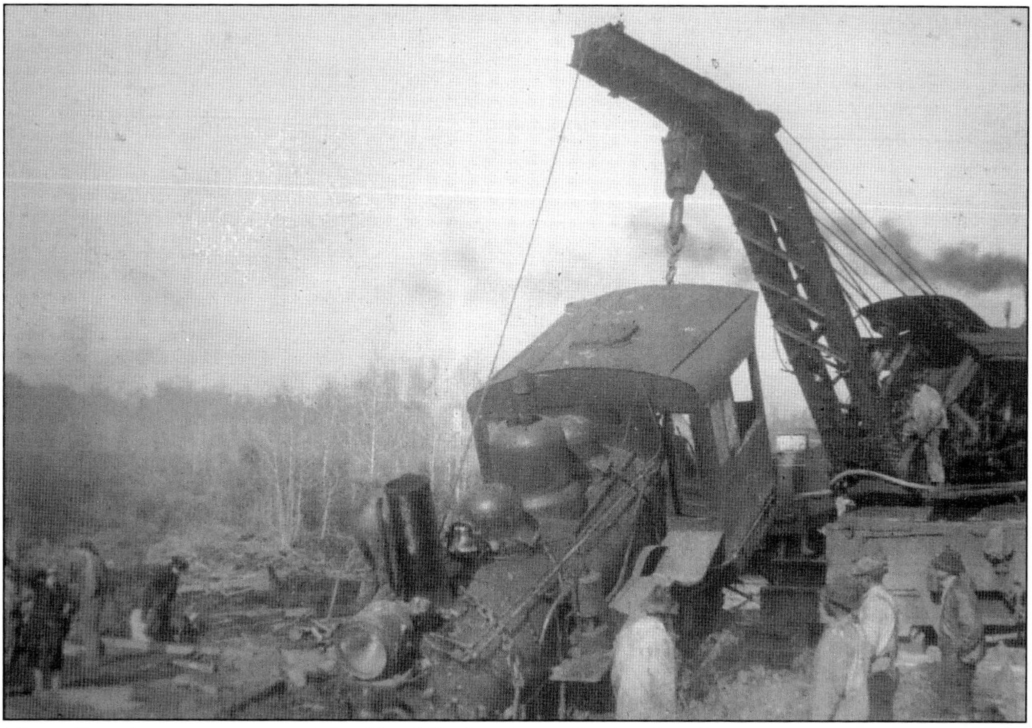

The railroad owners arranged for Norfolk Southern Railroad to bring in a rail crane mounted on a flatcar to lift the huge steam locomotive back onto the tracks. (Courtesy of Geoffrey and Gerald Furbee.)

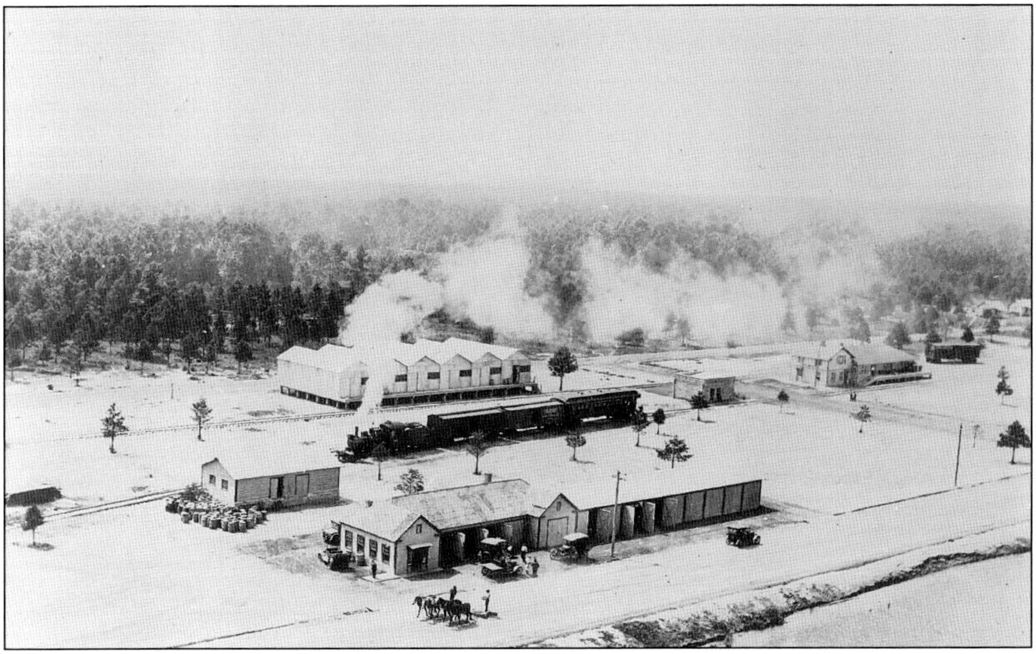

The New Holland, Higginsport and Mt. Vernon Railroad locomotive #100 arrives in New Holland on a snowy day. Snow is rare in Hyde County. The engine is towing two boxcars and one passenger car. Note the 12-bay automotive garage in the foreground, the depot in the upper right, and the workmen leveling the main road, c. 1923. (Courtesy of Carolyn Ponzer Taylor.)

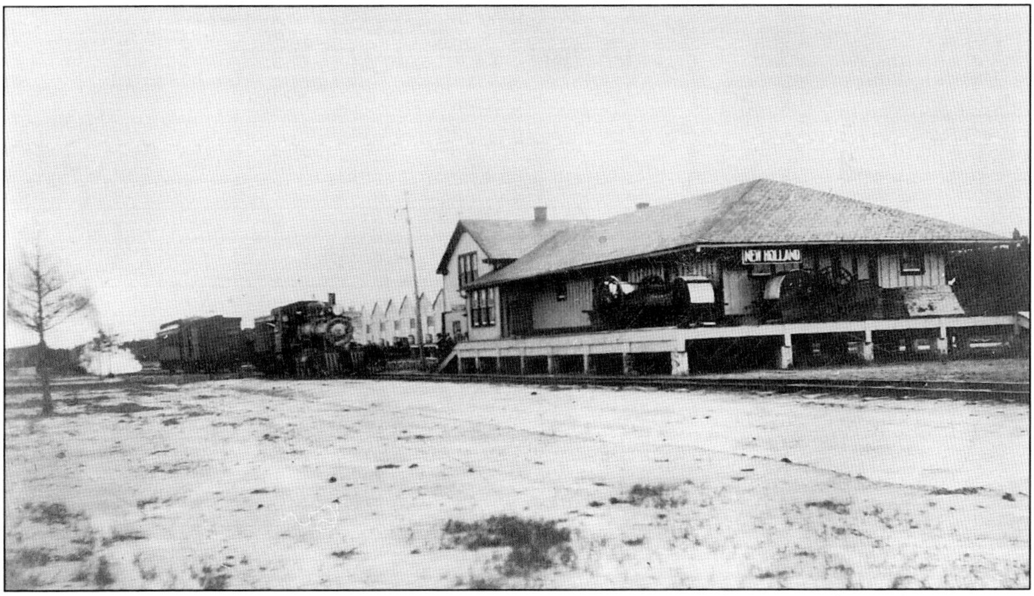

The depot at New Holland is seen here with engine #100 heading west from the pumping plant. In the October 1921 issue of "The Official Guide of the Railways and Steam Navigation Lines of the United States," the New Holland railroad advertised, "Daily schedule between New Holland, N. C., and all points in connection with the Norfolk Southern Railroad and lines diverging." (Courtesy of Sybble Smithwick.)

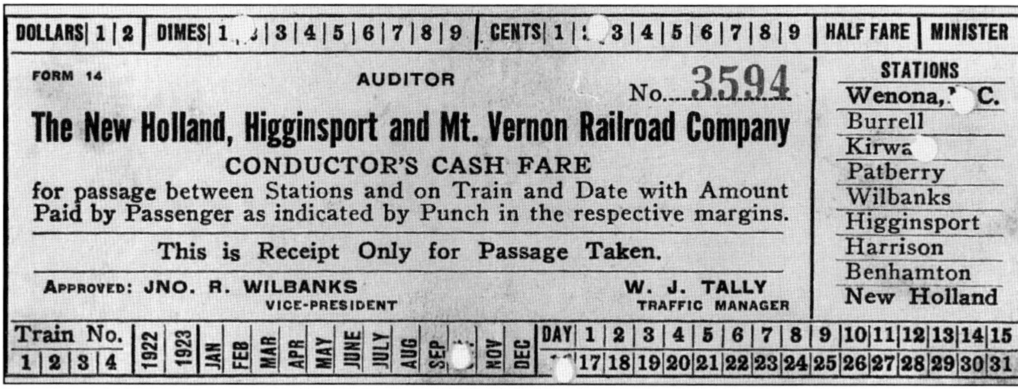

DOLLARS | 1 | 2 | DIMES | 1 | 2 | 3 | 4 | 5 | 6 | 7 | 8 | 9 | CENTS | 1 | 2 | 3 | 4 | 5 | 6 | 7 | 8 | 9 | HALF FARE | MINISTER

FORM 14

AUDITOR

No. 3594

The New Holland, Higginsport and Mt. Vernon Railroad Company

CONDUCTOR'S CASH FARE

for passage between Stations and on Train and Date with Amount Paid by Passenger as indicated by Punch in the respective margins.

This is Receipt Only for Passage Taken.

APPROVED: JNO. R. WILBANKS, VICE-PRESIDENT

W. J. TALLY, TRAFFIC MANAGER

STATIONS
Wenona, N. C.
Burrell
Kirwan
Patberry
Wilbanks
Higginsport
Harrison
Benhamton
New Holland

Train No. 1 | 2 | 3 | 4 | 1922 | 1923 | JAN | FEB | MAR | APR | MAY | JUNE | JULY | AUG | SEP | OCT | NOV | DEC

DAY | 1 | 2 | 3 | 4 | 5 | 6 | 7 | 8 | 9 | 10 | 11 | 12 | 13 | 14 | 15 | 16 | 17 | 18 | 19 | 20 | 21 | 22 | 23 | 24 | 25 | 26 | 27 | 28 | 29 | 30 | 31

Leaving New Holland, the train stopped at Benhampton, Harrison, Higginsport, Wilbanks, Patberry, and Kirwin before reaching its final stop at Wenona. The stops were named for principal investors in North Carolina Farms Company. Some stops had a water tank for the steam engines and a ramp for loading passengers and cargo. (Courtesy of Gloria Gray and Elbert Jones.)

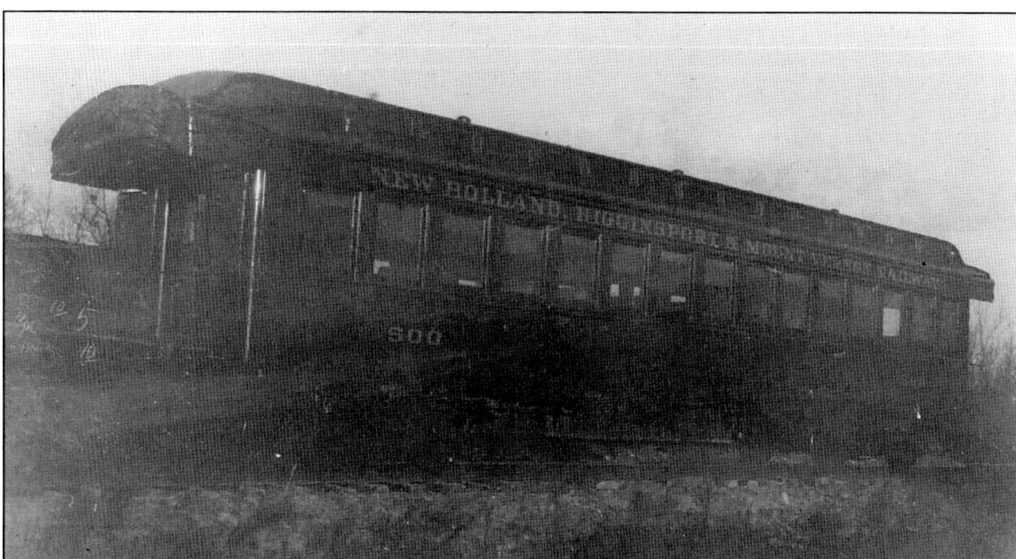

When North Carolina Farms Company went into bankruptcy in 1923, scheduled passenger service on the New Holland line ended forever. The next owner, New Holland Corporation, chose not to operate the railroad as a public carrier. (Courtesy of Carolyn Ponzer Taylor.)

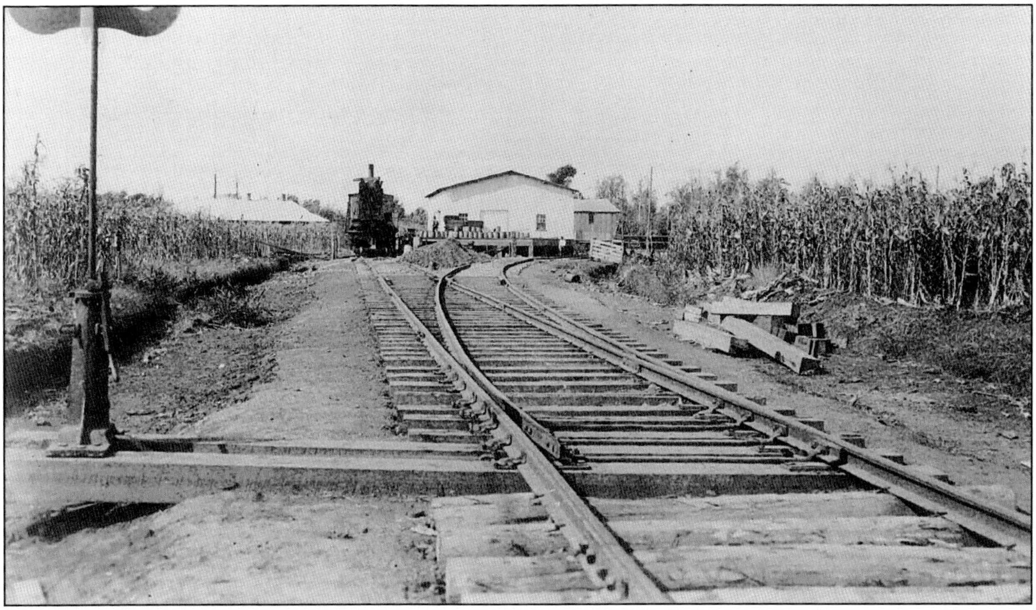

The train station at Wenona in Washington County included a storage barn, a small house for the train crew, a larger house called the "hotel" for other railroad personnel and occasional overnight guests, and an office for Ernest Rose, who was the Norfolk Southern Railroad Company agent. (Courtesy of Carolyn Ponzer Taylor.)

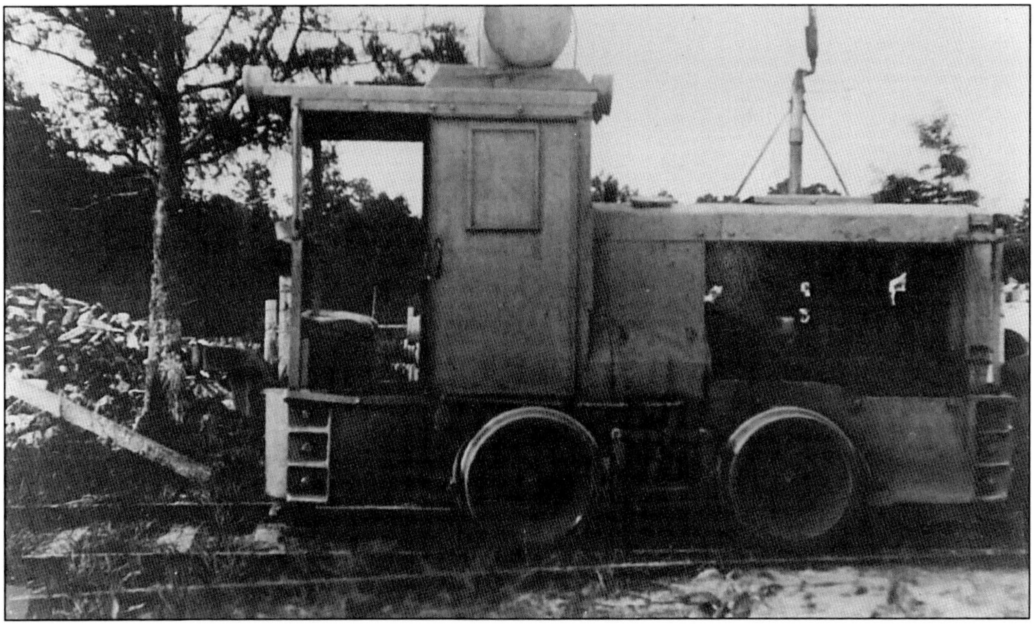

In January 1927, New Holland Corporation purchased this used 8-ton Plymouth gasoline-powered locomotive for $3,325. It became the main engine on the line, replacing the steam locomotives. The corporation eliminated scheduled passenger service and used the train strictly for hauling coal, freight, and farm products. (Courtesy of George R. Scott and Edna E. Harris.)

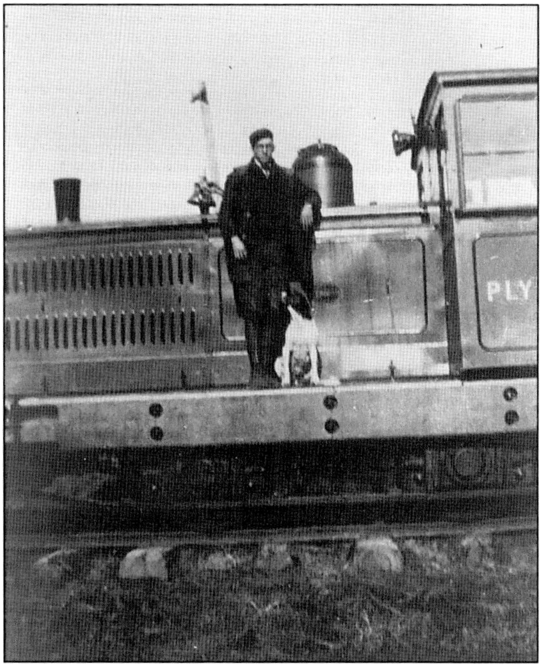

New Holland Corporation bought this 25-ton Plymouth diesel electric engine in the late 1920s, but it proved to be too heavy to be practical for the New Holland line. George R. Scott, shown in this photograph with his dog, was in charge of the New Holland Railroad. (Courtesy of Lennie Jones Christenson.)

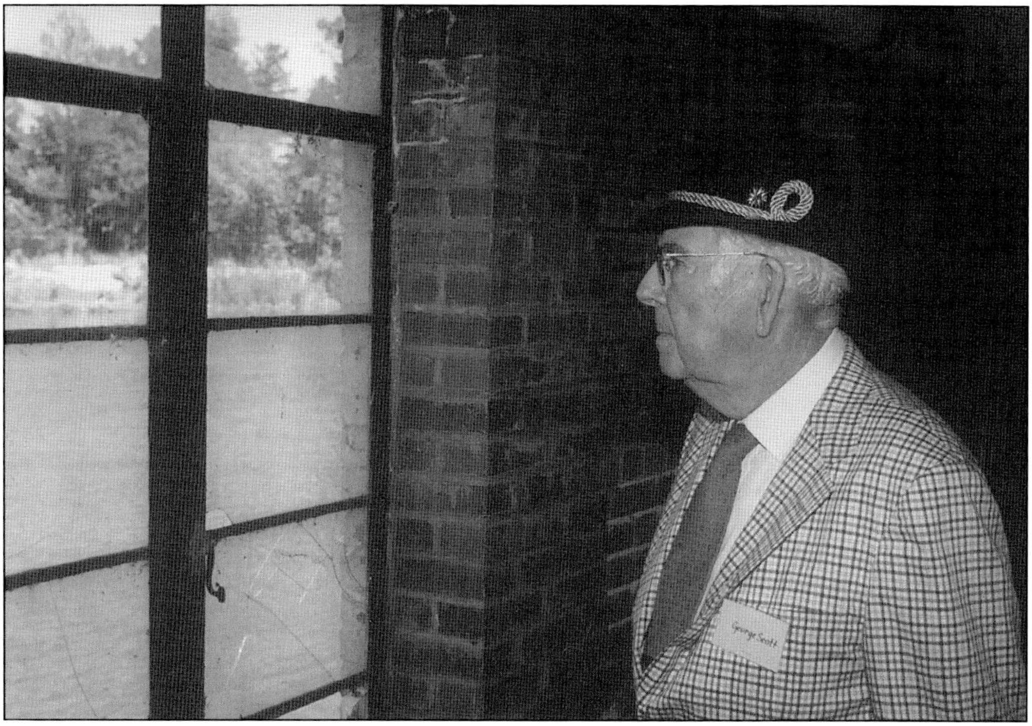

George R. Scott moved to New Holland in 1927, about a year after he earned his civil engineering degree from North Carolina State College (later University). He began as timekeeper for the New Holland Railroad. In 1928, Scott's title changed to general manager of the line. This photo was made at Lake Mattamuskeet in 1989, when Scott attended a reunion of former employees of New Holland Corporation. (Courtesy of Cliff Hollis.)

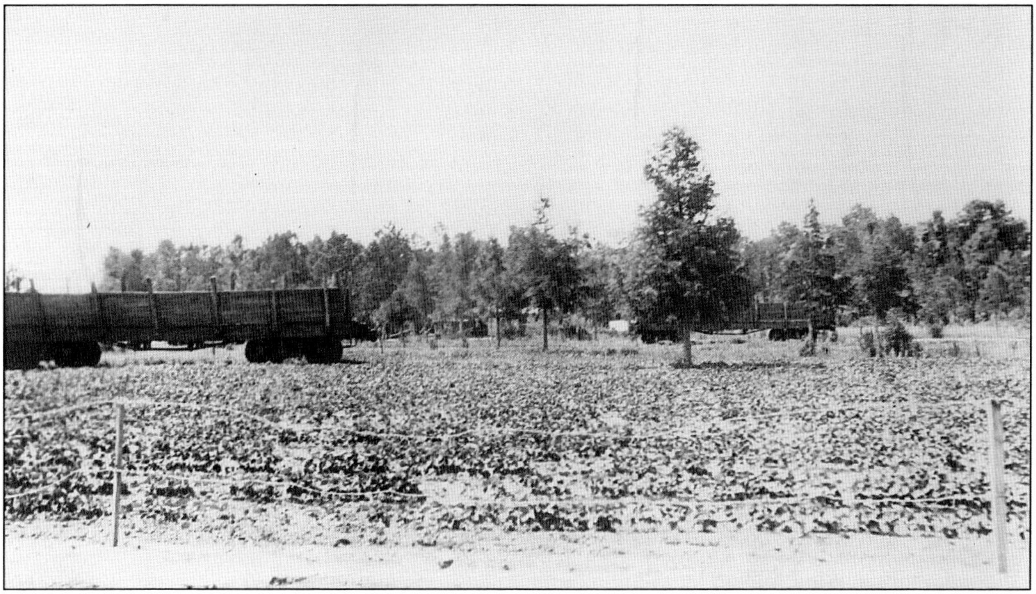

By the end of 1927, the small Plymouth engine was moving 200 tons of coal per week from Wenona to New Holland for the pumping plant. The drainage commissioners specified that coal had to be delivered in low-sided gondola cars to facilitate manual unloading. (Courtesy of Hal Swindell.)

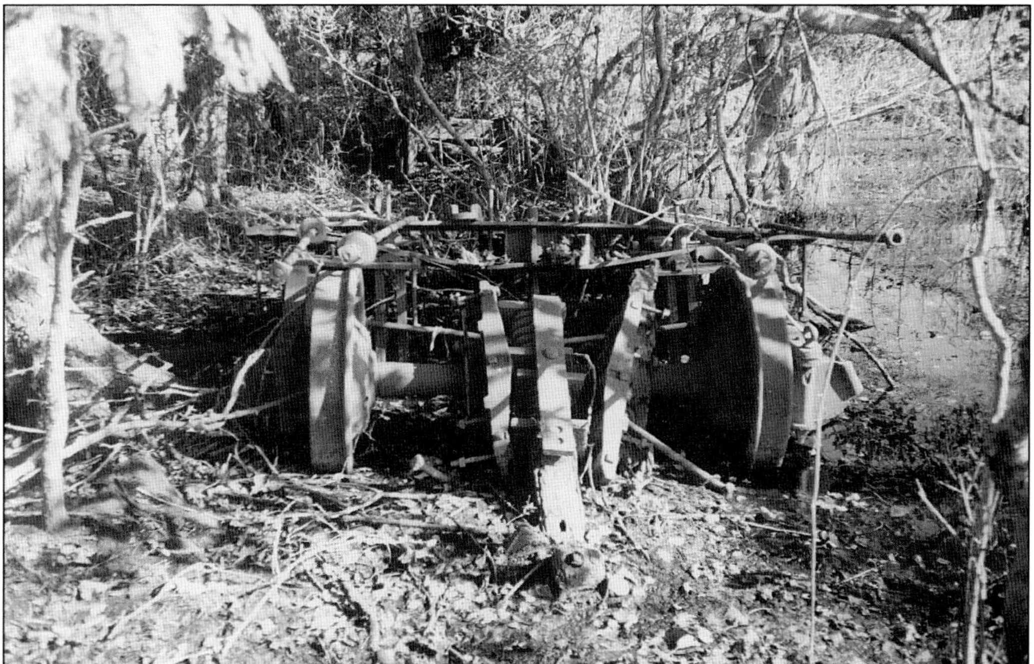

There are five islands in the west end of Lake Mattamuskeet. On old maps, they are called Heron Bay Island, Big Island, Head of Lake Island, House Island, and Topping Island. This October 1998 photo shows the remains of three gondola train cars rusting away on one of these islands. The cars transported coal to the pumping plant in the late 1920s. (Courtesy of Lewis Forrest.)

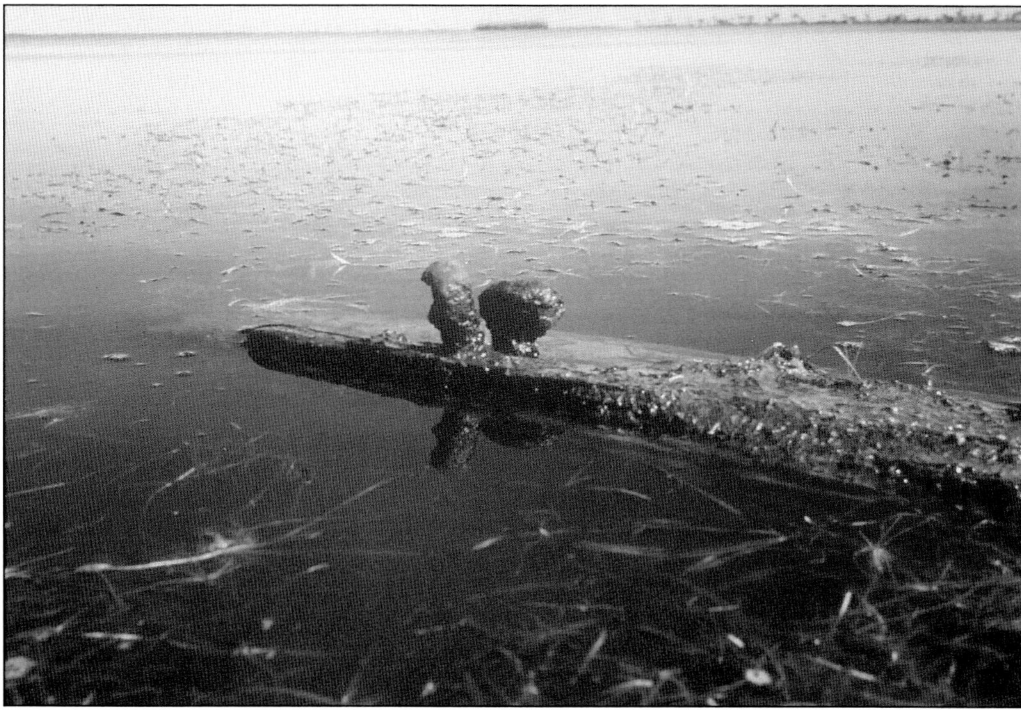

The railroad included 9 miles of track laid directly in the lake bed. When the drainage commissioners shut down the pumps in 1932 for the final time, that section of the railroad was soon under 1-2 feet of water. New Holland Corporation sold the rails and rolling stock for salvage. It is still possible to find red-heart Cyprus cross ties in the lake bed. (Courtesy of Cliff Hollis.)

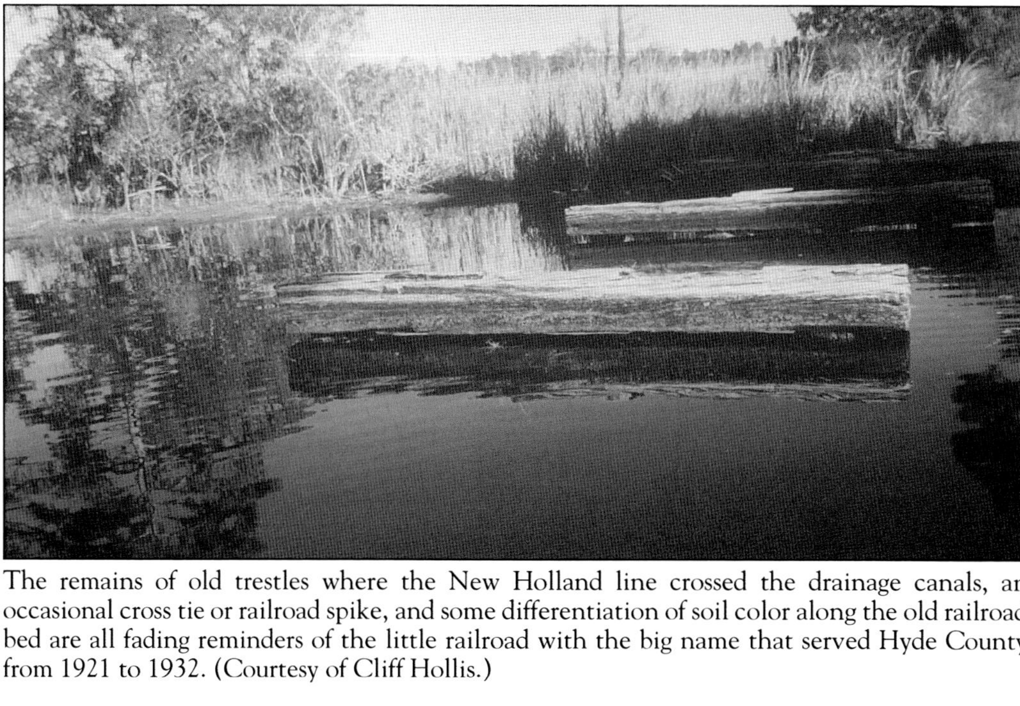

The remains of old trestles where the New Holland line crossed the drainage canals, an occasional cross tie or railroad spike, and some differentiation of soil color along the old railroad bed are all fading reminders of the little railroad with the big name that served Hyde County from 1921 to 1932. (Courtesy of Cliff Hollis.)

Seven

New Holland Corporation Farms the Dry Lake Bed

On May 19, 1925, August Heckscher of New York City, a wealthy real estate developer, purchased the bankrupt assets of North Carolina Farms Company. For $200,000, August Heckscher bought the 48,830-acre lake property, the New Holland Inn, the boarding house, the planing mill, the garage, the houses in New Holland, the general store, the usable equipment on the premises, and the New Holland Railroad that had cost nearly $1 million to build and equip.

Heckscher incorporated the new venture as New Holland Corporation and established a corporate office in New York City. He hired E.C. Stuckless as president to run the New York office and Douglas Nelson Graves as vice president and general manager to run the operation at New Holland. When Graves returned to the lake property in September of 1925, he brought back the vision for the lake development that he left behind in 1918.

Heckscher abandoned the earlier plan of subdividing the drained lake bed and selling it as a real estate project. Instead, he decided to turn the dry lake bed into a huge commercial farm.

New Holland Corporation paid the delinquent drainage taxes of North Carolina Farms Company that were incurred in buying the property and assets. Graves reorganized the board of drainage commissioners. At their first meeting under this period, the commissioners elected Graves as chairman. They began getting the pumps overhauled and back into operation. In 1926, the pumps drained Lake Mattamuskeet for the third and final time.

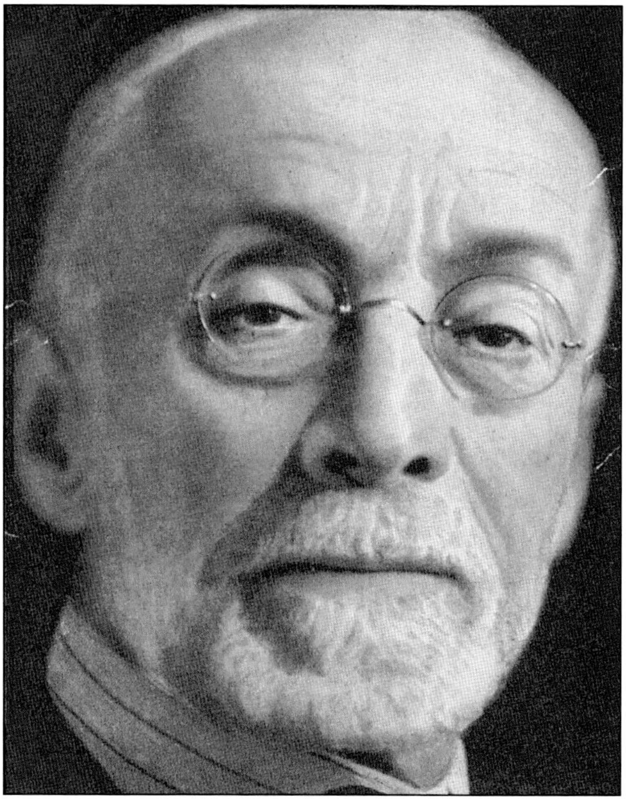

August Heckscher, a German from Hamburg, immigrated to the United States in 1867 at the age of 19. He became a multimillionaire because of his shrewd business skills, and when he bought Lake Mattamuskeet when he was 77 years old, he already owned major interests in a number of large corporations and was in the midst of a successful commercial real estate "second career" in New York City. (From the Mattamuskeet Records.)

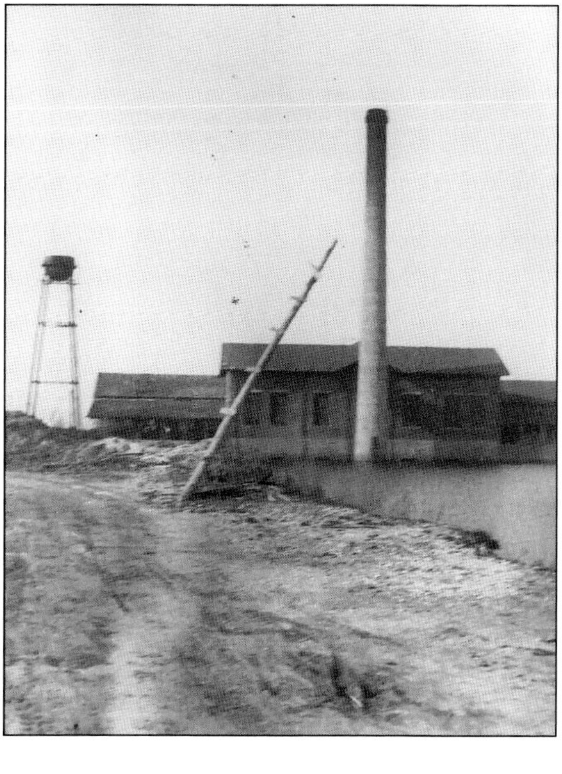

The only structure in New Holland that August Heckscher did not acquire ownership of in the purchase of the lake property was the pumping plant. The plant always belonged to the Mattamuskeet Drainage District. (Courtesy of Leon Ballance.)

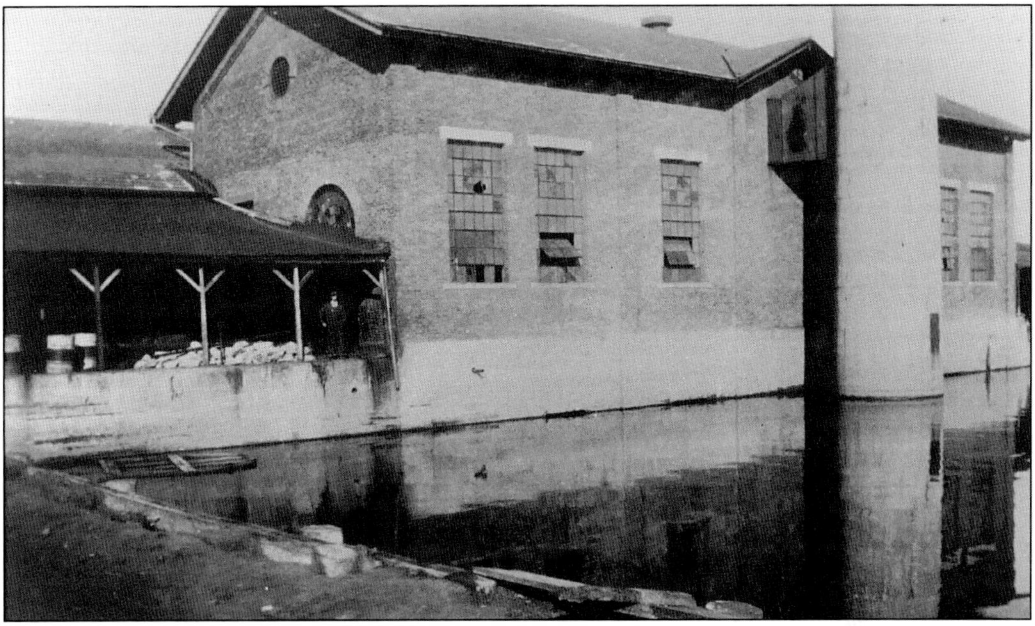

D.N. Graves returned to Hyde County in September 1925 as vice president and general manager of New Holland Corporation. With new money in the district from the New Holland Corporation, Graves quickly reorganized the drainage commissioners, and the court released the district from the receivers. The new drainage board elected Graves chairman and began planning how to get the pumps running again. (Courtesy of Lennie Jones Christenson.)

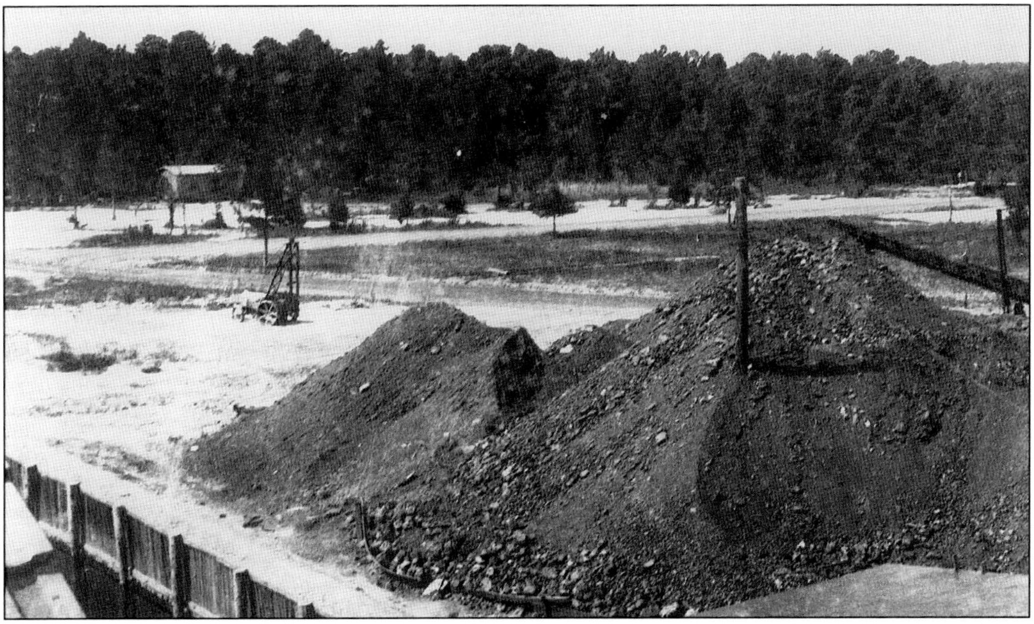

The commissioners paid overdue accounts carried forward from the bankrupt situation, hired a chief engineer for the pumping plant, began repairing the pumps, and began stockpiling coal (pictured here) at New Holland so there would be no delay in draining the lake as soon as the plant could begin operations. (Courtesy of Mattamuskeet National Wildlife Refuge, Donald E. Temple, manager.)

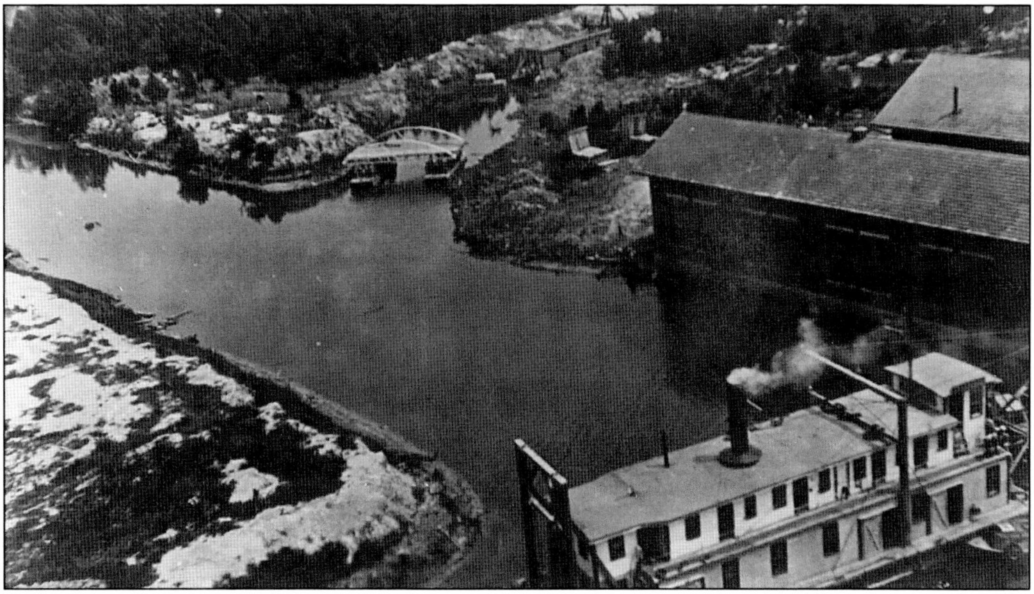

In late 1925, the drainage commissioners signed a dredging contract with S.J. Grove & Sons Company, of Minneapolis, Minnesota, who subcontracted the work to their partners, Wilson Brothers (John and Ernest Wilson). The commissioners directed the contractor to remove a silt bar that was blocking the mouth of Outfall Canal and then begin repairing other canals in the district. (Courtesy of George R. Scott and Edna E. Harris.)

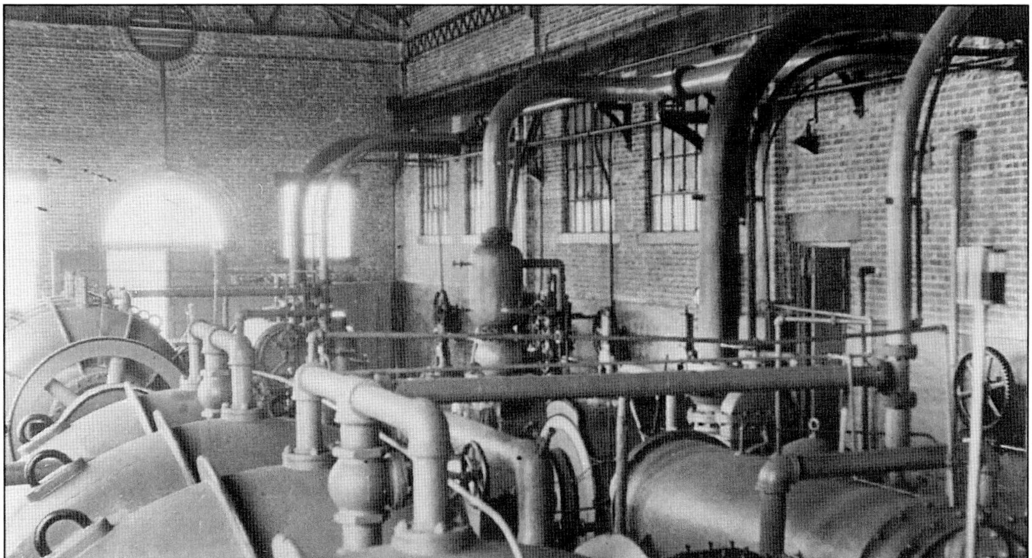

Before the district resumed pumping in 1926, Morris Machine Works and Erie City Iron Works installed the new impellers that were promised in 1917. This increased the pumps' performance to 1,200,000 gallons per minute, 33 percent above the contract specifications and 182 percent above the 1916–1917 performance. This involved 16 cast-iron impellers, 48 inches in diameter, 26 inches thick, and weighing about 1,800 pounds each. (Courtesy of Lennie Jones Christenson.)

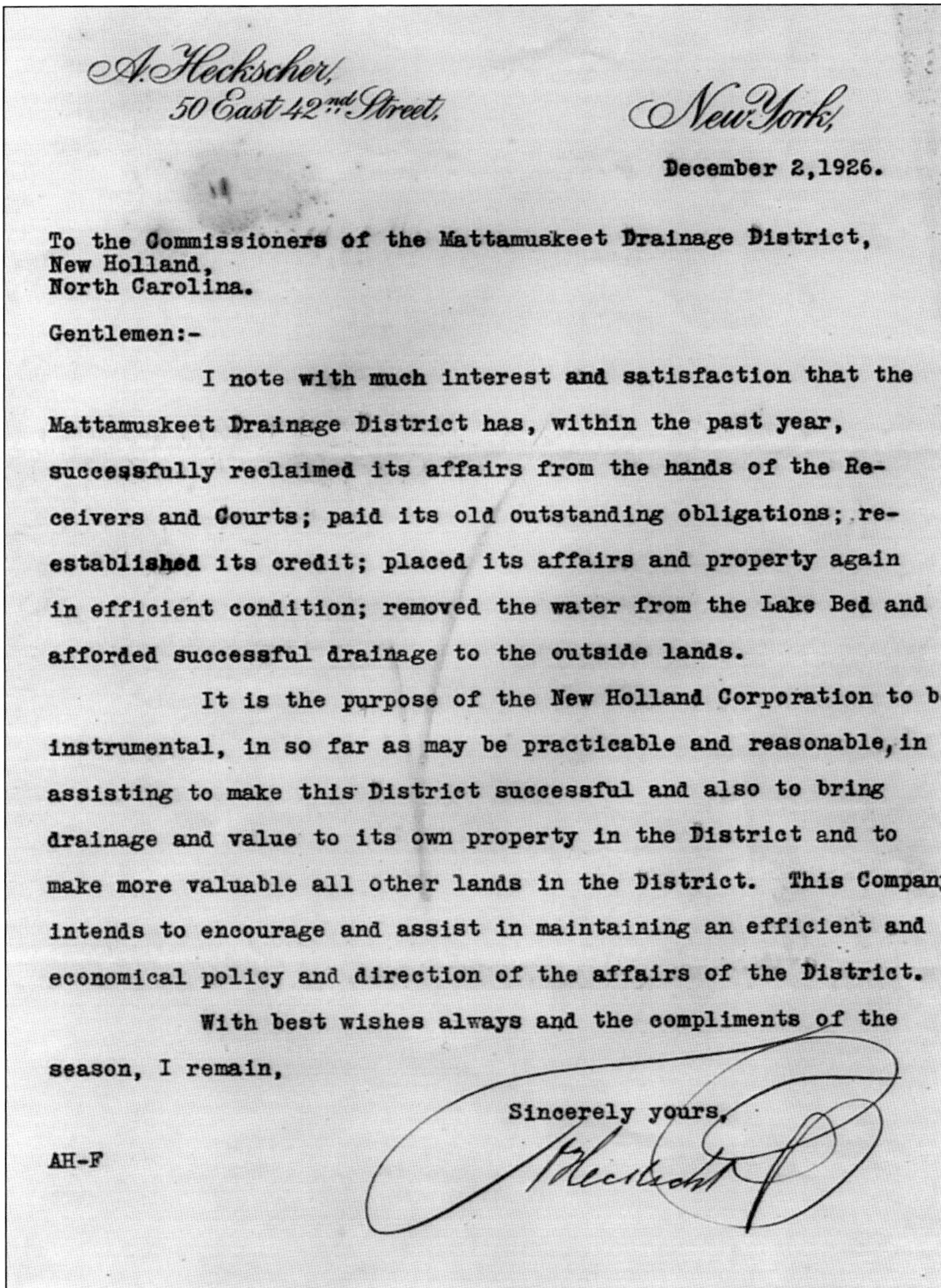

A. Heckscher,
50 East 42nd Street, New York,

December 2,1926.

To the Commissioners of the Mattamuskeet Drainage District,
New Holland,
North Carolina.

Gentlemen:-

I note with much interest and satisfaction that the Mattamuskeet Drainage District has, within the past year, successfully reclaimed its affairs from the hands of the Receivers and Courts; paid its old outstanding obligations; re-established its credit; placed its affairs and property again in efficient condition; removed the water from the Lake Bed and afforded successful drainage to the outside lands.

It is the purpose of the New Holland Corporation to be instrumental, in so far as may be practicable and reasonable, in assisting to make this District successful and also to bring drainage and value to its own property in the District and to make more valuable all other lands in the District. This Company intends to encourage and assist in maintaining an efficient and economical policy and direction of the affairs of the District.

With best wishes always and the compliments of the season, I remain,

Sincerely yours,

A. Heckscher

AH-F

On June 1, 1926, the commissioners of the Mattamuskeet Drainage District repaid the last of the bonds issued by the district in 1913 to raise $500,000 to dredge the canals and build the pumping plant. August Heckscher complimented the commissioners on this accomplishment. (From the Mattamuskeet Records.)

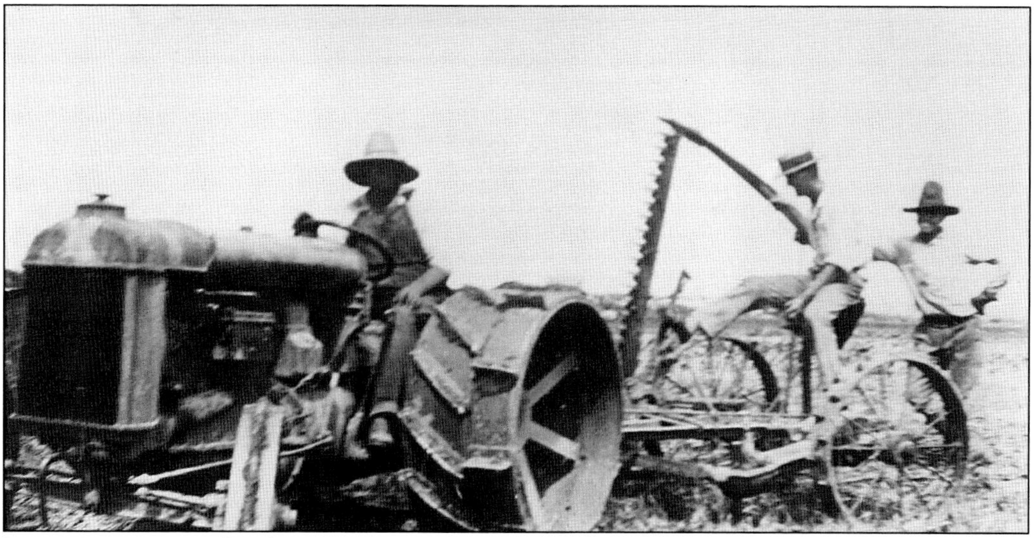

By 1932, New Holland Corporation owned 51 tractors, including 22 Farmall Regulars, 12 Oliver Hart-Parr Model 28-44s, 8 Case Model-Ks, 1 McCormick Deering 15-30, 1 Caterpillar "60," 1 Caterpillar "30," and 5 Caterpillar "20s." They inherited one old Fordson, Model F, pictured here, from North Carolina Farms Company. (Courtesy of George R. Scott and Edna E. Harris.)

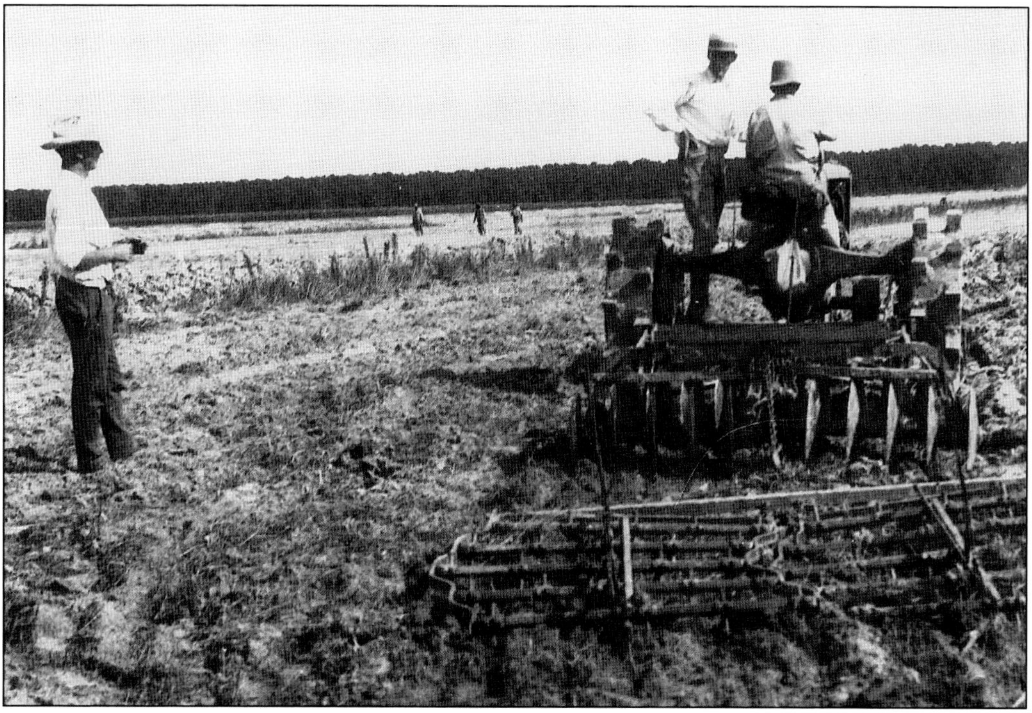

The North Carolina State Prison Department built a camp at New Holland and entered into a contract for the inmates to work on the farm in the lake bed. New Holland Corporation paid the State's Prison Department 25¢ per hour for each inmate's eight-hour day and paid the individual inmates for overtime hours. (Courtesy of Mattamuskeet National Wildlife Refuge, Donald E. Temple, manager.)

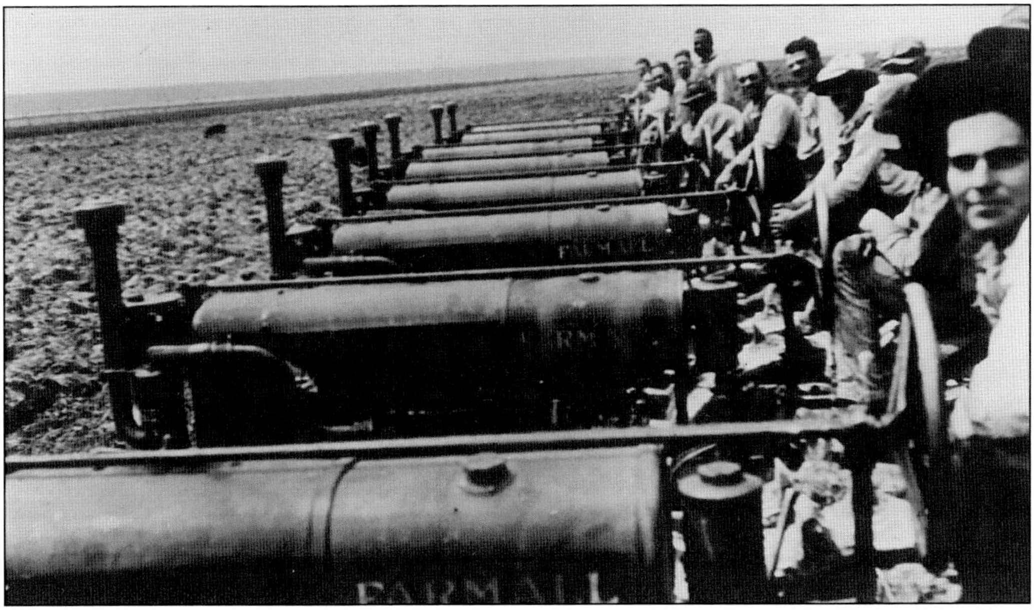

On this occasion, operators lined up eight of the 22 Farmall Regulars owned by New Holland Corporation for a photograph. Most of these operators were inmates from the New Holland Prison Camp. Honor-grade prisoners who had experience operating tractors or other machinery were selected from other camps and sent to New Holland. (Courtesy of George R. Scott and Edna E. Harris.)

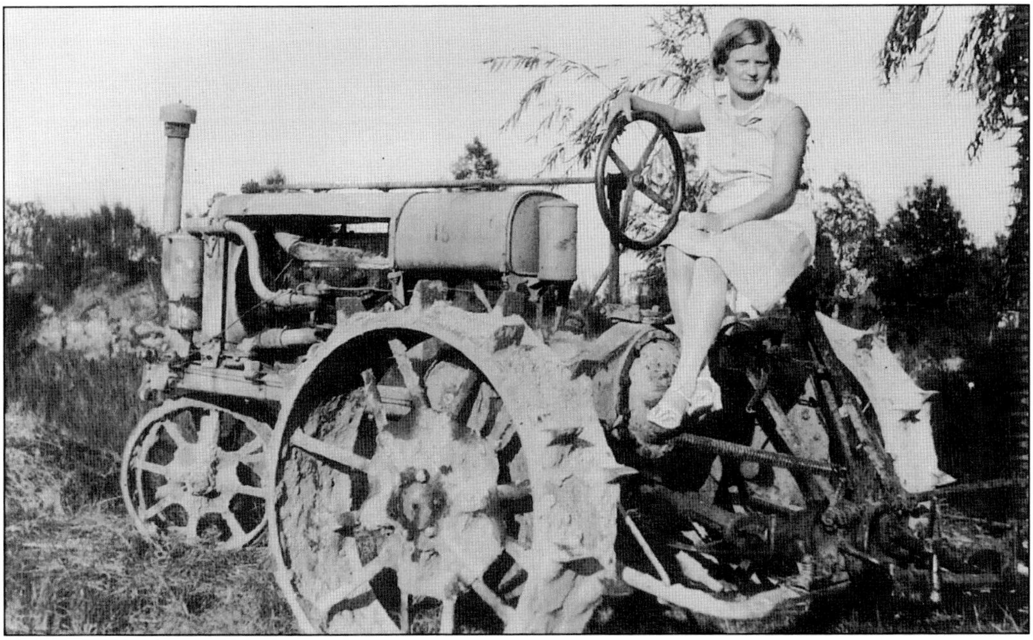

Steel-wheeled tractors worked well in the lake in dry weather but mired to their axles after a heavy rain. The average annual rainfall of Hyde County was 60 inches. Gladys Allen, a waitress from the New Holland Inn, poses on one of the 22 Farmall Regulars owned by New Holland Corporation. (Courtesy of Mattamuskeet National Wildlife Refuge, Donald E. Temple, manager.)

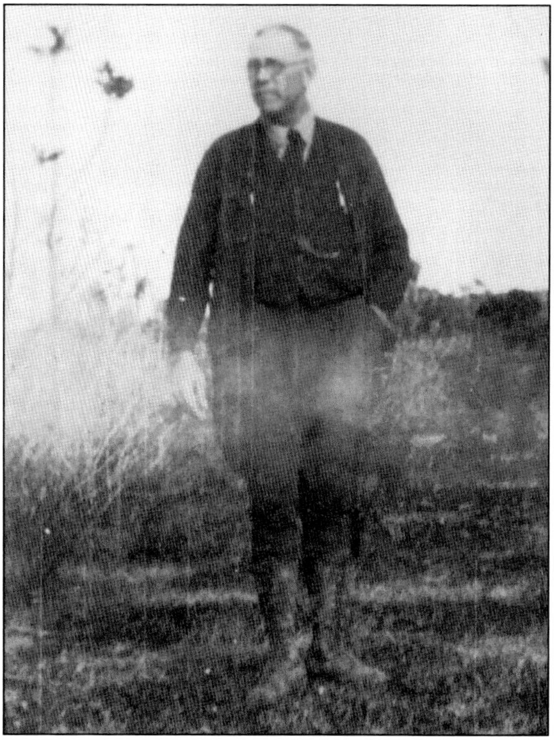

From 1926 through 1929, Mr. C.F. Patten was the foreman of the farming operation in the lake bed. His wife, Martha M. Patten, managed the New Holland Inn. (Courtesy of Lennie Jones Christenson.)

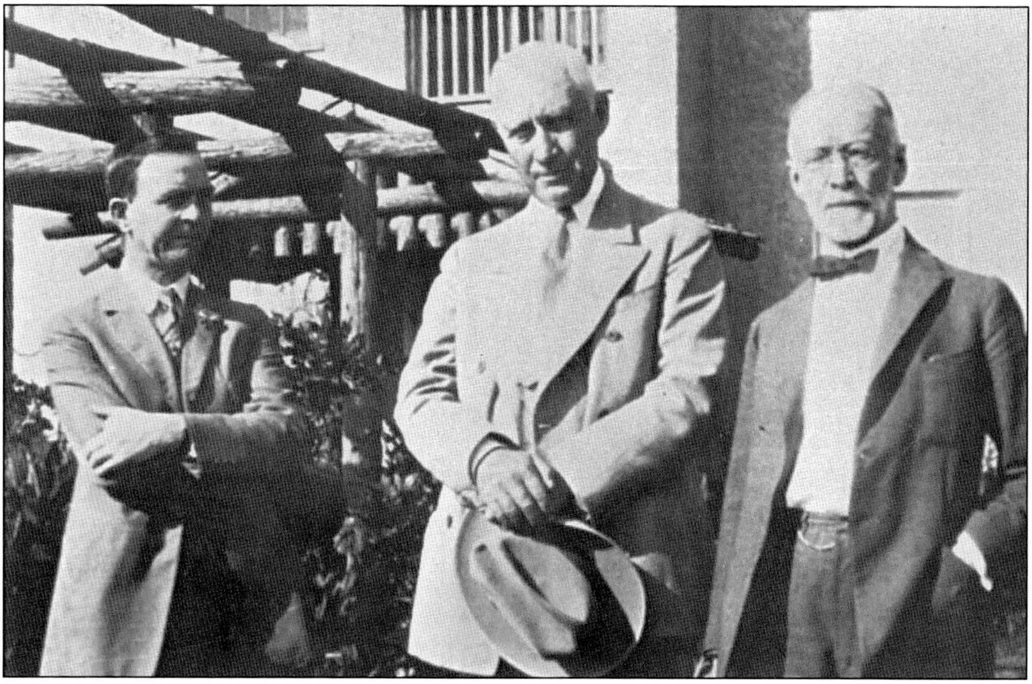

This *c.* 1928 photo was taken during the only visit August Heckscher ever made to his property in Hyde County. From left to right are E.C. Stuckless, president of New Holland Corporation; Douglas Nelson Graves, vice president and general manager; and August Heckscher, owner. (Courtesy of George R. Scott and Edna E. Harris.)

In November 1929, Thomas Donald Campbell (right), president of Campbell Farming Company and the world's most renowned authority on wheat production, and John S. "Jack" Fisher (left), auditor for the New Holland Corporation, visited Douglas N. Graves (center) at New Holland. Graves showed off corn from the lake farm that was 15 feet tall with ears beyond a man's reach. (Courtesy of George R. Scott and Edna E. Harris.)

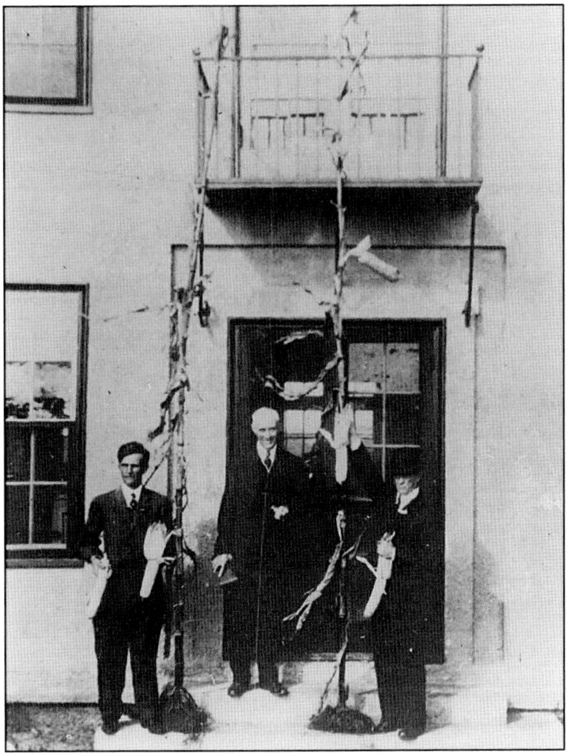

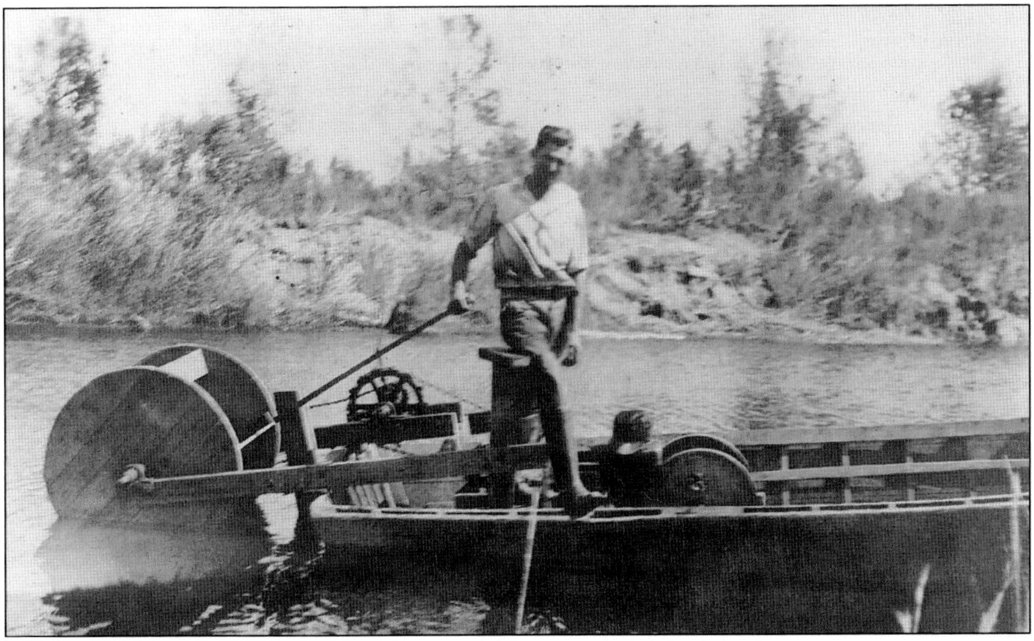

In January 1930, Jack Fisher became vice president and Tom Campbell became general manager of New Holland Corporation's Hyde County operations, replacing D.N. Graves. Campbell sent J.R. Taylor from Wisconsin to be the farm manager, and Alfred J. Schmitt (pictured here) and Carl D. Miller were foremen. Campbell Farming Company operated the lake farm through March 1931. (Courtesy of Alfred J. Schmitt Jr.)

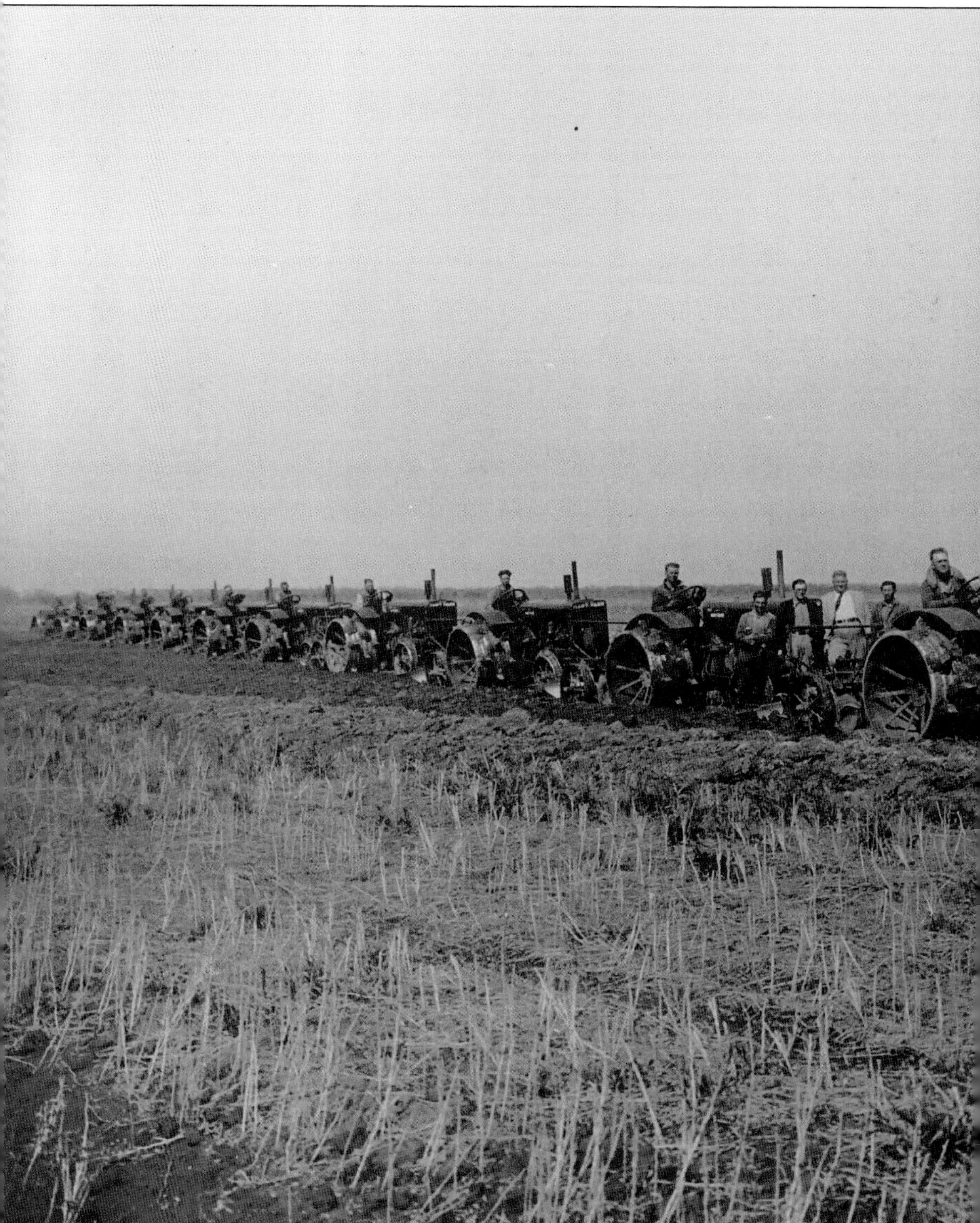

These 12 1930 Oliver Hart-Parr, Model 28-44 tractors were the last new tractors bought by New Holland Corporation. Built in 1930, the tractors came straight from the factory in Charles

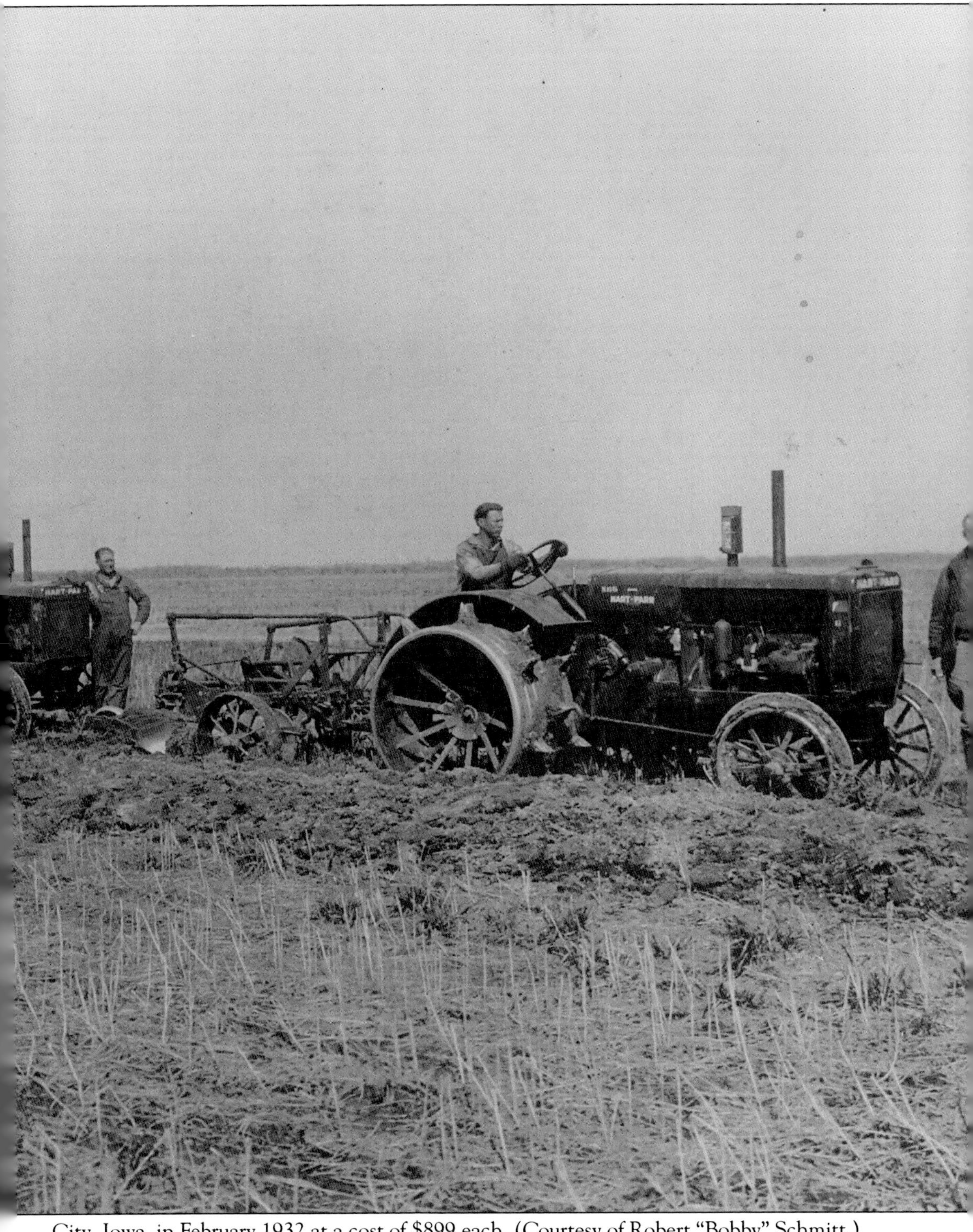

City, Iowa, in February 1932 at a cost of $899 each. (Courtesy of Robert "Bobby" Schmitt.)

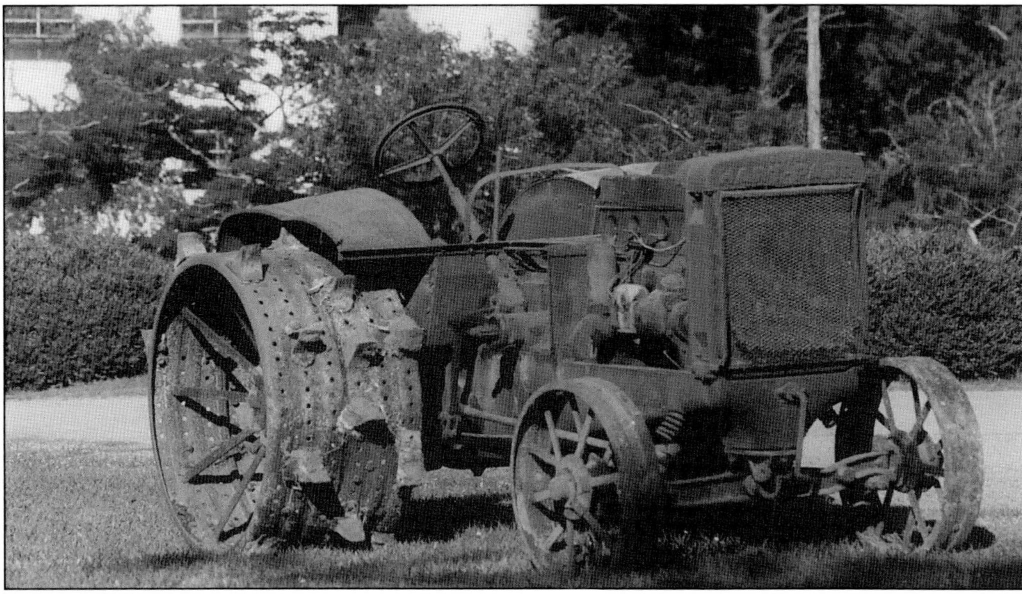

The family of Reubin Bennett Stotesbury donated this tractor to The Mattamuskeet Foundation in 1996. Pictured here in 1989, this old Oliver Hart-Parr, Model 28-44, Serial # 500723, is one of the 12 bought by New Holland Corporation in January 1932. In 1999, Joe Gress of Shreve, Ohio, completely restored the tractor for use by The Mattamuskeet Foundation in interpreting the history of Lake Mattamuskeet. (Courtesy of Lewis Forrest.)

SHIPPING ORDER—INVOICE COPY

OLIVER FARM EQUIPMENT SALES COMPANY

SHIPPING DATE

PLANT INV. NO. — INVOICE NO. C-491

CHARGE TO New Holland Corp
New Holland NC

DATE 2/23/32

SHIPPED FROM CHARLES CI

TERRITORY 33

PLANT CAR NO. — R. R. CAR NO. — ENTERED 1/29/32 — TERMS: NET CASH

BRANCH CAR NO. CC-21 — WEIGHT — CUSTOMER ORDER 1/28/CT

SHIP TO: New Holland Corp
Wenona NC

VIA NS Delvy
Prepaid & Absorb

ORDER NO.

		Hart Parr		
	6	Oliver Hart Parr 28x44 Tractors with A-956-B 6" Spade lugs & A-730-A 3" skids bands with one set (2) A-1225-A 12" extension rims complete less lugs,		
		Serial Numbers 500463-500717 500723-500744 501021-501122	899.00	5394.00

These are shipping documents for six of the Oliver Hart-Parr 28-44 tractors delivered to New Holland Corporation in February 1932, including the one now owned by The Mattamuskeet Foundation with Serial #500723. (From the Mattamuskeet Records.)

New Holland Corporation owned 13 of these Case Model-P, 12-foot combines for picking soybeans and other grain crops. The beans were bagged, dropped off the combine onto the ground, and then collected at the end of the day. L. Hoffman, seen here, was the Case representative, and he spent considerable time at New Holland setting up the combines and working to improve their efficiency. (Courtesy of Lennie Jones Christenson.)

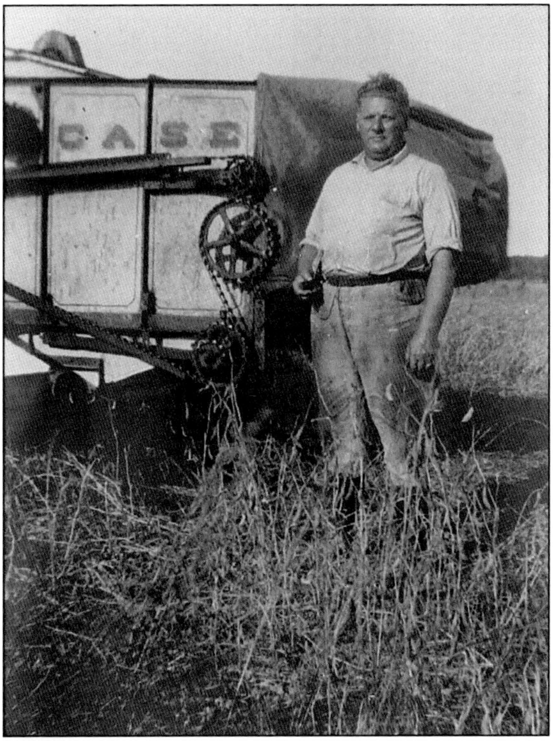

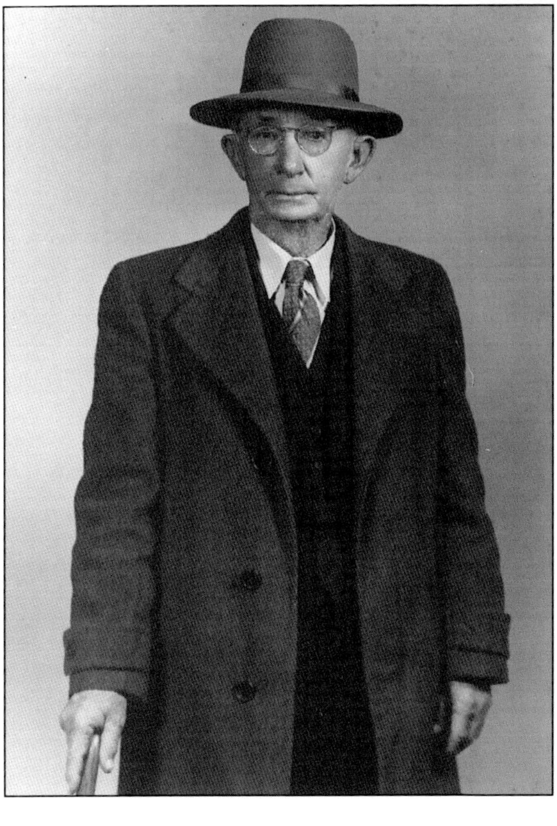

Fred Phineas Latham was a successful farmer from the Belhaven community, 30 miles west of New Holland. Widely regarded as an expert on the drainage of farm lands and hybrid corn production, he served as a consultant for the New Holland Corporation. On April 21, 1931, Latham became the last superintendent in charge of the farming operation at New Holland (see page 125). (Courtesy of Seth David Latham.)

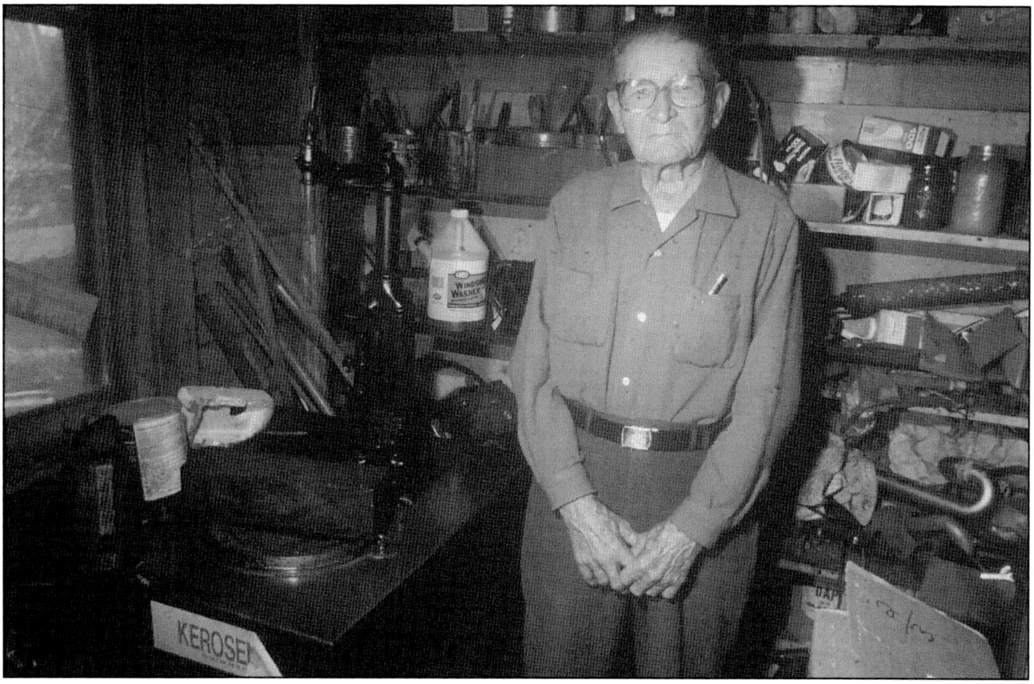

Huron Jefferson Gibbs of the Middletown community in Hyde County was the last chief engineer at the pumping plant. He started out as an oiler in 1926 and progressed to chief engineer by the second half of 1932. Huron Gibbs died on January 8, 1999, at the age of 95. (Courtesy of Cliff Hollis.)

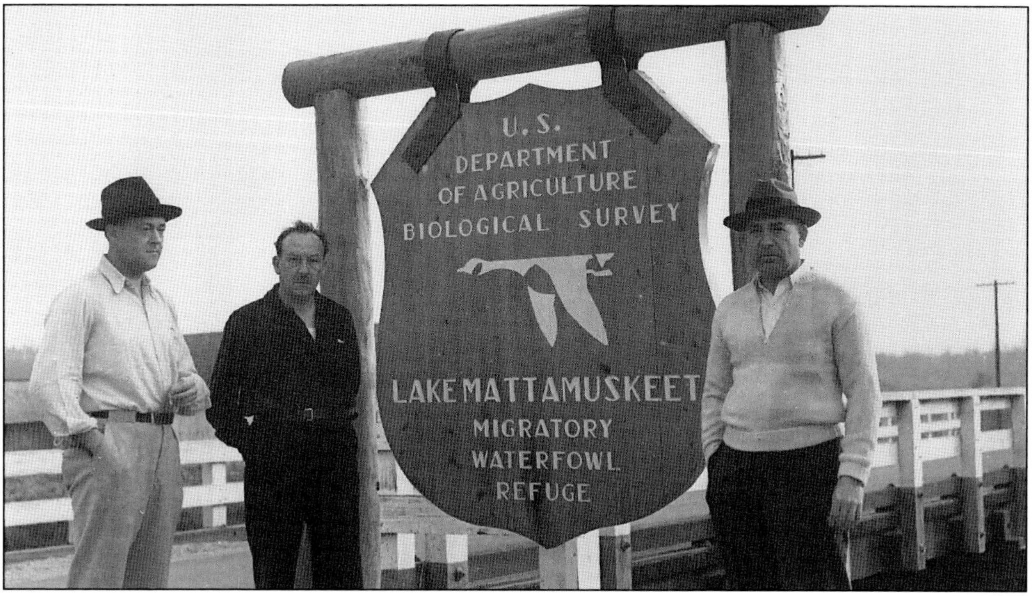

New Holland Corporation shut down its farming operation in the fall of 1932 and sold the lake property to the U.S. government, ending the drainage era at Lake Mattamuskeet. On December 18, 1934, the U.S. government declared the property the "Mattamuskeet Migratory Waterfowl Refuge." Pictured, from left to right, are Chet Smith, John Mock, and Victor Showbert. (Courtesy of North Carolina Division of Archives and History.)

Eight

CCC Boys Convert Lake Farm to Waterfowl Refuge

President Franklin D. Roosevelt's administration established the Civilian Conservation Corps (CCC) in 1933 to combat unemployment in the United States during the Great Depression. The program enrolled unemployed single young men to work on conservation and resource-development projects. Enrollees received food, lodging, other necessities, and a small monthly salary. The CCC program lasted until 1942.

On June 29, 1933, Company 424 of the CCC from Fort Bragg, North Carolina, consisting of about 200 enrollees, landed by boat off Bell Island on the Swanquarter Migratory Waterfowl Refuge in Hyde County. There was no wharf and the water was too shallow for the boat to get to shore so the men undressed and waded 100 or more yards to shore, carrying their belongings over their heads. This was the beginning of the CCC in Hyde County history. First known as "Swanquarter Camp," located on Bell Island, Company 424 later relocated to New Holland and was renamed "Mattamuskeet Camp." The Mattamuskeet Camp was located adjacent to Highway 264 just south of the old pumping plant and was officially designated Mattamuskeet Camp, BS-3, North Carolina.

The CCC camps were in Hyde County for nine years, and the enrollees completed numerous projects in developing Mattamuskeet and Swan Quarter Migratory Waterfowl Refuges. The project that stands as a memorial to the hard work of the CCC boys in Hyde County is Mattamuskeet Lodge, which they created by renovating the old pumping plant that had belonged to the 550-575 landowners of the Mattamuskeet Drainage District.

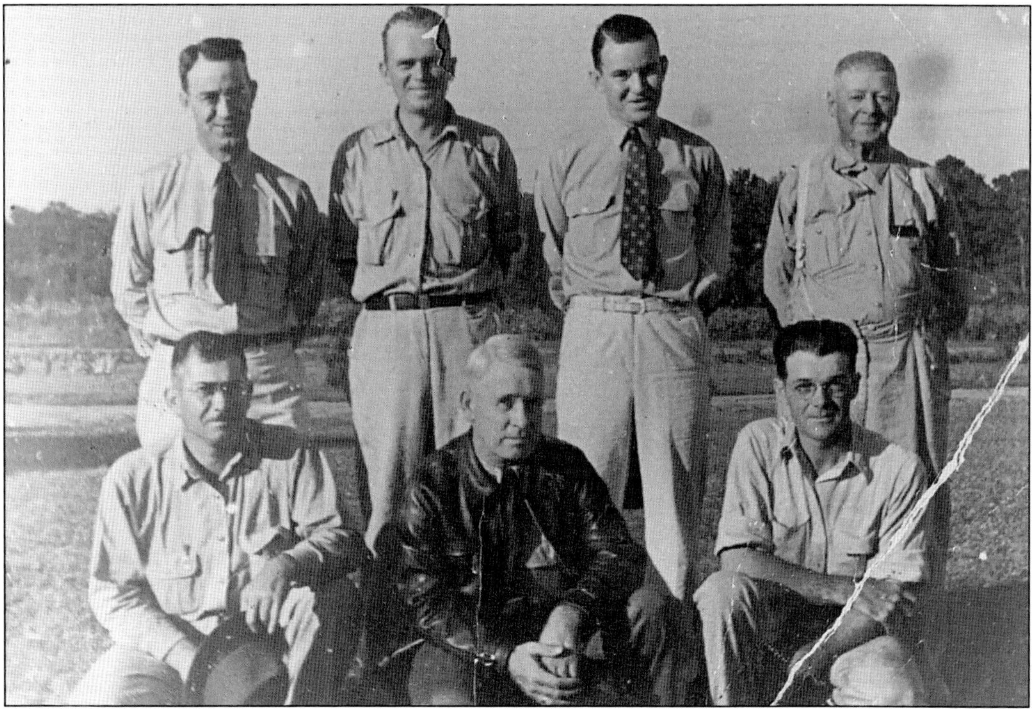

The project superintendent and his staff for CCC Company 424 included the following, from left to right: (front row) John Lawrence Jr., junior foreman; Joseph S. Mann, project superintendent; and Leland Carawan, foreman; (second row) Hugh Wyatt, foreman; Stacy Lupton, foreman; Cecil Winstead, clerk; and John R. Wheeler, foreman. (Courtesy of CCC Company 424 Archives.)

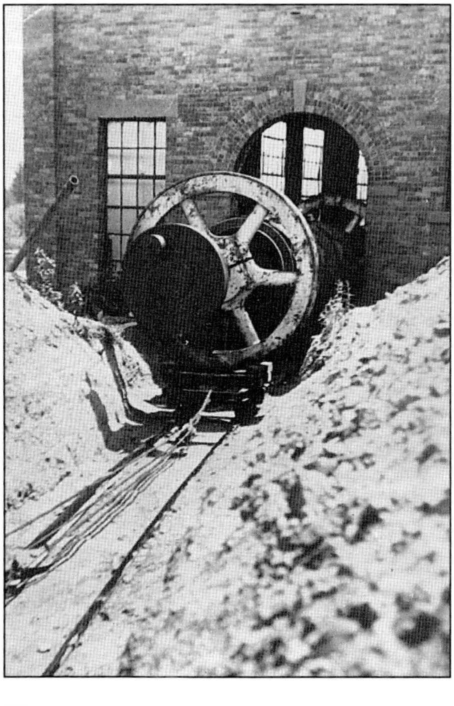

The landmark project completed by the CCC boys of Company 424 was the conversion of the old pumping plant into a rustic hunting lodge, complete with a restaurant, sleeping rooms, and public gathering space. The CCC boys began the project by removing the pumps and boilers from the building for disposal as scrap metal. (Courtesy of Hal Swindell.)

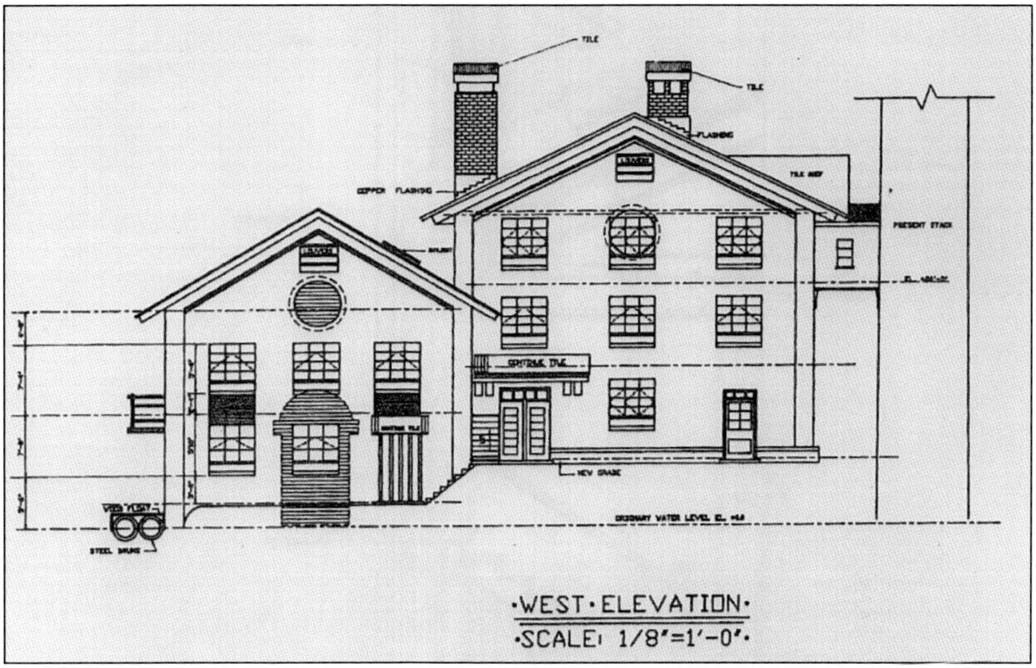

Compare this west-end elevation and cross section from the 1935 plans for Mattamuskeet Lodge with the cross section of the pumping plant shown on page 36. Notice how the renovation plan specified the addition of floors to provide two levels in the north wing (left) and three levels in the south wing (right). (Courtesy of Regional Development Institute, East Carolina University.)

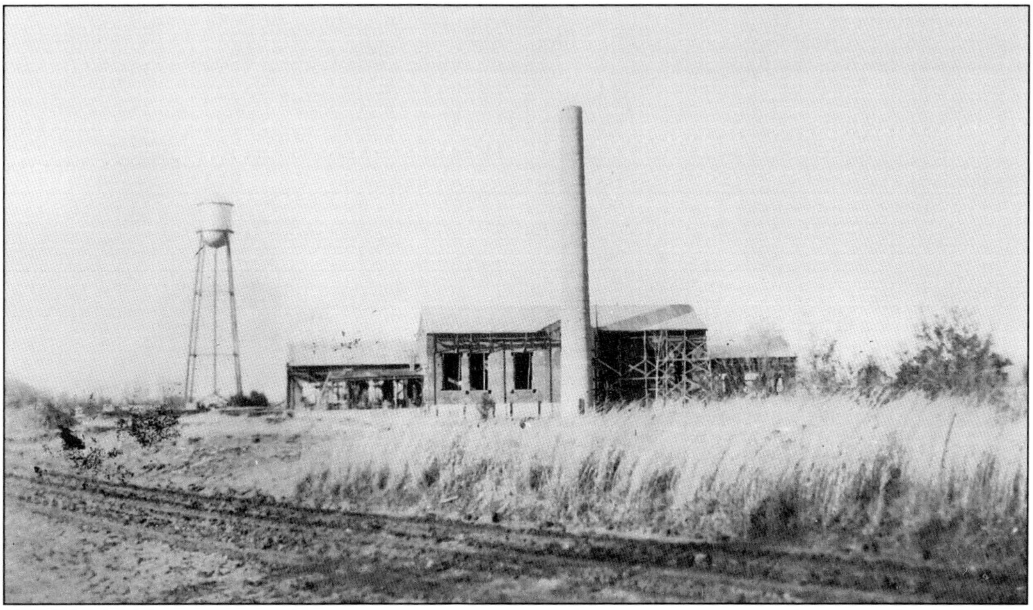

Having removed the pumps and boilers, the next task was cleaning and painting the steel roof girders, followed by removing the tall windows, which were to be replaced with smaller windows that would correspond to the floors the CCC boys would add to the building. (Courtesy of Mattamuskeet Wildlife Refuge, Donald E. Temple, manager.)

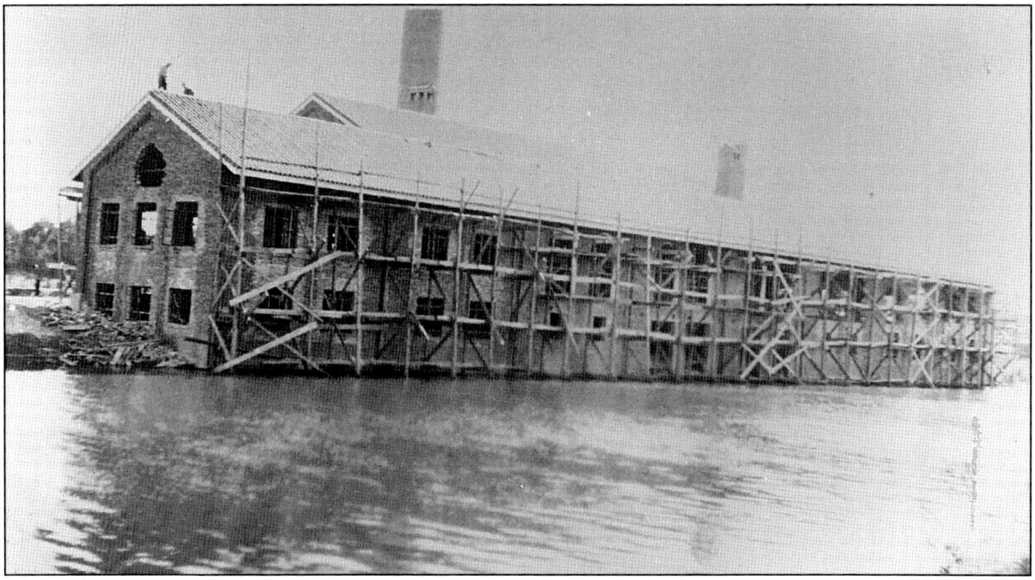

After installing the floors, the CCC boys erected scaffolding on both sides of the building to fit the new windows and paint the structure. (Courtesy of Hal Swindell.)

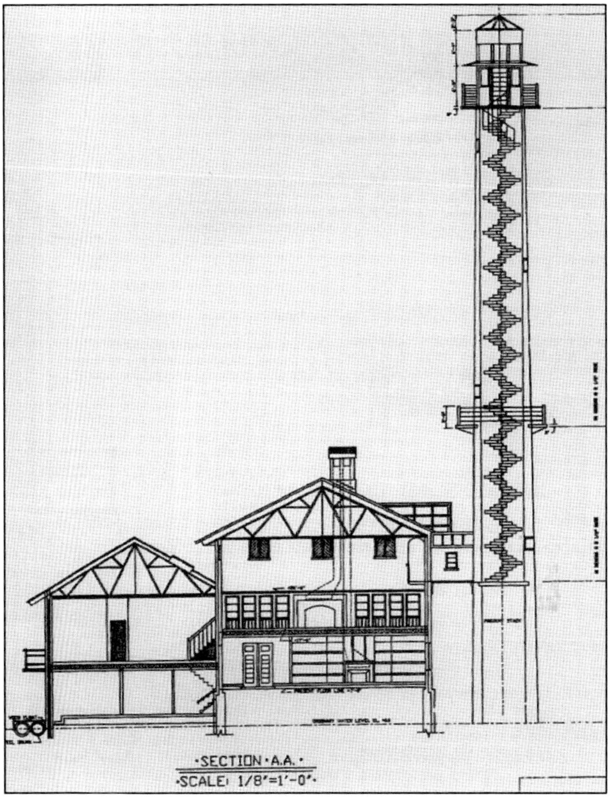

This drawing shows how the old smokestack of the pumping plant was to be converted to an observation tower. The observation tower is entered from the second story of the Mattamuskeet Lodge, 26.5 feet above sea level. There are 121 iron steps spiraling upward to a height of 112 1/2 feet above sea level. (Courtesy of Regional Development Institute, East Carolina University.)

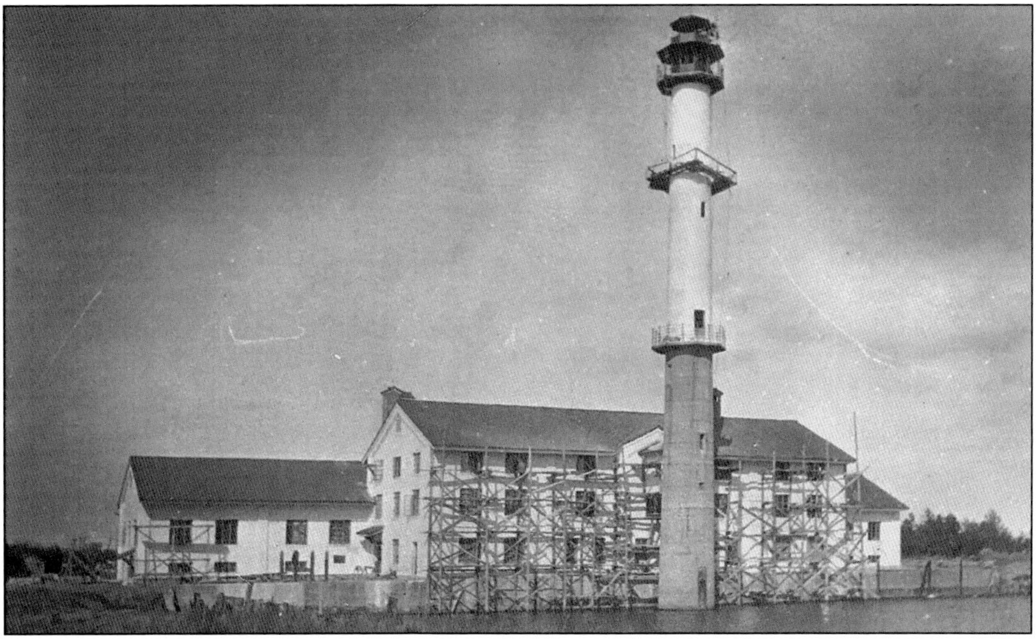

During September 1936, plasterers were busy finishing the inside walls of Mattamuskeet Lodge, and painters were busy finishing the exterior of the building. To cover the red bricks of the old pumping plant, the CCC boys used white cement paint and kept it wet for several days, hoping that the slow drying would add to the life of the exterior finish. (Courtesy of CCC Company 424 Archives.)

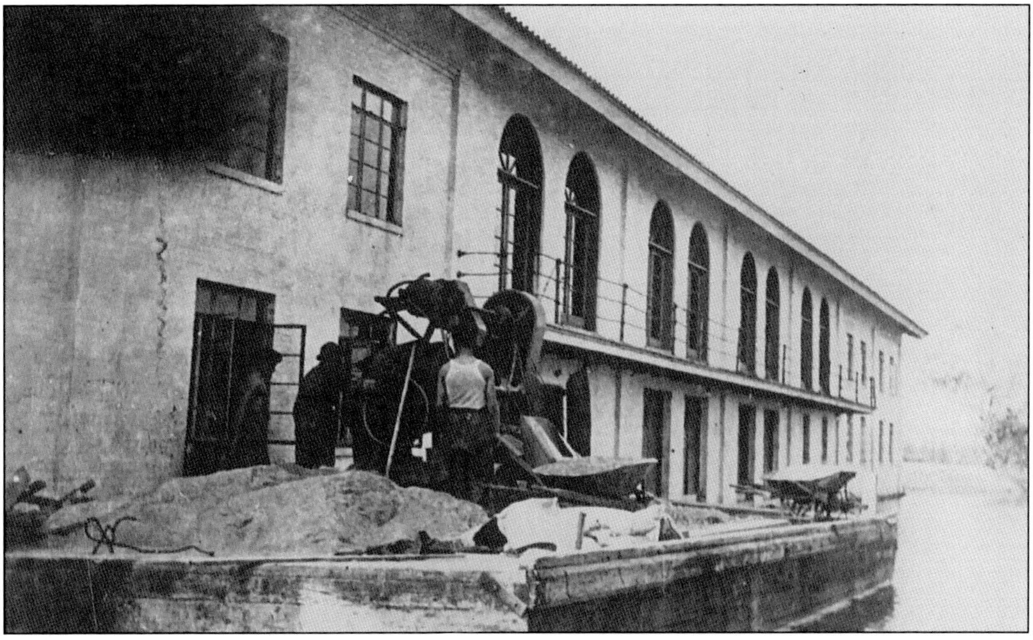

On September 25, 1936, the CCC boys completed pouring new concrete floors in the lower level of the building where the pumps had been. The new floor was elevated at least 6 feet above the original floor. The lower halves of the pump housings were left below the new suspended floor. (Courtesy of CCC Company 424 Archives.)

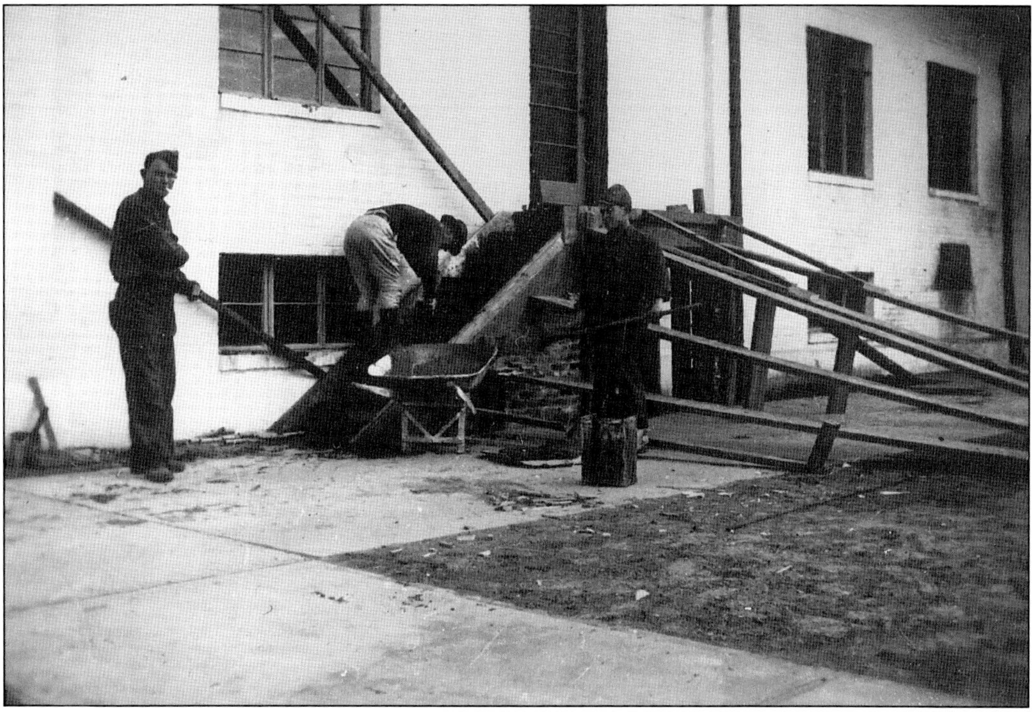

CCC boys built steps to the refuge manager's office on the west end of the Headquarters Building (Mattamuskeet Lodge). (Courtesy of CCC Company 424 Archives.)

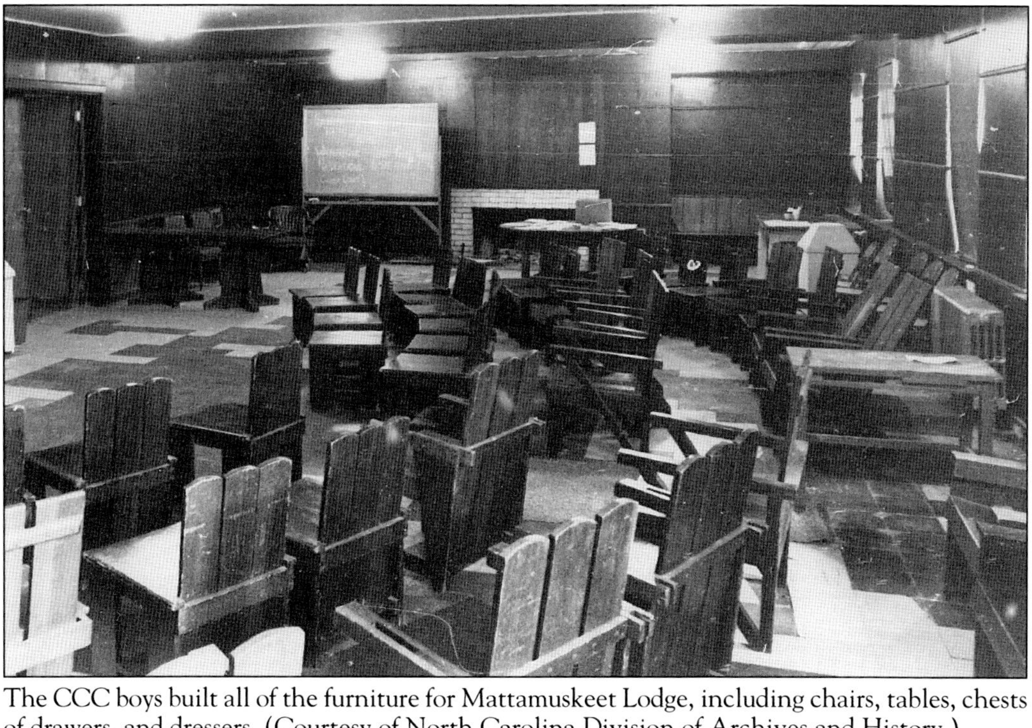

The CCC boys built all of the furniture for Mattamuskeet Lodge, including chairs, tables, chests of drawers, and dressers. (Courtesy of North Carolina Division of Archives and History.)

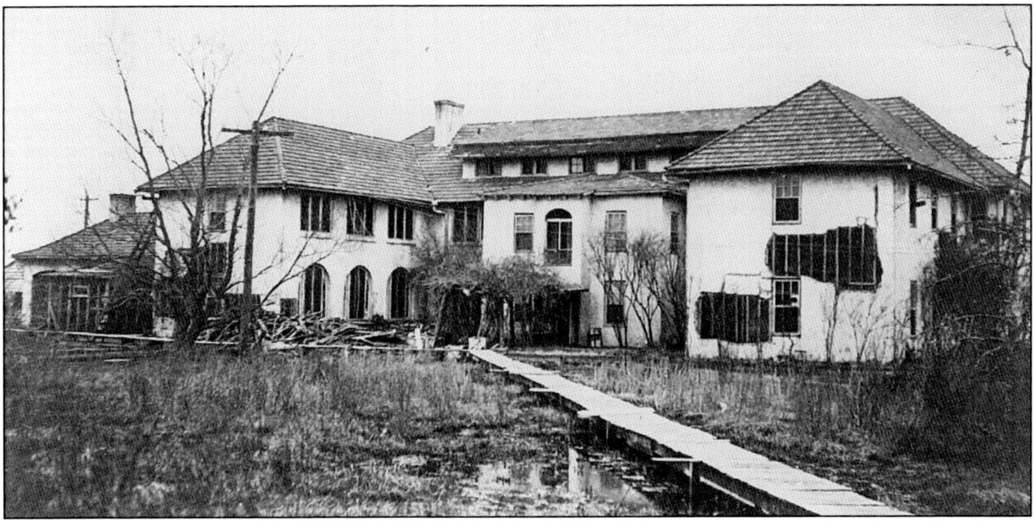

In September 1936, the CCC boys completed tearing down the old New Holland Inn. They salvaged 4,500 board feet of lumber to be reused in buildings for the Wildlife Refuge, and they hauled away 97 loads of trash, lumber, cement, and plaster from the old hotel. After the lake refilled, when the wind blew from the northeast, the water was 2 feet deep in the lobby. (Courtesy of Hal Swindell.)

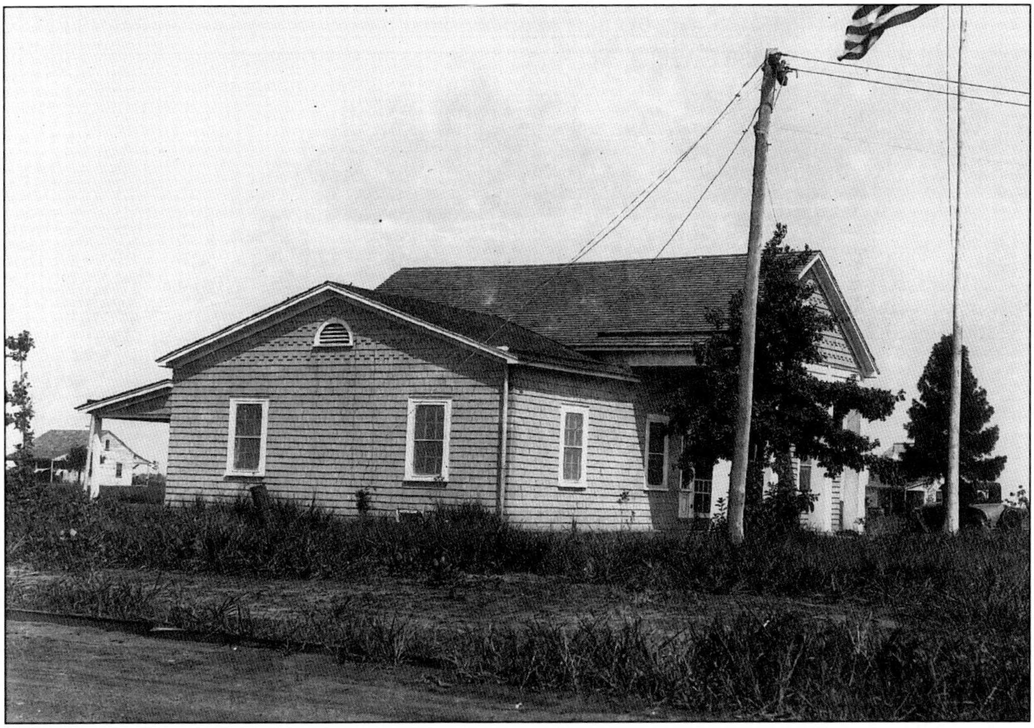

In June of 1937, the CCC boys demolished the old administrative building and an equipment garage. These buildings were built by North Carolina Farms Company in the early 1920s and were also used by New Holland Corporation. Fortunately, Fred P. Latham removed the business records from the administrative building before the demolition began (see page 125). (Courtesy of Mattamuskeet National Wildlife Refuge, Donald E. Temple, manager.)

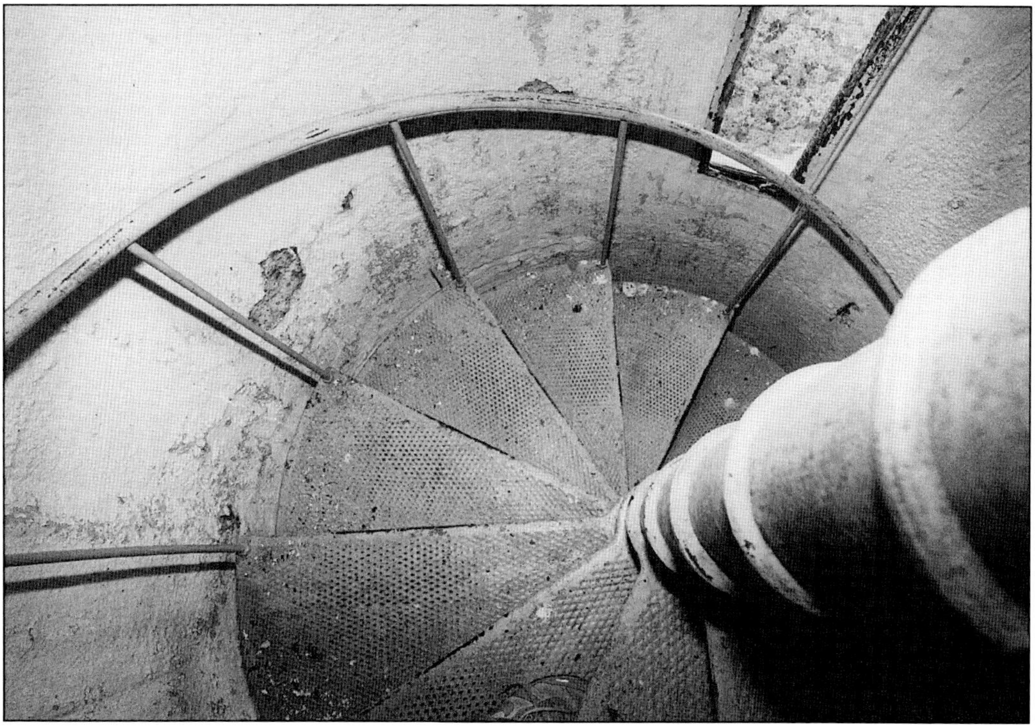

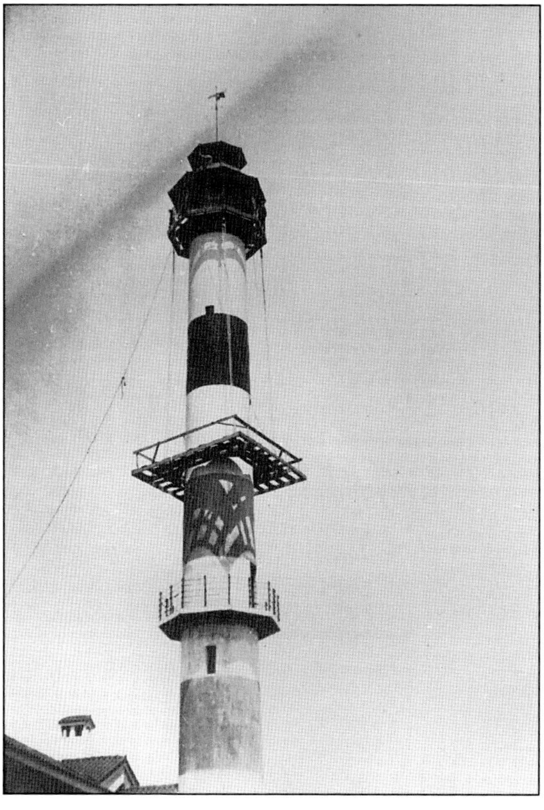

In February 1937, CCC boys began painting the spiral stairway in the observation tower (smokestack), and they completed painting the inside walls of the tower with two coats of thin concrete paint. (Courtesy of Cliff Hollis.)

During April 1937, the CCC boys painted the blue stripes on the smokestack (observation tower). The CCC personnel who painted the 112-1/2-foot tower worked from a swinging hanging scaffold and wore a safety line in case they were to fall. (Courtesy of CCC Company 424 Archives.)

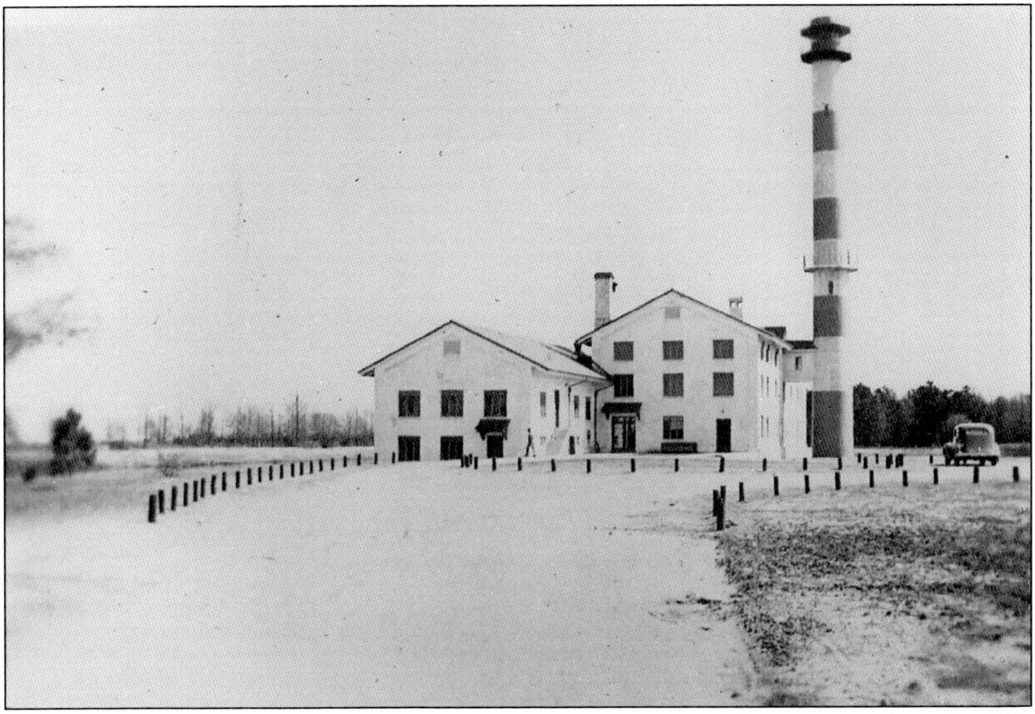

Mattamuskeet Lodge opened for its first guests with ten rooms ready on November 26, 1937. Between November 1937 and July 1942, the CCC boys completed an additional nine guest rooms. This photo was taken during the late summer of 1937, shortly before the lodge was ready for its first guests. (Courtesy of CCC Company 424 Archives.)

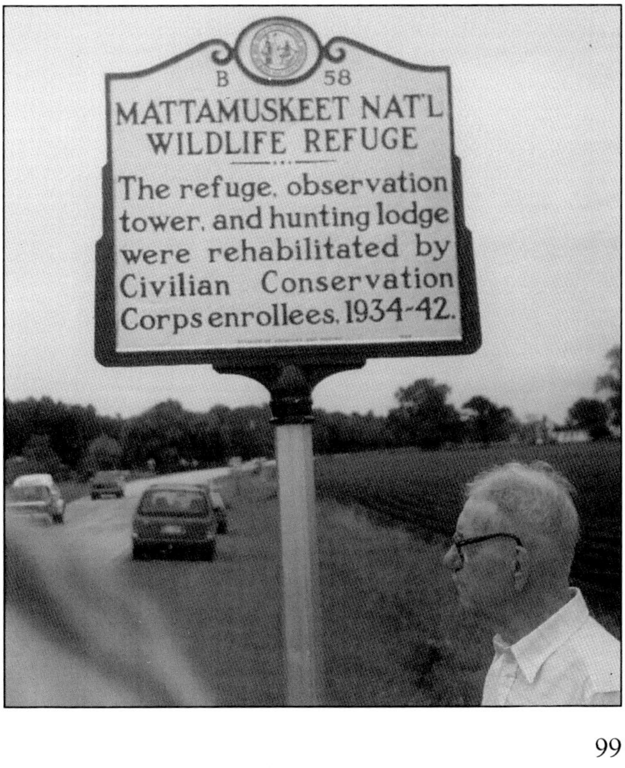

On June 3, 1995, this historical marker was erected by the State of North Carolina to recognize the contribution of the two CCC Company 424 Camps in Hyde County in converting the commercial farm that operated in Lake Mattamuskeet during the drainage era into Mattamuskeet Migratory Waterfowl Refuge and the pumping plant into Mattamuskeet Lodge. (Courtesy of Lewis Forrest.)

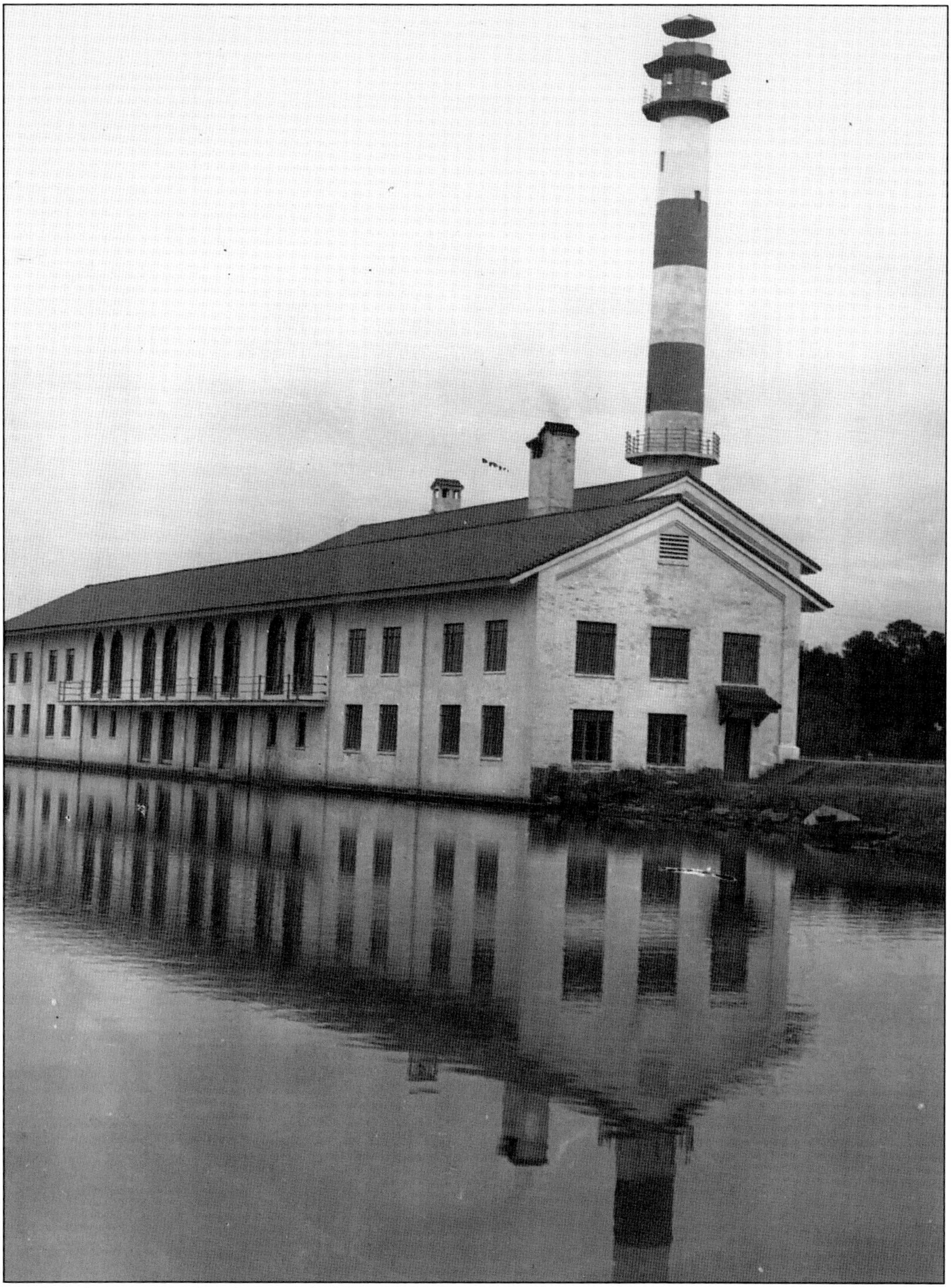

In October 1935, the first scaffolding had been erected to begin work on the conversion of the pumping plant building into Mattamuskeet Lodge. From that point forward, 7,403 CCC enrollee man-days were expended in reconstructing the building and its immediate grounds. This view of Mattamuskeet Lodge shows how it looked in 1938, shortly after it was opened to guests. (Courtesy of North Carolina Division of Archives and History.)

Nine

Pumping Plant Becomes Mattamuskeet Lodge

Mattamuskeet Lodge welcomed its first hotel and restaurant guests on November 26, 1937. For 37 years, the building operated as a lodge and gained a reputation as one of the favorite hunting lodges in the country. Had the migration patterns of Canada geese remained unchanged, it might still be operating as a lodge.

During its heyday, Mattamuskeet Lodge guests included governors, senators, congressmen, state representatives, lawyers, doctors, and the wealthy, but it was never a place that catered primarily to the rich or influential. Its doors were always open to anyone who wished to come, and within its historic walls, a sense of hospitality and cooperation always prevailed.

Douglas Nelson Graves poured 20 years of his life into the pumping plant that provided the foundation and shell for Mattamuskeet Lodge. Had he lived beyond January 1931, he would have been proud of the role the building played as a center for community and sporting activities. He would also approve of the nonprofit events and fund-raising activities that are currently held there because he believed in the spirit of cooperation and service.

Mattamuskeet Lodge ceased being a hotel in 1974. Its future is in its educational value, as a reminder of the lake drainage history and a time when Lake Mattamuskeet was the "Canada Goose Hunting Capital of the World." The building barely escaped demolition in 1979–1980, but its future looks bright as the community works together to preserve and renovate it without destroying its historical character and charm.

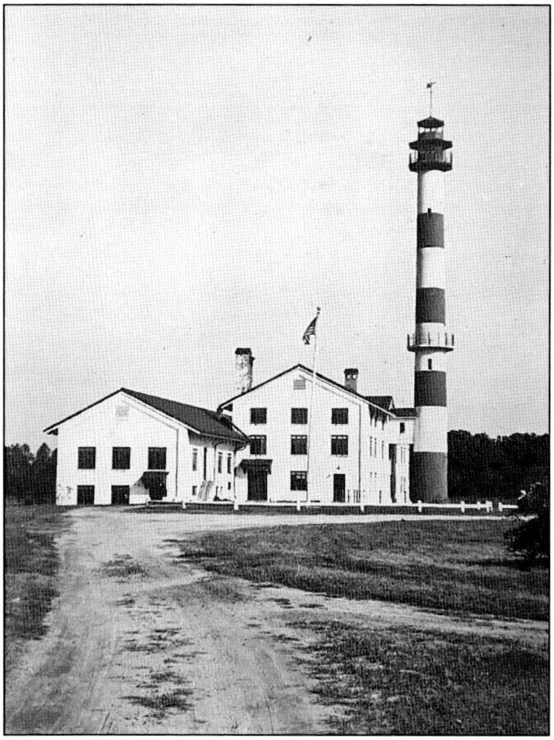

The higher roof line on the south wing of the structure made it possible to install two floors, making that side a three-story structure. An entrance hallway, public restrooms, a kitchen, and a dining room were on the first floor. On the second floor, there was a large assembly room that also served as a dining room. There were sleeping rooms and baths on the third floor. (Courtesy of CCC Company 424 Archives.)

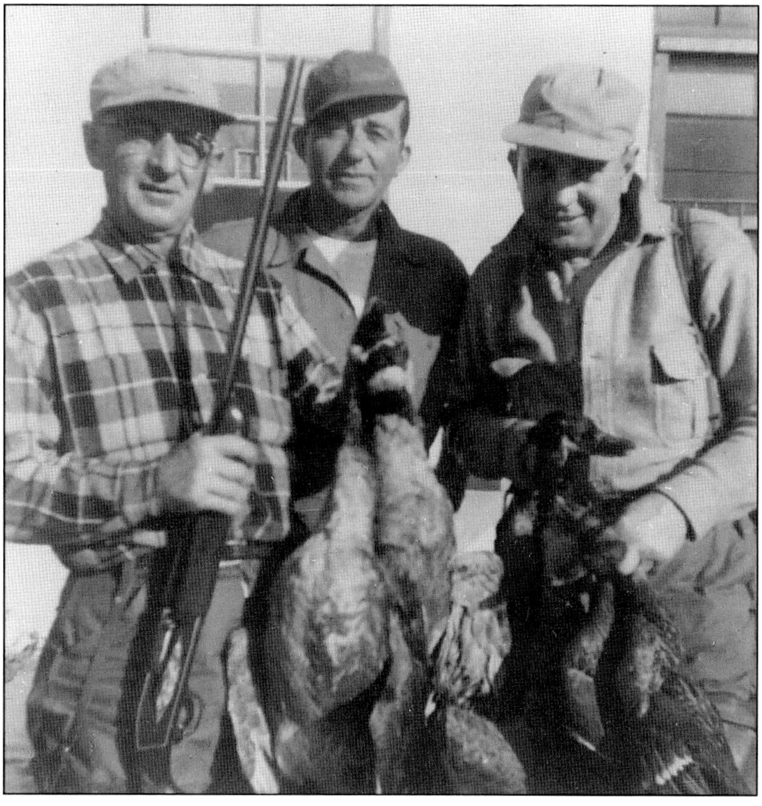

During the glory days at Lake Mattamuskeet when the hunting of Canada geese was permitted on the refuge, John Harold Swindell of Swindell's Fork Community in Hyde County was a well-known guide for hunters staying at Mattamuskeet Lodge. Swindell (middle) poses with two satisfied hunters. (Courtesy of Janie Cutrell Swindell.)

North Carolina secretary of conservation Claude Wickard and his wife head out early from Mattamuskeet Lodge in 1941 for a morning of shooting. Each has a bag lunch prepared by the lodge staff. Most hunters reportedly ate their lunch before 9 a.m. (Courtesy of North Carolina Division of Archives and History.)

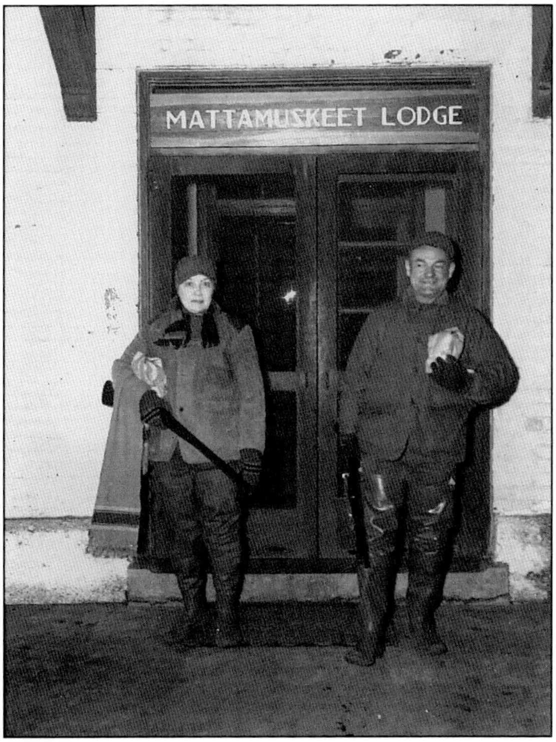

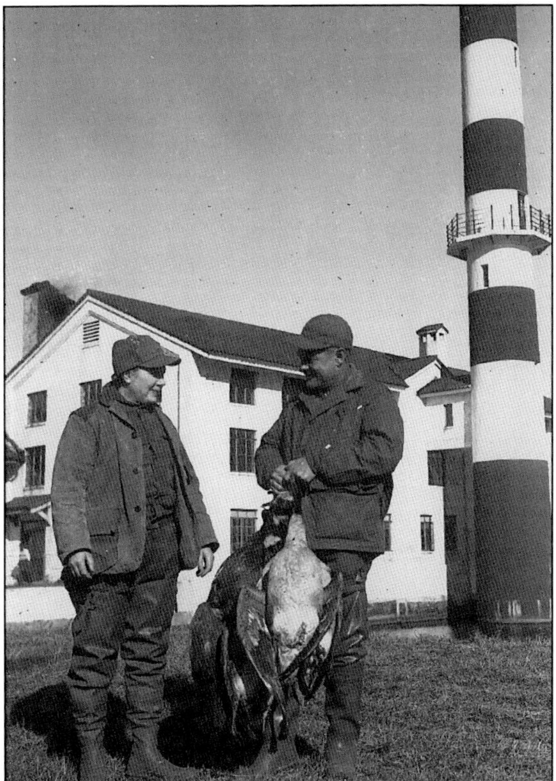

Claude Wickard and his wife return to Mattamuskeet Lodge after a successful day of shooting on Lake Mattamuskeet. (Courtesy of North Carolina Division of Archives and History.)

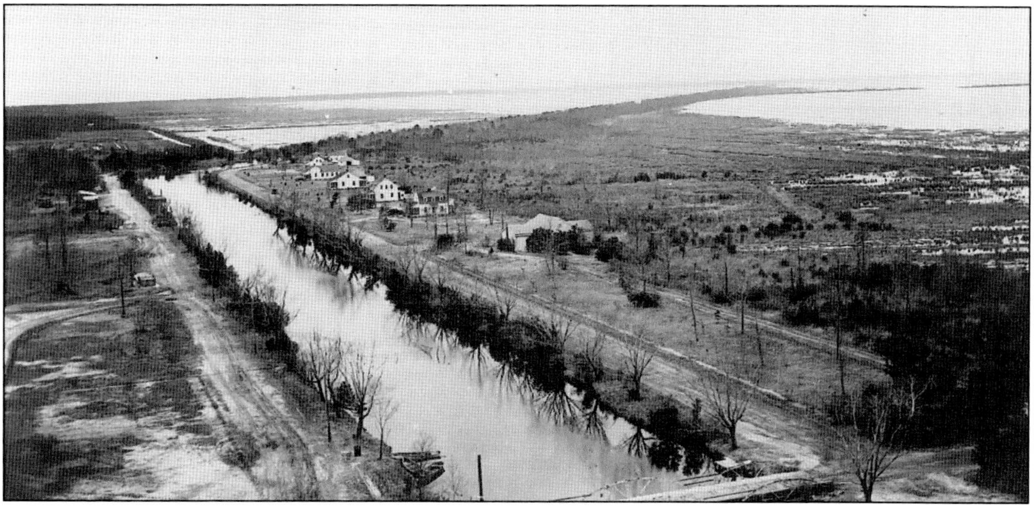

This is a 1938 view from the observation tower at Mattamuskeet Lodge, looking west. Note the width of West Main Canal from the drainage era. The houses on the north side of the canal were built by North Carolina Farms Company between 1920 and 1923 and were moved to the canal bank by the CCC boys during the period between 1935 and 1942. (Courtesy of North Carolina Division of Archives and History.)

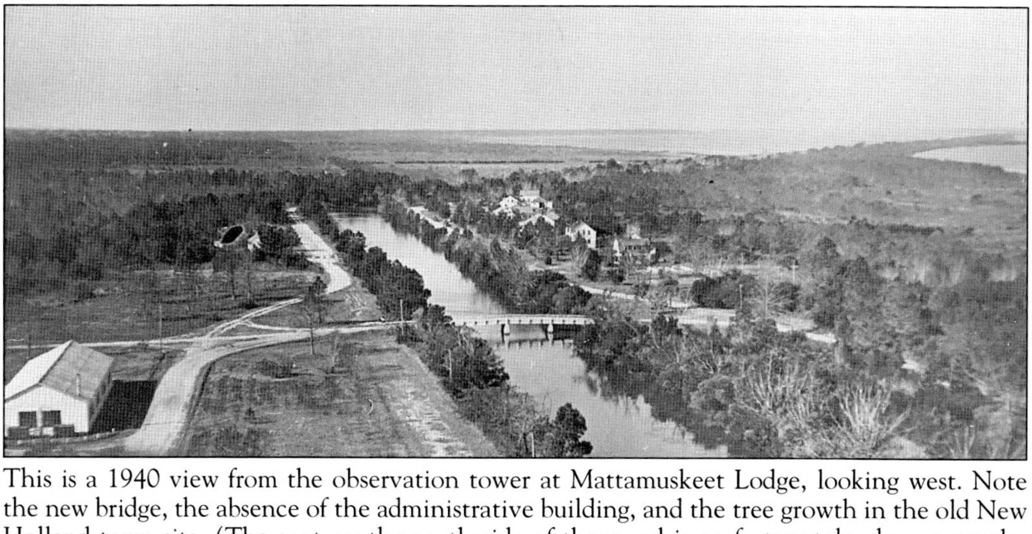

This is a 1940 view from the observation tower at Mattamuskeet Lodge, looking west. Note the new bridge, the absence of the administrative building, and the tree growth in the old New Holland town site. (The spot on the south side of the canal is, unfortunately, damage to the original photo.) (Courtesy of Hal Swindell.)

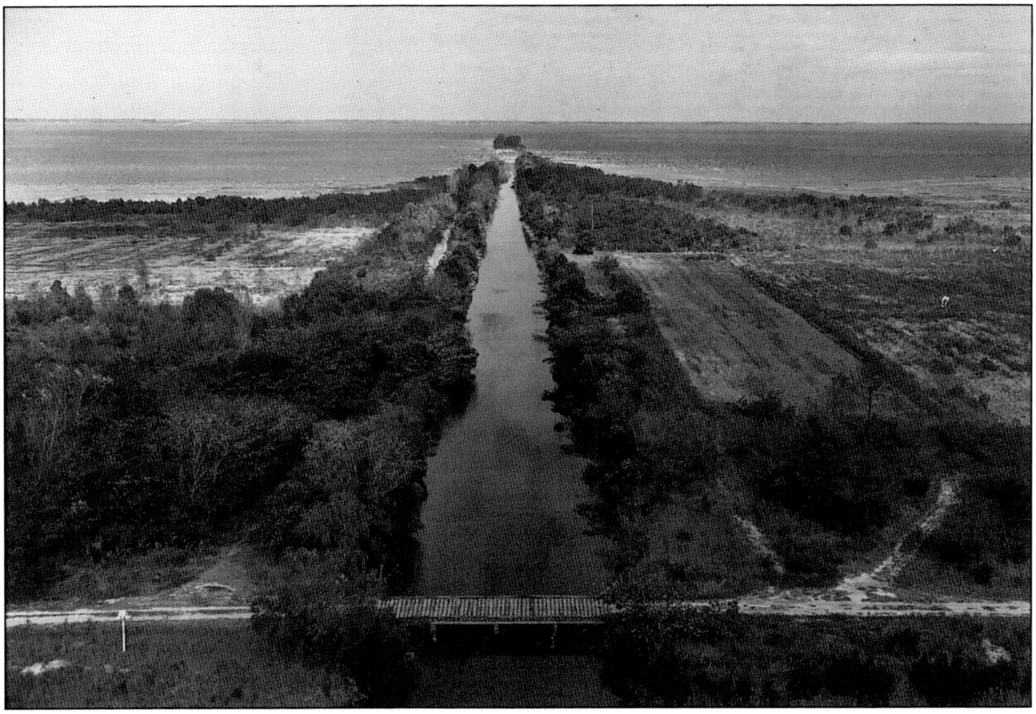

This 1944 view of Central Canal leading into Lake Mattamuskeet north from Mattamuskeet Lodge is a breathtaking sight from the upper level of the observation tower. This vantage point offers a panoramic view of much of the 18-mile length from west to east and the 7-mile width from south to north. (Courtesy of North Carolina Division of Archives and History.)

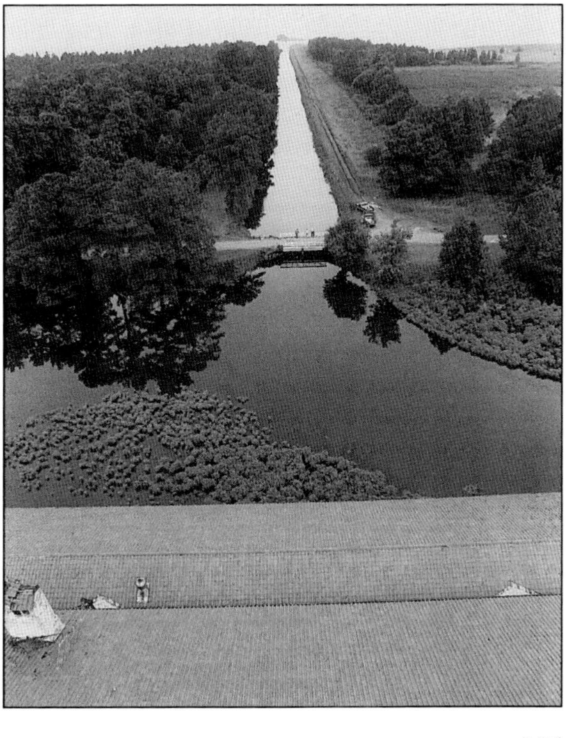

This 1989 view of Central Canal from the observation tower at Mattamuskeet Lodge contrasts the growth of trees in the old town site of New Holland. The old New Holland Inn, the administrative building, the boarding house, and a number of small houses were west (to the left) of Central Canal. (Courtesy of Cliff Hollis.)

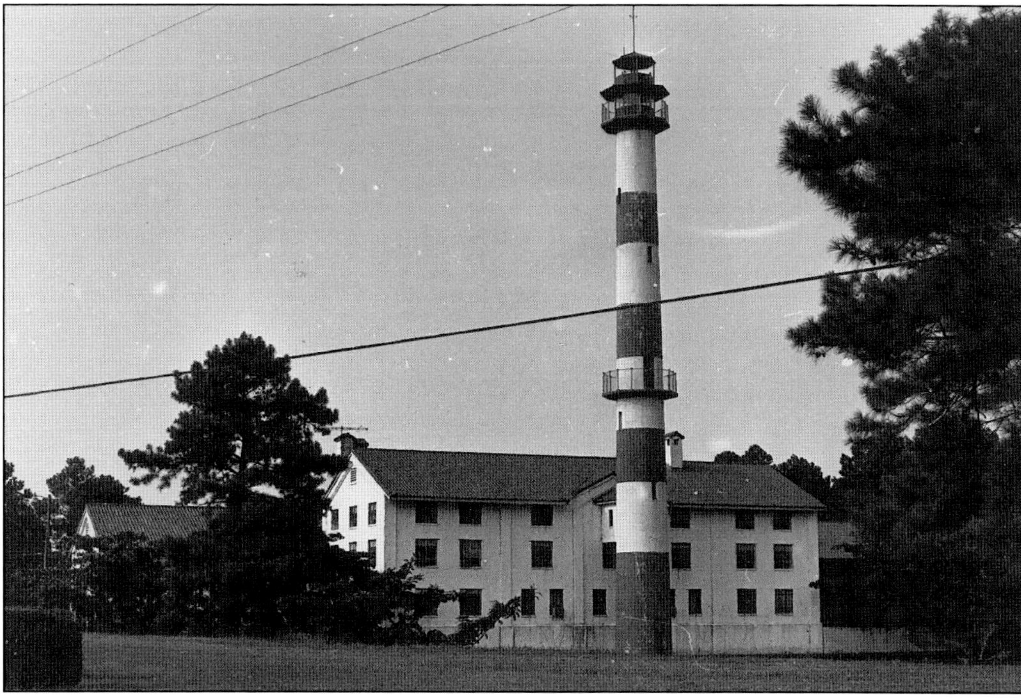

Mattamuskeet Lodge is seen here as it appeared in 1976, just two years after the U.S. Fish and Wildlife Service closed it as a hotel and restaurant operation for hunters and other visitors to the lake. (Courtesy of North Carolina Division of Archives and History.)

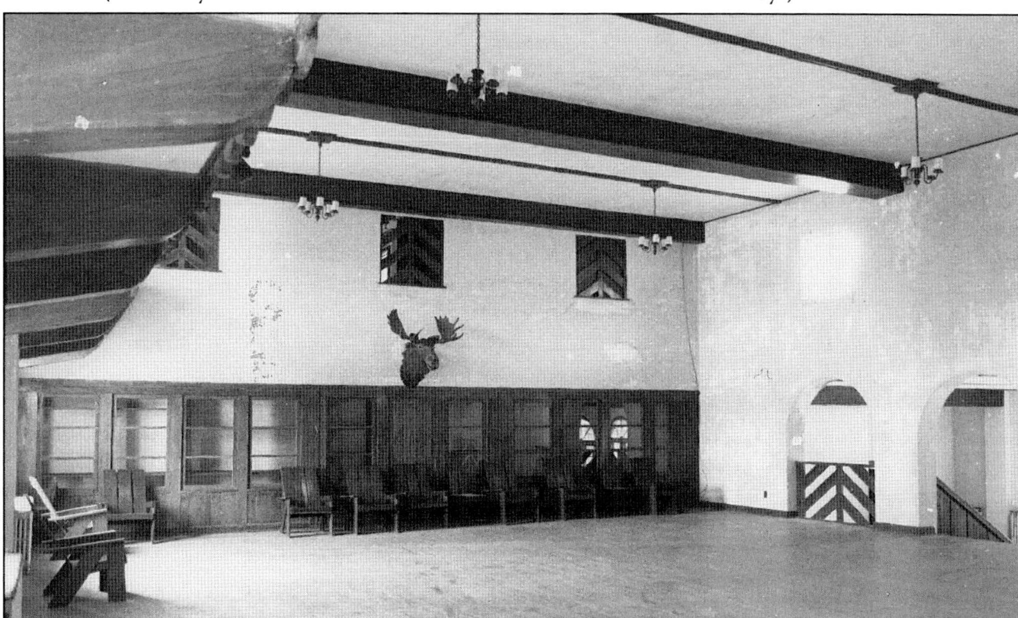

The "assembly room" in old Mattamuskeet Lodge (now referred to as the "ballroom") on the second floor of the south side of the historic building is pictured here in 1980 when the building was being considered for the National Register of Historic Places. The moose is not among Hyde County's wildlife. (Courtesy of North Carolina Division of Archives and History.)

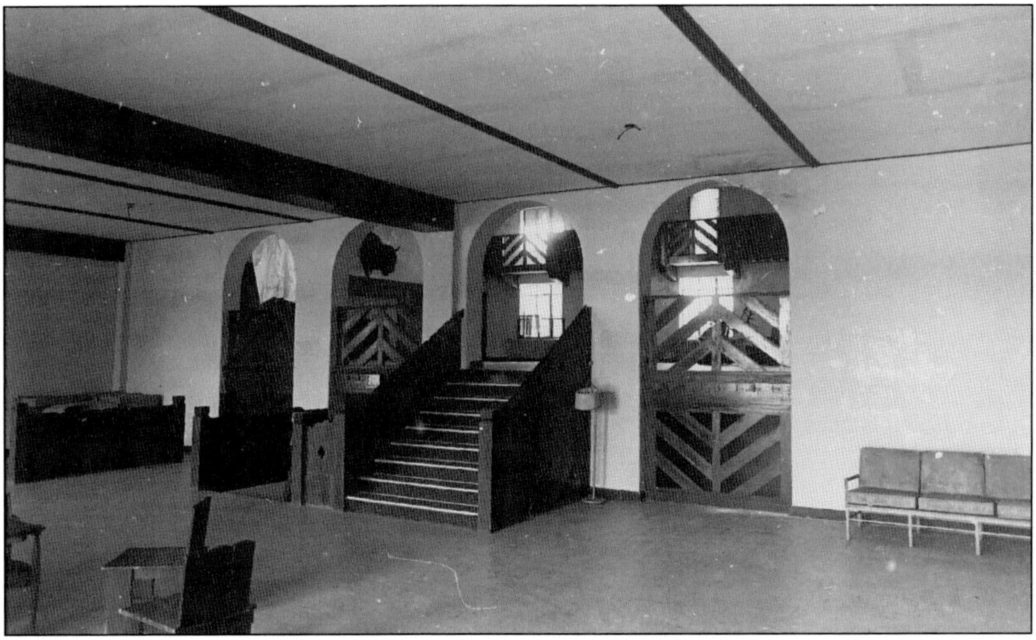

This 1980 image was taken from the "lounge" level in old Mattamuskeet Lodge (now referred to as the "mezzanine") on the second floor of the north side of the structure, looking up the steps to the "assembly room" ("ballroom"). This side of the building originally housed the huge pumps that once moved millions of gallons of water from Lake Mattamuskeet. (Courtesy of North Carolina Division of Archives and History.)

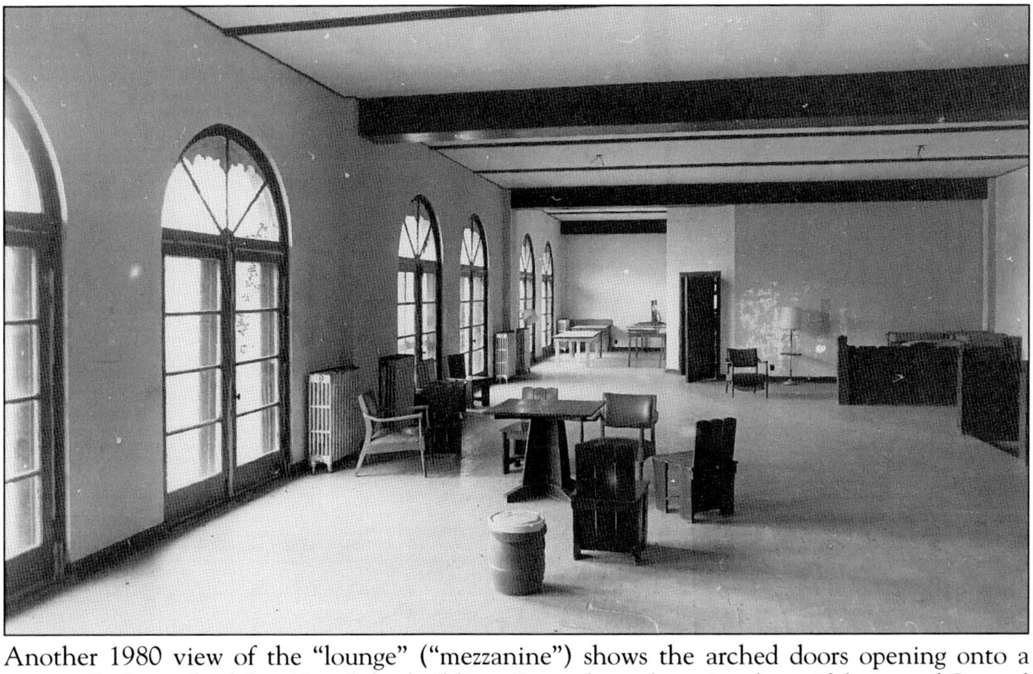

Another 1980 view of the "lounge" ("mezzanine") shows the arched doors opening onto a narrow deck on the lake side of the building. From these doors is a beautiful view of Central Canal. The wooden chairs in the foreground were made by the CCC boys in the late 1930s. (Courtesy of North Carolina Division of Archives and History.)

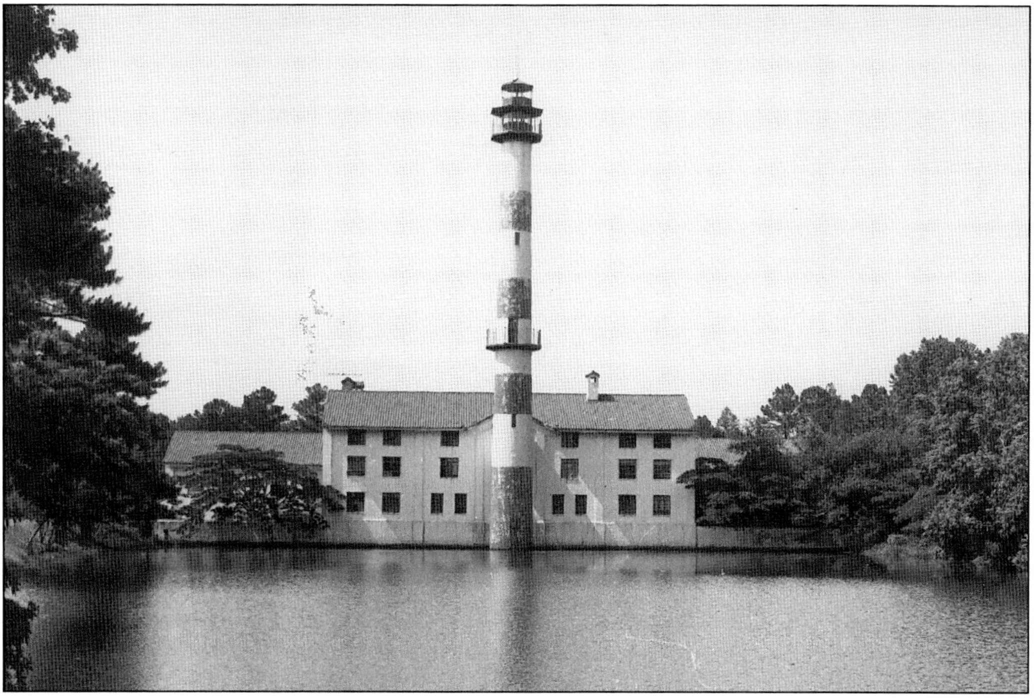

The south side of Mattamuskeet Lodge is pictured here in 1980, when a group of concerned citizens from Hyde County applied to have the building placed on the National Register of Historic Places. It received the designation in 1981. (Courtesy of North Carolina Division of Archives and History.)

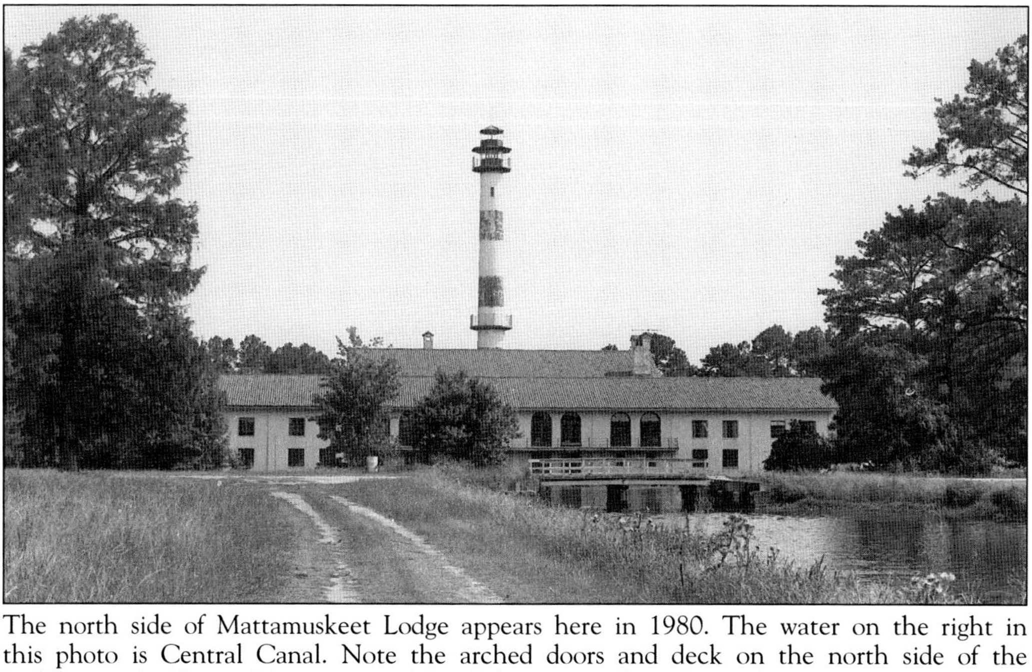

The north side of Mattamuskeet Lodge appears here in 1980. The water on the right in this photo is Central Canal. Note the arched doors and deck on the north side of the building on the "lounge" ("mezzanine") level. (Courtesy of North Carolina Division of Archives and History.)

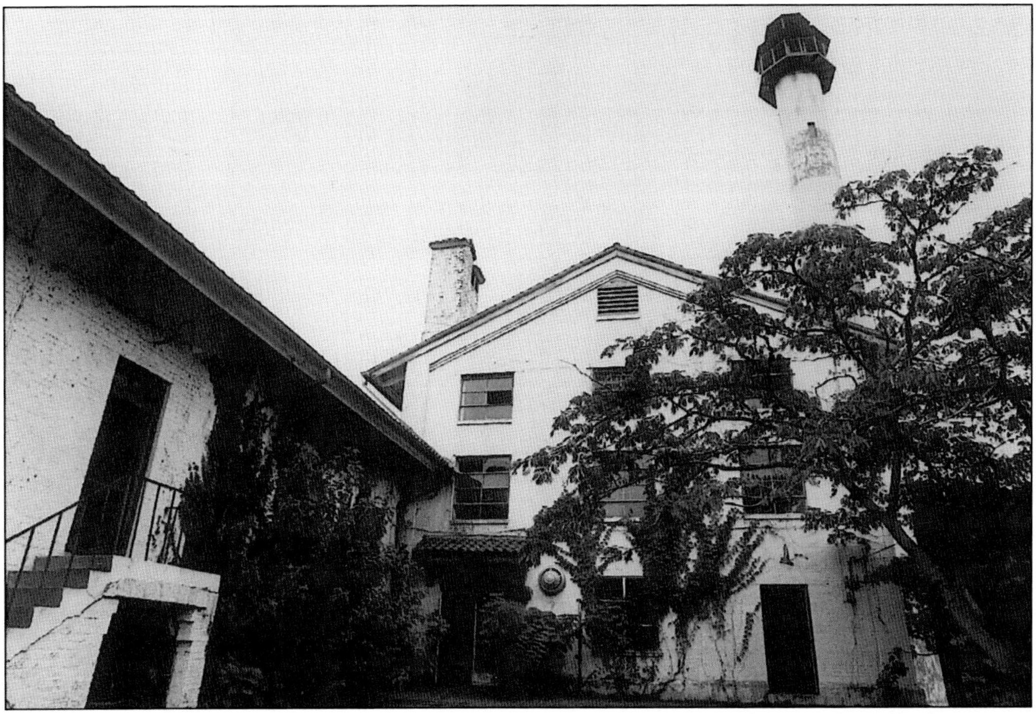

This, another photo of the west end of Mattamuskeet Lodge, was taken in the fall of 1988, 14 years after the U.S. Fish and Wildlife Service discontinued using the building as the headquarters for Mattamuskeet National Wildlife Refuge and a hunting lodge. (Courtesy of Cliff Hollis.)

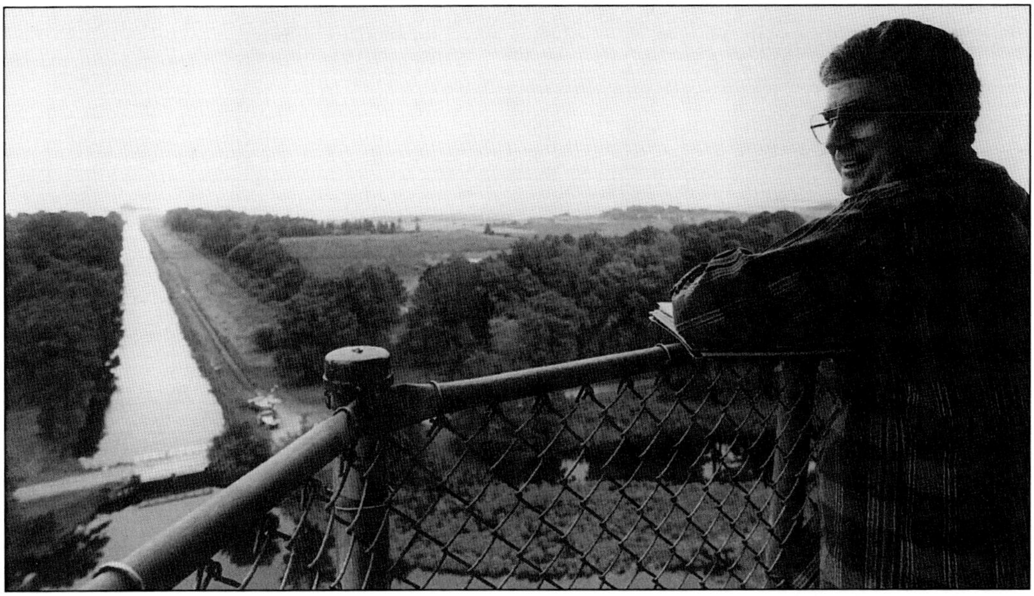

Here is another view from the top of the observation tower. With this beautiful view of Central Canal, the old town site of New Holland, and the wide expanse of the lake, it was easy to forget in 1988, when this photo was made, that the historic structure below was leaking badly, overgrown with vines, and in danger of being lost forever. (Courtesy of Cliff Hollis.)

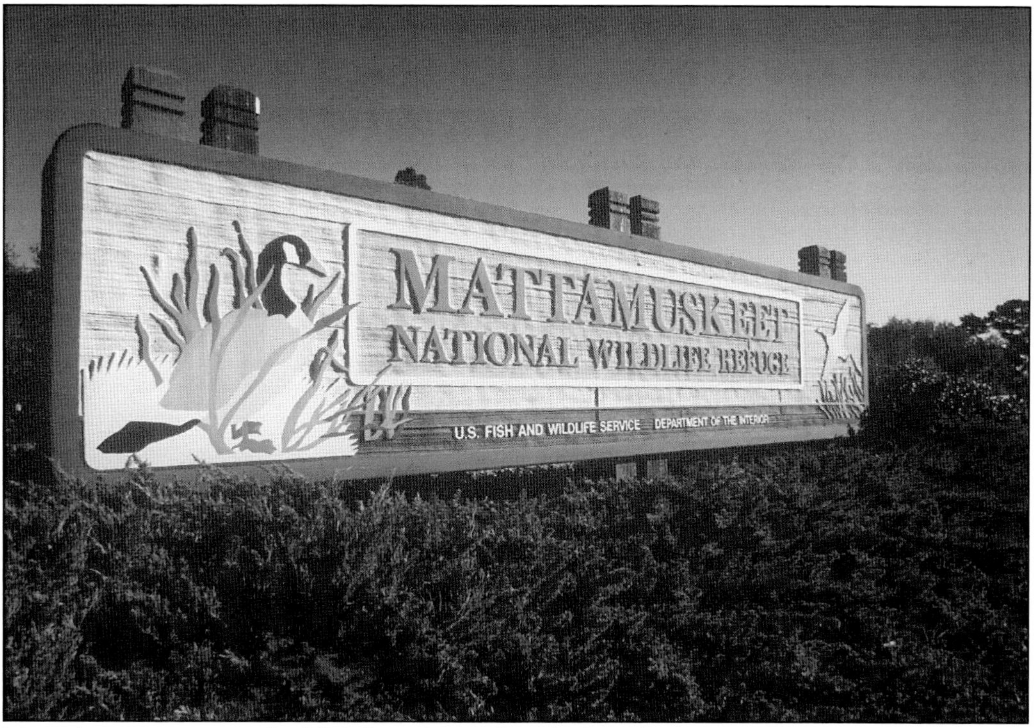

More than 800 species of wildlife have been identified on the Mattamuskeet National Wildlife Refuge. Fresh water anglers regard the refuge as one of the best places to fish for bass on the East Coast. Hunting is restricted to white tail deer and ducks, and then only by special permit under a closely controlled lottery system. Bird watchers and nature lovers find plenty to do at the refuge, and it is a wonderful place to spend the day with the entire family. (Courtesy of Cliff Hollis.)

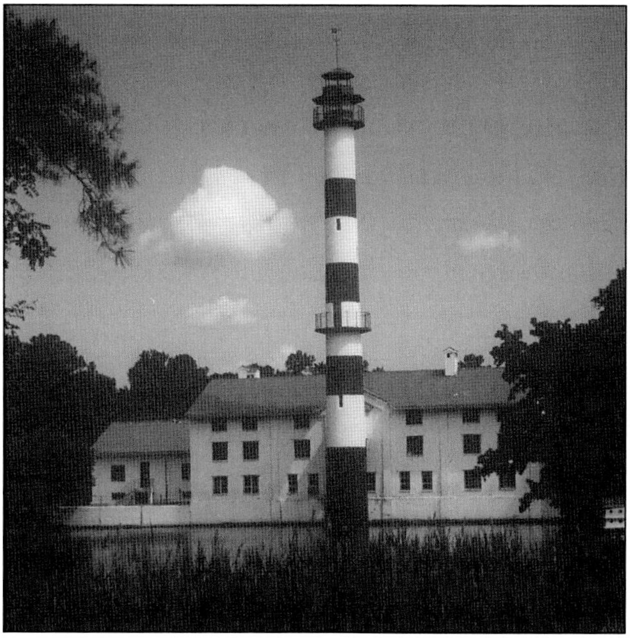

Mattamuskeet Lodge is one of the most photographed structures in the State of North Carolina and is seen here *c.* 1996. The observation tower has often been mistaken for a lighthouse, since it is painted in the same pattern as the Bodie Island Lighthouse on the Outer Banks of North Carolina. (Courtesy of Lewis Forrest.)

Ten

Hunters and Fishermen at Lake Mattamuskeet

Lake Mattamuskeet has been a hunter's paradise since long before recorded history. On July 11 and 12, 1585, 60 English gentlemen who were part of Ralph Lane's company's attempt to establish a colony on Roanoke Island, paid the first recorded visit by white men to the land that is now Hyde County. Leaving Ocracoke in three small pinnaces, these men sailed and rowed to Wysocking Bay on the Pamlico Sound, just south of Lake Mattamuskeet. They walked from the bay to the huge inland sea the Native Americans called "Paquippe." The next day, they visited a large palisaded Indian village that the English artist John White called "Pomeiock." White painted about 20 watercolors of what the Englishmen saw during that two-day excursion. The paintings that have survived include swans, geese, ducks, and other birds and wildlife that are still found in abundance in Hyde County.

During the lake drainage era, New Holland Corporation operated its farm in the lake bed as a private hunting refuge. Hunters stayed at the New Holland Inn, and the farming company provided guides and special hunting permits for the duration of the hunters' stay.

After the lake drainage era, hunting on Mattamuskeet Migratory Waterfowl Refuge was a special treat for men and women alike until the U.S. Fish and Wildlife Service outlawed the shooting of Canada geese on the refuge in 1972. Today, the refuge has a lottery system that permits limited duck and deer hunting on Mattamuskeet National Wildlife Refuge.

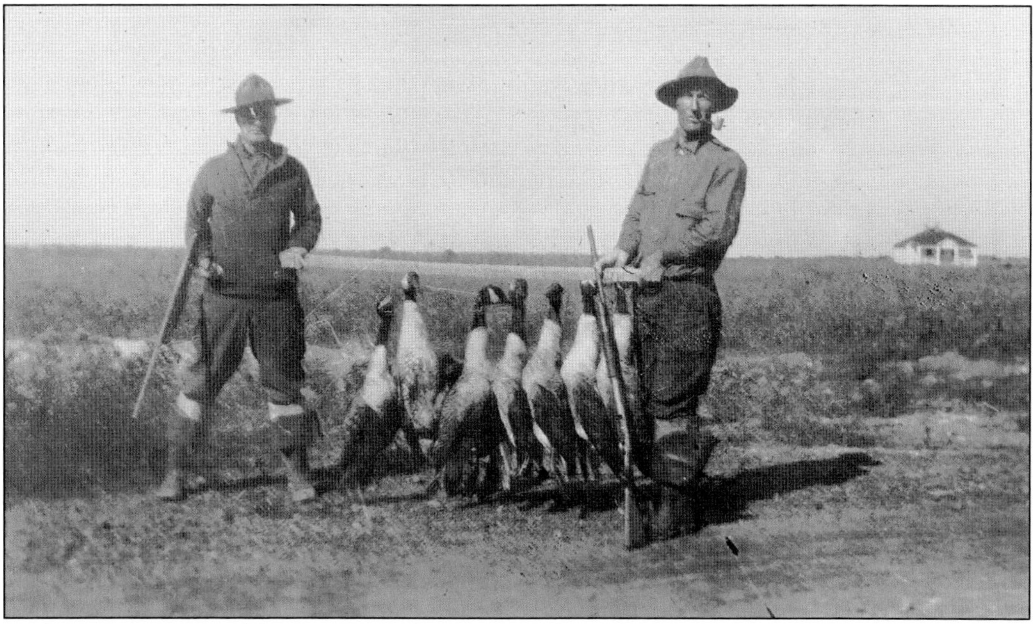

Karl L. Ponzer enjoyed hunting on Lake Mattamuskeet during the six years he worked at New Holland as a civil engineer for North Carolina Farms Company from 1918 to 1924. According to his granddaughter, Ponzer used to brag that he could stand on his front porch in New Holland and shoot seven geese with one shot. (Courtesy of Carolyn Ponzer Taylor.)

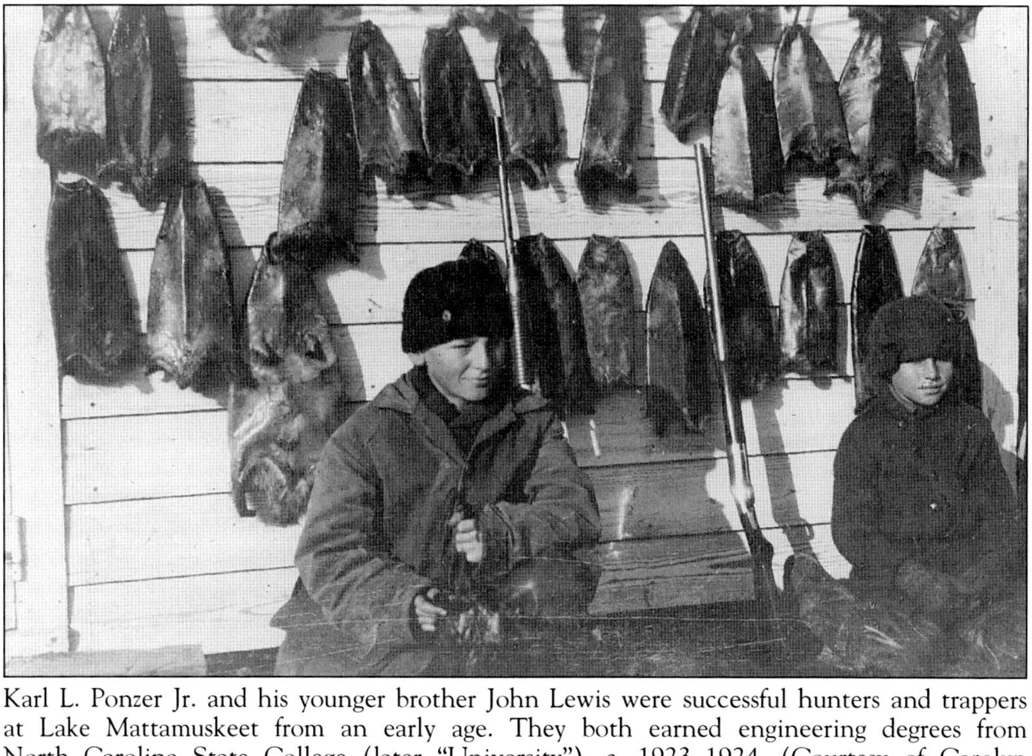

Karl L. Ponzer Jr. and his younger brother John Lewis were successful hunters and trappers at Lake Mattamuskeet from an early age. They both earned engineering degrees from North Carolina State College (later "University"), *c.* 1923–1924. (Courtesy of Carolyn Ponzer Taylor.)

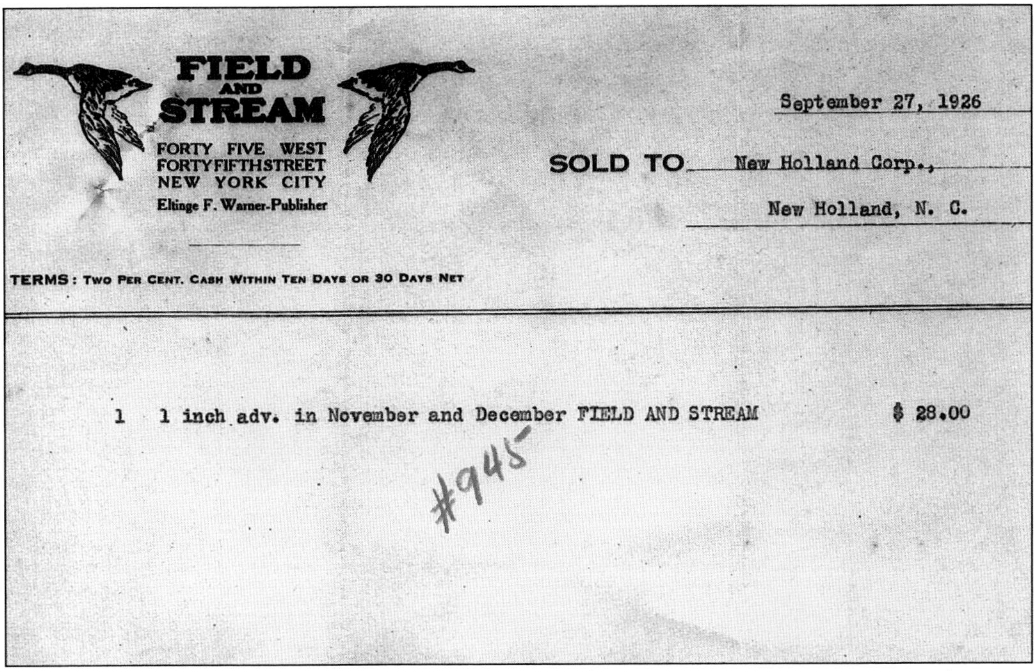

FIELD AND STREAM
FORTY FIVE WEST FORTYFIFTHSTREET
NEW YORK CITY
Eltinge F. Warner-Publisher

September 27, 1926

SOLD TO New Holland Corp.,
New Holland, N. C.

TERMS: Two Per Cent. Cash Within Ten Days or 30 Days Net

1 1 inch adv. in November and December FIELD AND STREAM $ 28.00

#945

In the fall of 1926, New Holland Corporation began advertising its property as a private hunting preserve. The first ads in *Field & Stream Magazine* ran in November 1926. Hunters came from as far away as Canada and Louisiana to shoot Canada geese and ducks in the bed of Lake Mattamuskeet. (From the Mattamuskeet Records.)

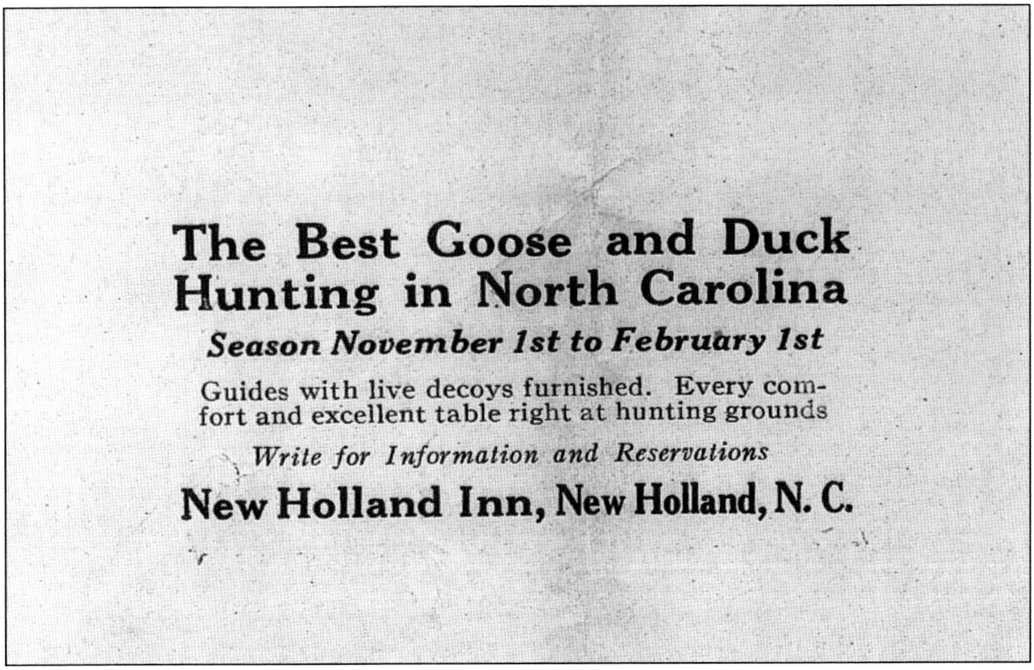

The Best Goose and Duck Hunting in North Carolina

Season November 1st to February 1st

Guides with live decoys furnished. Every comfort and excellent table right at hunting grounds

Write for Information and Reservations

New Holland Inn, New Holland, N. C.

This is the proof of the ad that appeared in *Field and Stream Magazine* in 1926. Notice the promise of live decoys. The use of live decoys was popular at the time. (From the Mattamuskeet Records.)

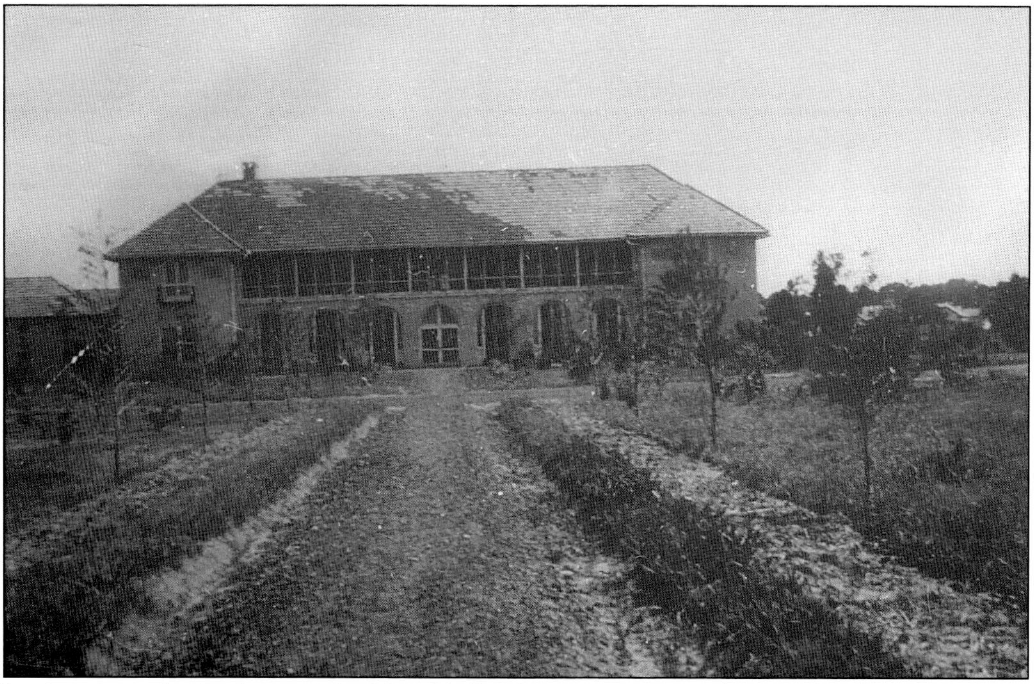

In describing the facilities of the New Holland Inn, prospective hunters for the 1926 season were informed that "We feel we can make you perfectly comfortable at our New Holland Inn which is located right on our hunting preserve, where you will find good table, electric lights, steam heat, and hot and cold water." (Courtesy of the Hyde County Historical and Genealogical Society.)

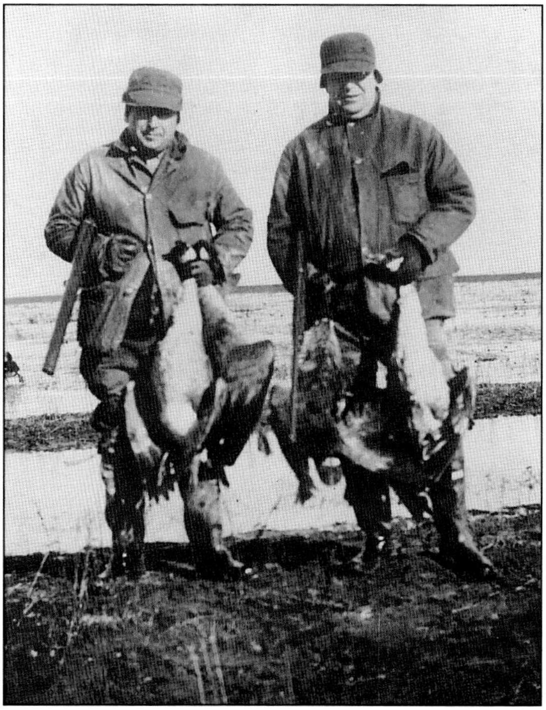

The original caption under this 1931 photo read, "Uncle Lloyd and Tom gets in a nice broadside at a close flock and done right well." Lloyd Kinsey (left) and Tom Nicholson (right) stayed at the New Holland Inn, and their party included Elmer Geisler, Jack Scott, and E.S. Kenny. Using live decoys, the five hunters took home 60 Canada geese. (Courtesy of John R. "Jack" Pyburn Jr.)

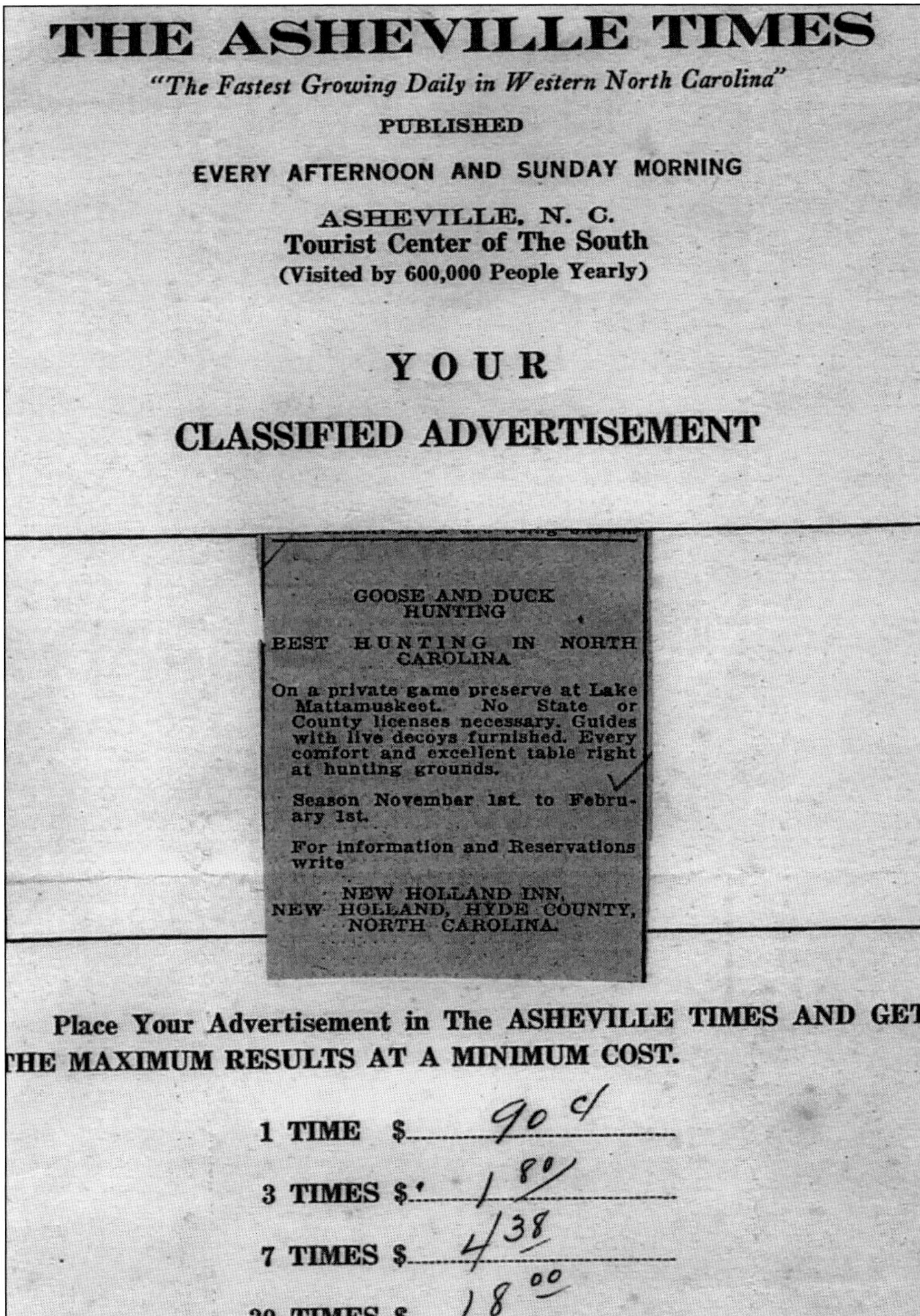

THE ASHEVILLE TIMES

"The Fastest Growing Daily in Western North Carolina"

PUBLISHED

EVERY AFTERNOON AND SUNDAY MORNING

ASHEVILLE, N. C.

Tourist Center of The South

(Visited by 600,000 People Yearly)

YOUR

CLASSIFIED ADVERTISEMENT

GOOSE AND DUCK HUNTING

BEST HUNTING IN NORTH CAROLINA

On a private game preserve at Lake Mattamuskeet. No State or County licenses necessary. Guides with live decoys furnished. Every comfort and excellent table right at hunting grounds.

Season November 1st. to February 1st.

For information and Reservations write

NEW HOLLAND INN,
NEW HOLLAND, HYDE COUNTY,
NORTH CAROLINA.

Place Your Advertisement in The ASHEVILLE TIMES AND GET THE MAXIMUM RESULTS AT A MINIMUM COST.

1 TIME $ 90¢

3 TIMES $ 1.80

7 TIMES $ 4.38

30 TIMES $ 18.00

During the three-month 1929–1930 migratory waterfowl hunting season, the guides working for New Holland Corporation reported that their hunting parties killed 1,867 Canada geese and 615 ducks while hunting in the drained bed of Lake Mattamuskeet. J. Byron Hodges of Swan Quarter was the chief guide that year. This *Asheville Times* advertisement comes from the Mattamuskeet Records.

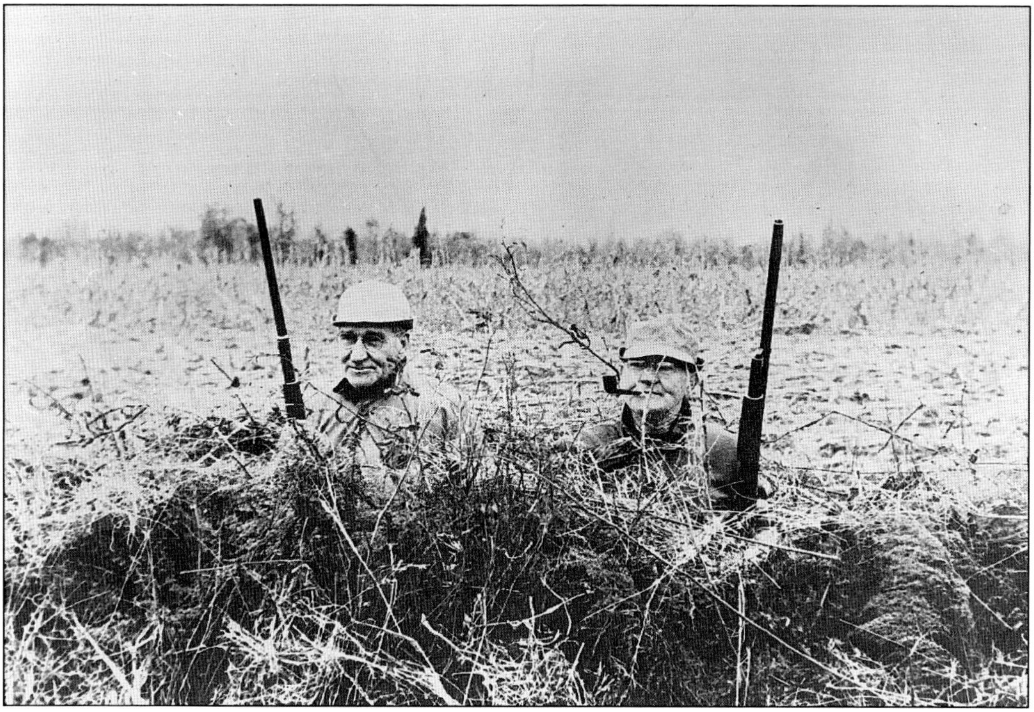

Since the lake was drained in 1930, the birds would come into the fields to feed during the days and then fly to the nearby Pamlico Sound for the night and return to the fields again early in the morning. Hunters were out early to shoot birds as they flew over the blinds on the way to the fields. (Courtesy of Lizzie Mae Credle Britton.)

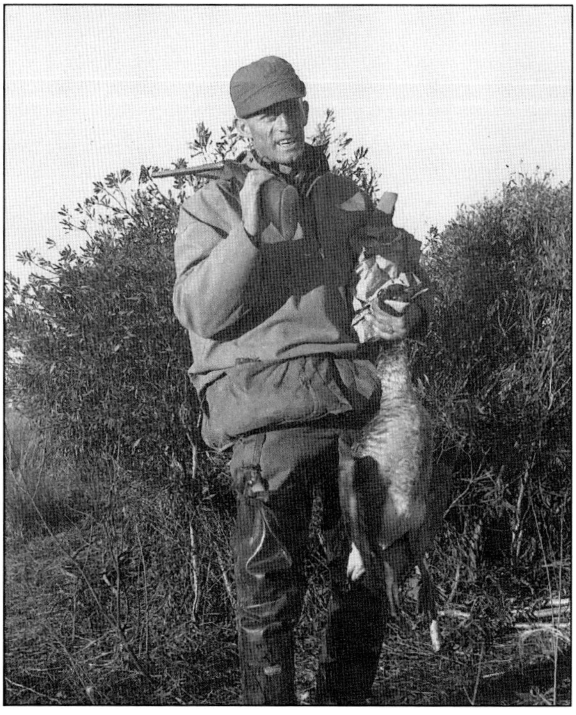

This unidentified hunter bagged a Canada goose at Lake Mattamuskeet during the 1941 season. Canada geese migrated to the lake by the tens of thousands between 1940 and 1960. Lake Mattamuskeet was the favorite wintering spot in the Atlantic Flyway for Canada geese in those years. Since then, shifts in migratory patterns have reduced the number of Canada geese at Mattamuskeet. (Courtesy of North Carolina Division of Archives and History.)

Tom and John Prudens (left to right), sons of Bill Prudens, of Plymouth, North Carolina, are pictured here after a successful goose hunt in Hyde County, guided by John Harold Swindell. (Courtesy of Janie Cutrell Swindell.)

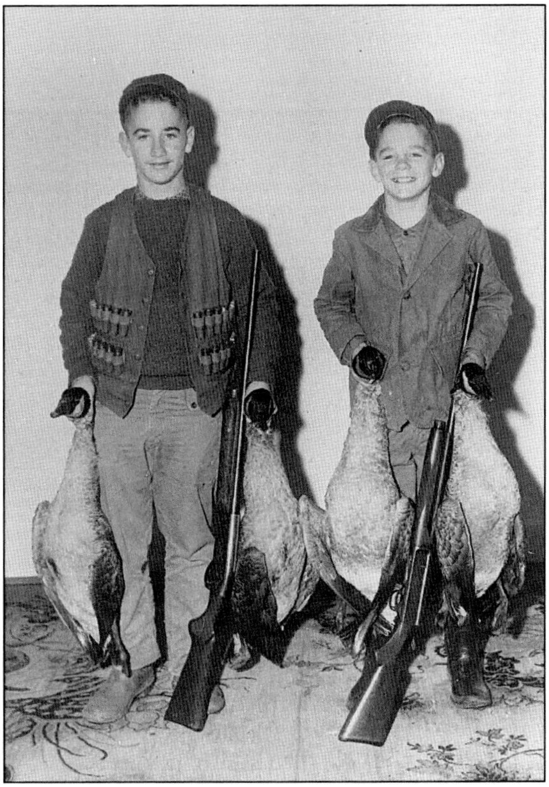

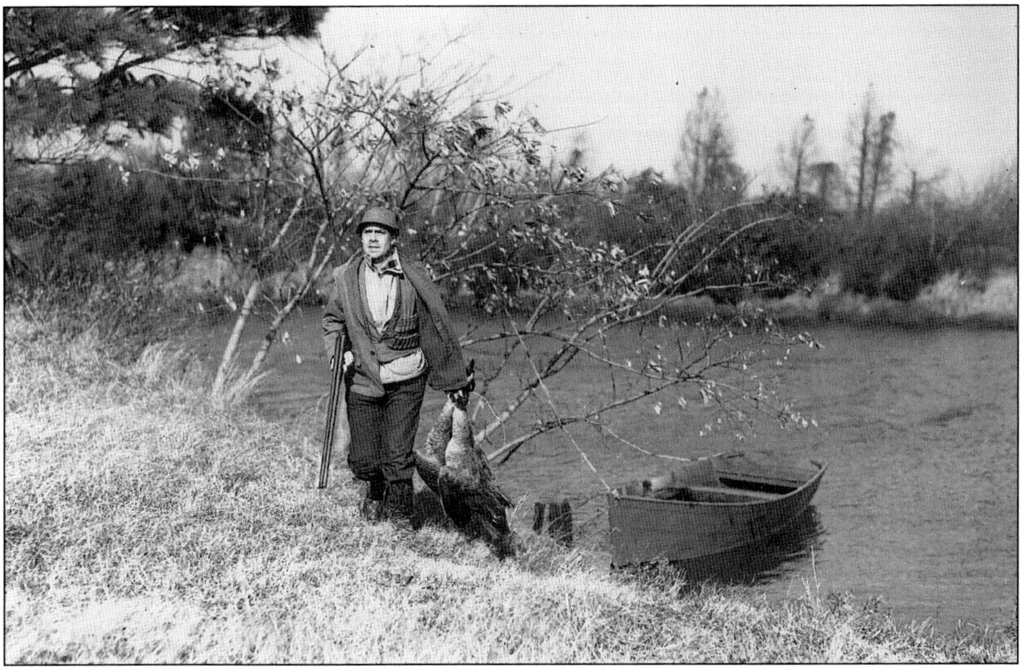

An unidentified hunter returns from a successful hunt on Lake Mattamuskeet in 1944, having accessed his blind by wooden skiff and the old drainage canals. (Courtesy of North Carolina Division of Archives and History.)

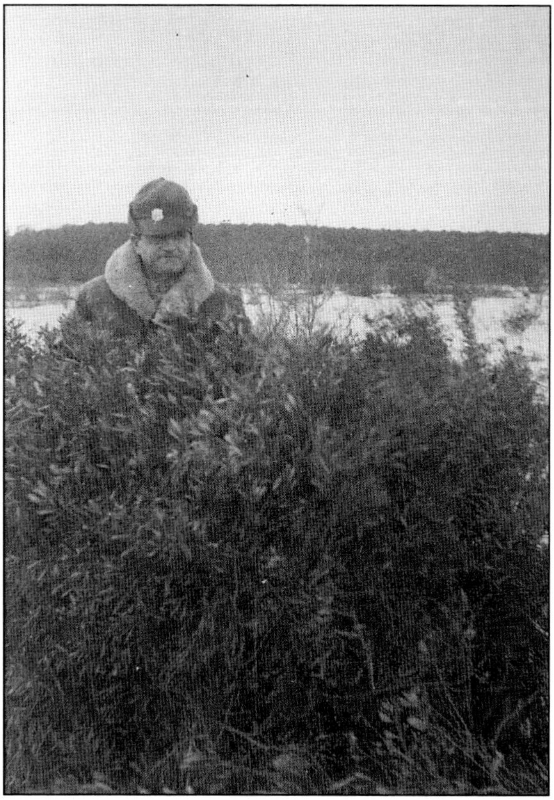

Oscar Chadwick was one of the early game wardens who kept a watchful eye on the hunters at Lake Mattamuskeet. This photo was taken in December 1938, during the CCC era, just one year after Mattamuskeet Lodge opened to host hunters who wanted to shoot birds on the new Mattamuskeet Migratory Waterfowl Refuge. (Courtesy of North Carolina Division of Archives and History.)

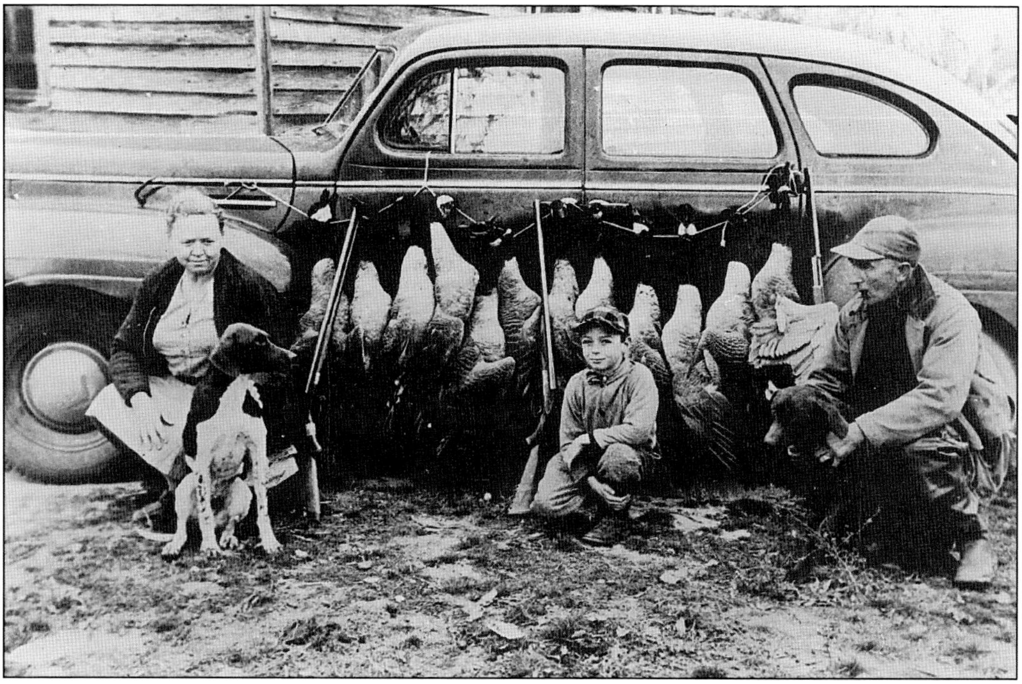

Beatrice Credle Williams, Richard (Dick) Powers Credle, and Samuel Robert Williams pose for a photograph after a successful hunt in Hyde County. (Courtesy of Lizzie Mae Credle Britton.)

The shallow waters of Lake Mattamuskeet made retrieving game without a dog rather easy, unless you foolishly chose to hunt over an area where 12-18 inches of soft silt on the lake bottom resulted in miring to your knees with every step. This unidentified hunter is pictured *c.* 1944. (Courtesy of North Carolina Division of Archives and History.)

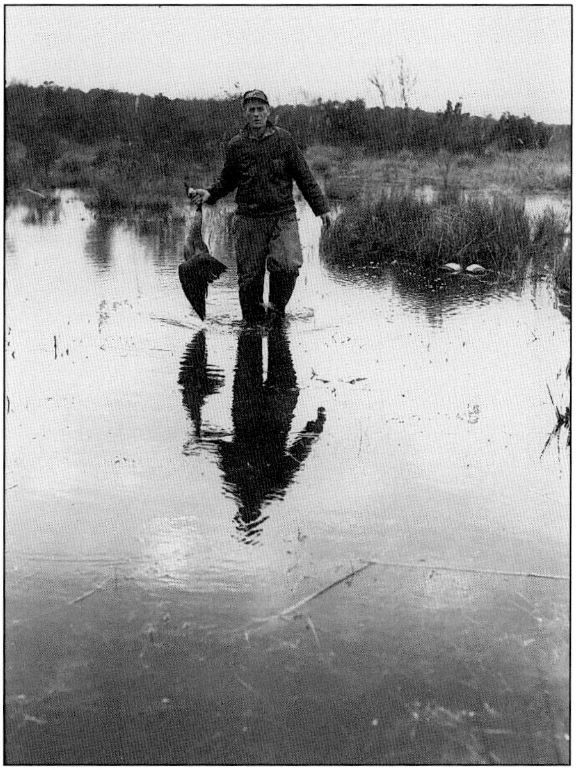

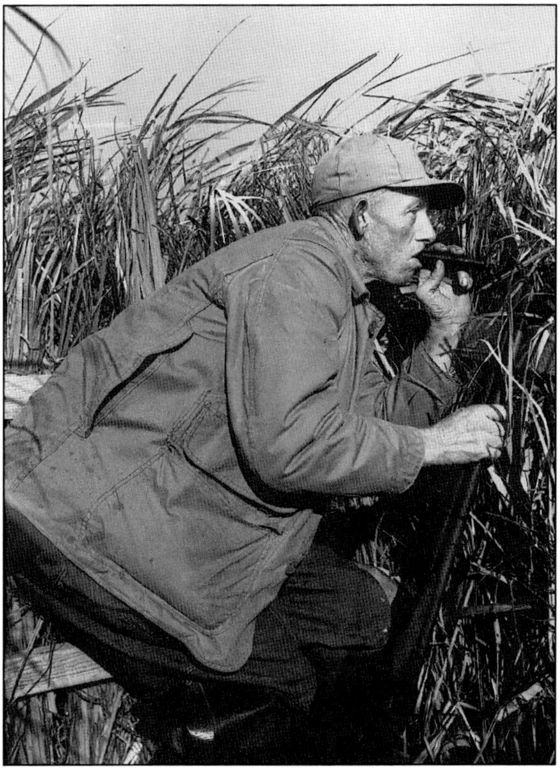

This unidentified hunter in 1944 calls in the birds from the protection of his blind. Hunters at Lake Mattamuskeet in the 1940s usually stayed at Mattamuskeet Lodge or one of the many "hunter's motels," private hunting camps, or in the private home of their guide. (Courtesy of North Carolina Division of Archives and History.)

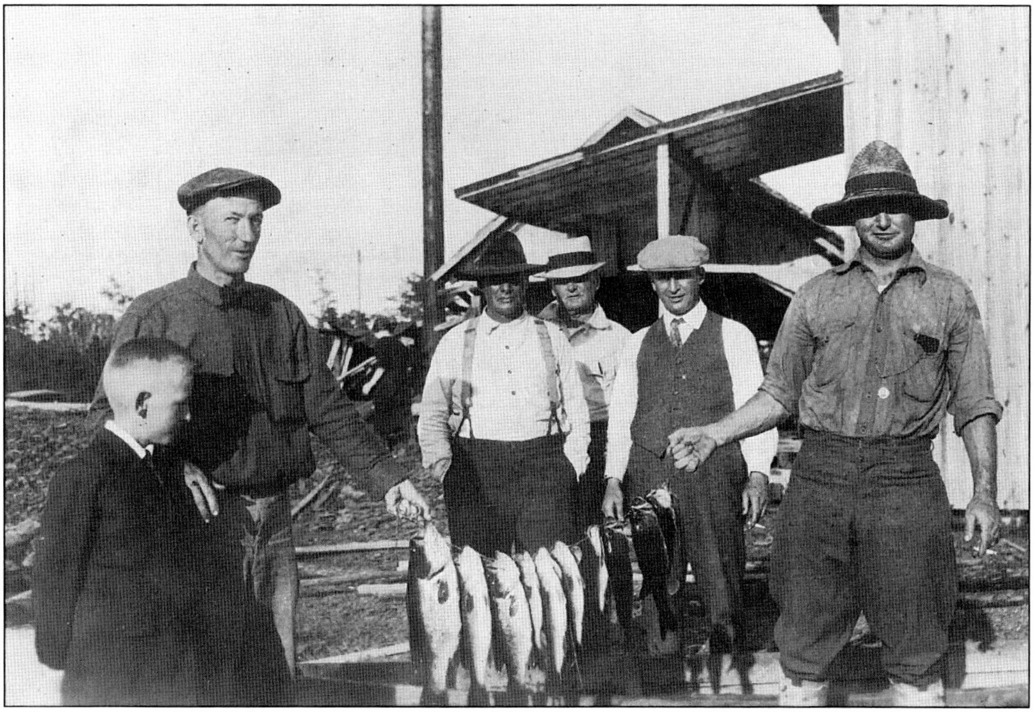

Karl L. Ponzer, his son Karl Lewis Jr. (both left), and a group of friends display their catch from the canals of Lake Mattamuskeet during the early 1920s when the lake was drained. (Courtesy of Carolyn Ponzer Taylor.)

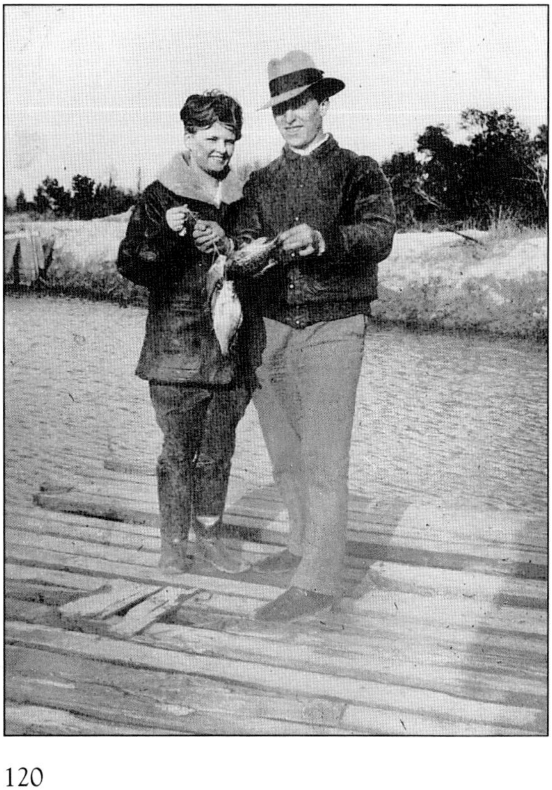

Gladys Allen, a waitress at the New Holland Inn, and an unidentified friend display their catch from the outfall basin on the south side of the pumping plant sometime around the late 1920s or early 1930s. (Courtesy of Patricia Auman, daughter of Gladys Allen.)

Danny Hembree, grandson of CCC Company 424 commanding officer Captain Hembree, proudly displays this bass caught in a Mattamuskeet canal in 1937. (Courtesy of CCC Company 424 Archives.)

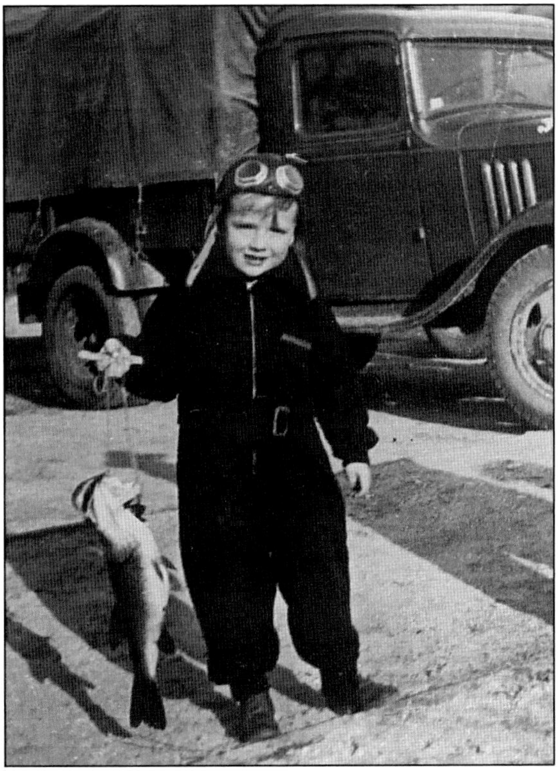

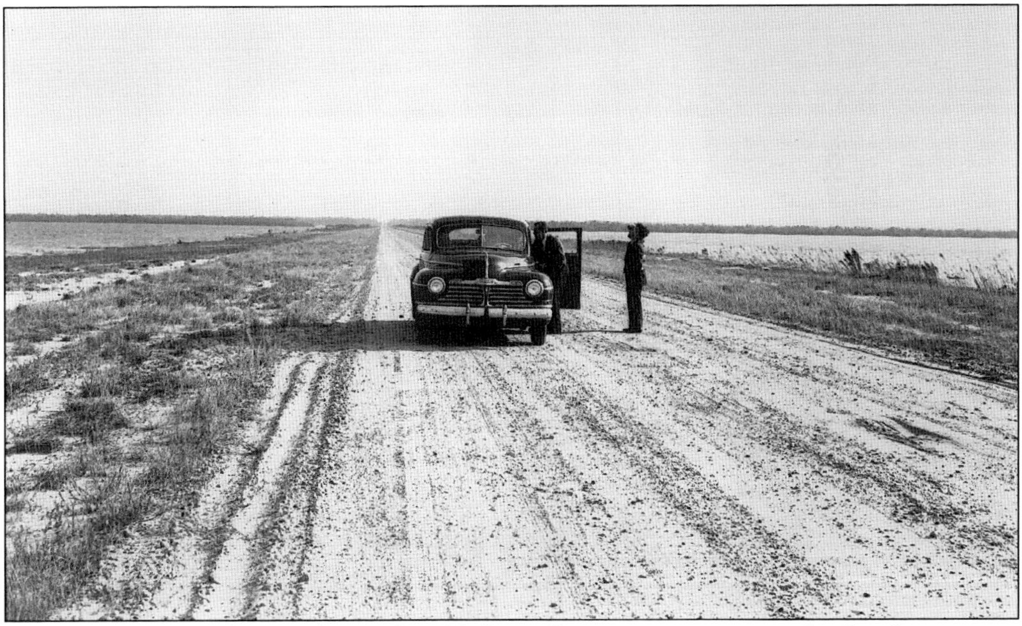

During 1940–1942, the North Carolina Highway Department constructed a 7-mile causeway across the middle of Lake Mattamuskeet from the Lake Comfort community on the south shore to Fairfield on the north shore. The causeway is part of North Carolina's Highway 94 that extends from Lake Comfort in Hyde County to Columbia in Tyrrell County. (Courtesy of North Carolina Division of Archives and History.)

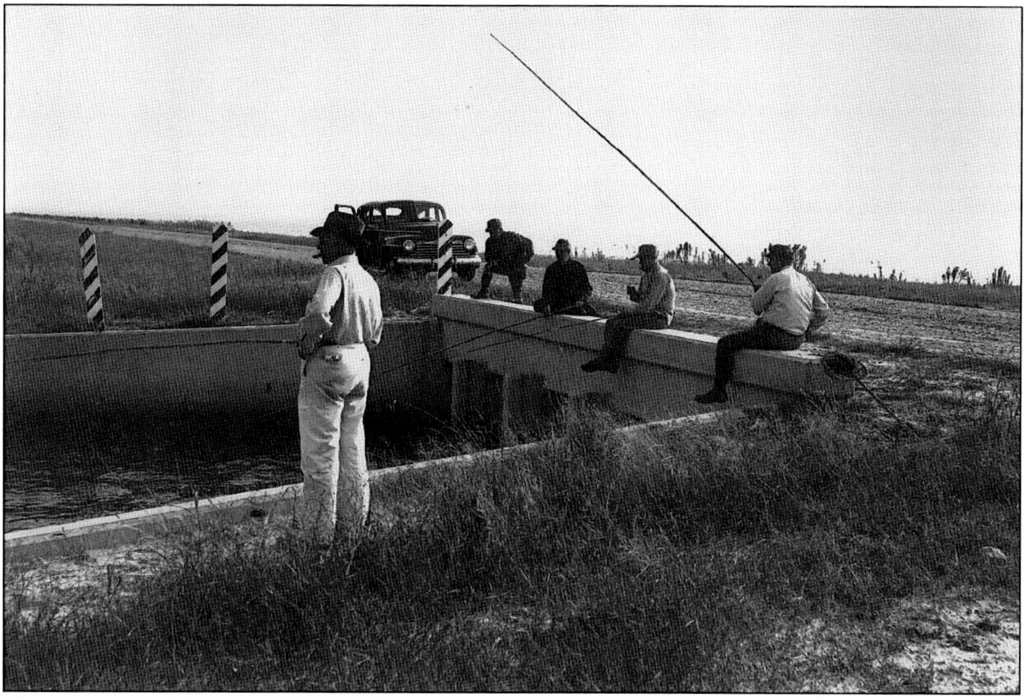

These men are fishing in 1944 at one of the culverts that allows water to pass under the causeway (Highway 94). (Courtesy of North Carolina Division of Archives and History.)

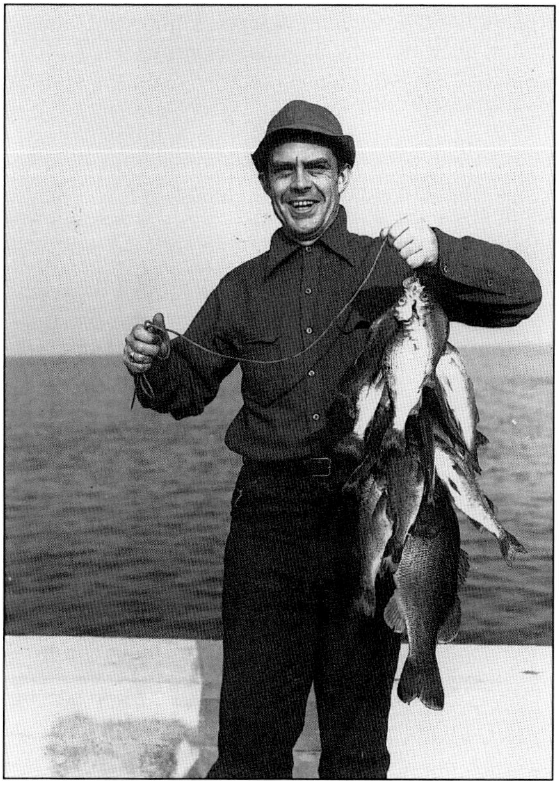

The smile says everything in this c. 1944 image! (Courtesy of North Carolina Division of Archives and History.)

EPILOGUE

Future Plans for Mattamuskeet Lodge

Mattamuskeet Lodge served as a hotel for hunters and other guests until 1974 when the U.S. Fish and Wildlife Service closed it because it was no longer financially viable. From 1974 to 1980, the empty building deteriorated. In 1980, Hyde County citizens were successful in having Mattamuskeet Lodge placed on the National Register of Historic Places. However, the building continued to deteriorate for ten more years.

In 1988, North Carolina Senator Marc Basnight and Representative Howard Chapin co-sponsored a bill that funded a study to assess the feasibility of adapting the lodge for some new purpose. The Regional Development Institute of East Carolina University coordinated the study and declared the building structurally sound and worth saving. The prospect of re-opening Mattamuskeet Lodge awakened a new spirit among the people of Hyde County.

In June of 1989, the Swan Quarter Home Demonstration Club sponsored a reunion at the lodge for former employees of the companies involved directly in the lake drainage and personnel from the two CCC Company 424 Camps. Several hundred survivors, families, and friends attended. The next year a group of Hyde County citizens formed a committee called "The Friends of Mattamuskeet Lodge" to spearhead efforts to save and renovate the building.

Since 1989, volunteers have worked thousands of hours with the Mattamuskeet Refuge staff and have made considerable improvements to the building. As funds have become available, contractors have replaced electrical wiring, plumbing, windows, floor coverings, and the heating system to make the building safer and more useful. While its renovation is not complete, the building serves as a community center for Hyde County and houses a Coastal Studies Field Station for East Carolina University. There is a full-time lodge coordinator on site to schedule groups who want to use the building and to provide tours for visitors.

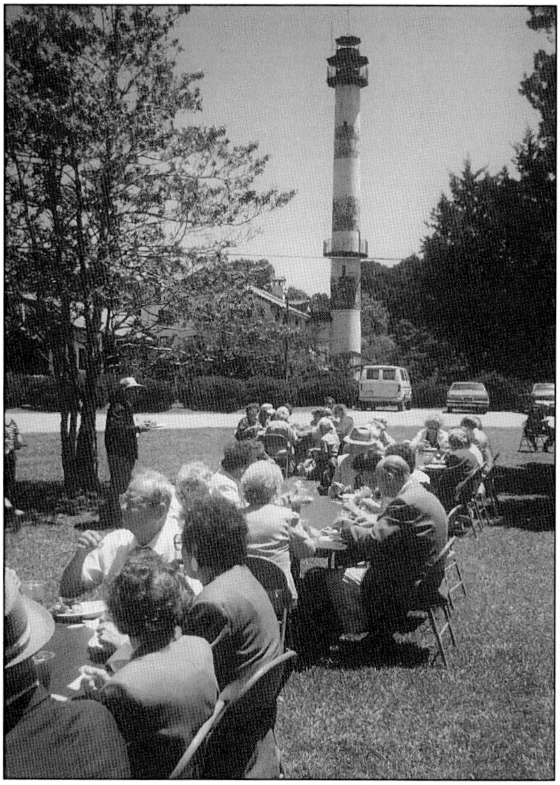

Former employees of the Mattamuskeet Drainage District, North Carolina Farms Company, New Holland Corporation, Morris Machine Works, and personnel from the two CCC Company 424 Camps gathered with families and friends at Mattamuskeet Lodge to renew their memories and stories of old New Holland during May 27–28, 1989. The CCC boys continue to hold an annual reunion at the lodge the first weekend in June. (Courtesy of Cliff Hollis.)

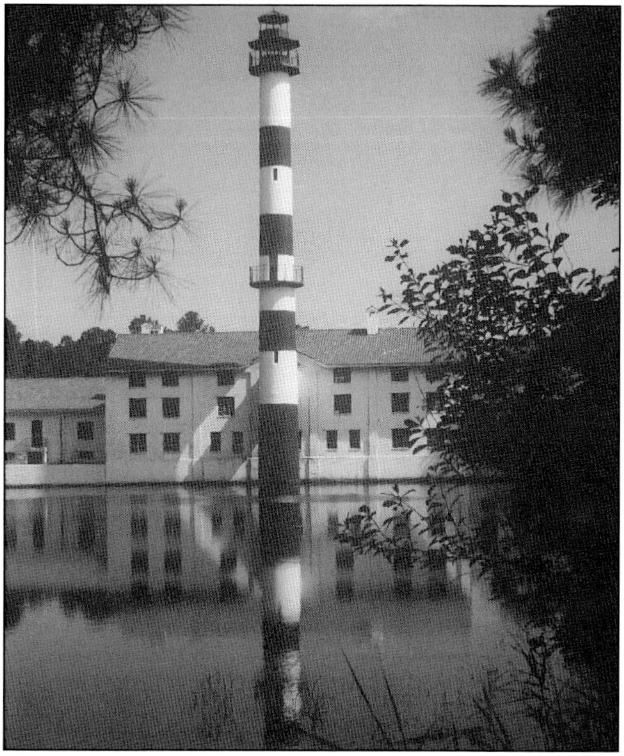

Renovation plans for Mattamuskeet Lodge are now under the leadership of the Partnership for the Sounds, a 501(c)(3) nonprofit organization, in cooperation with the U.S. Fish and Wildlife Service. Plans call for converting the building into an environmental and cultural resource center at a cost of about $4.5 million. The historical features of the building will be protected in the renovation. (Courtesy of Lewis Forrest.)

SOURCES

The Mattamuskeet Records

When the drainage project at Lake Mattamuskeet ended with the sale of the lake to the U.S. government in 1934, Fred Phineas Latham, the last superintendent of New Holland Corporation's farming operation at the lake, closed down the farm. Latham boxed the records from the administrative building at New Holland and moved them to his own farm east of Belhaven, North Carolina, where he stacked them in his barn.

In the fall of 1988, Lewis Forrest and Cliff Hollis visited Latham's granddaughter, Jane Latham Dilday, to inquire whether she knew anything about her grandfather's participation in the New Holland project. She led Forrest and Hollis to the old barn and showed them five large wooden boxes. She explained that, as a child, she and her friends climbed on the boxes to jump down on the hay. Some of the boxes were torn open and documents were scattered onto the floor. Fortunately, most were in place. They had been in the barn for 56 years.

Forrest inspected a file from one of the boxes. The contents were from the late 1920s and dealt with soybean sales to a company in Richmond. The second file dealt with Farmall tractors. Forrest immediately realized these were the records from the lake. Mrs. Dilday told Forrest that she and her husband, Marion, were planning to tear down the old barn and that if Forrest wanted the records, he was welcome to them. The next day, Forrest and Hollis moved the records to Forrest's home. For 11 years, Forrest has sorted, cleaned, and preserved the records. There are nearly 30,000 pages of letters, invoices, contracts, bank statements, and canceled checks plus about 40 bound ledgers and journals, which are the source of most of the facts stated in this book. These records make it possible to accurately interpret what occurred at Lake Mattamuskeet from 1911 to 1932 for the following entities:

—Board of Commissioners of the Mattamuskeet Drainage District
—Southern Land Reclamation Company/New Holland Farms, Inc.
—North Carolina Farms Co. and New Holland, Higginsport & Mt. Vernon Railroad
—New Holland Corporation and New Holland Railroad

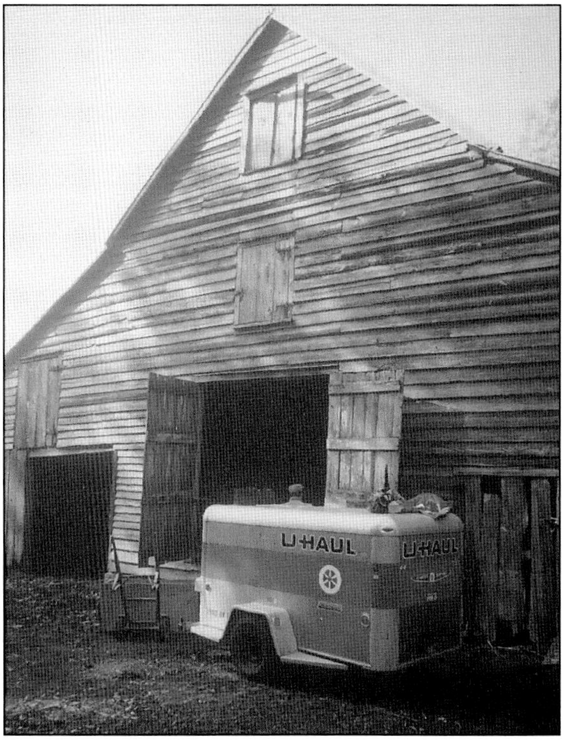

This is the barn where the Mattamuskeet records remained for 56 years from 1932 to 1988 and were exposed to mice and insects. Fortunately, the valuable records survived 56 years of unprotected storage. (Courtesy of Cliff Hollis.)

The records are pictured here in October 1988 when Lewis Forrest and Cliff Hollis visited Jane Latham Dilday and she gave Forrest the records with his assurance that he would preserve them and tell the stories of the history of the lake drainage. (Courtesy of Cliff Hollis.)

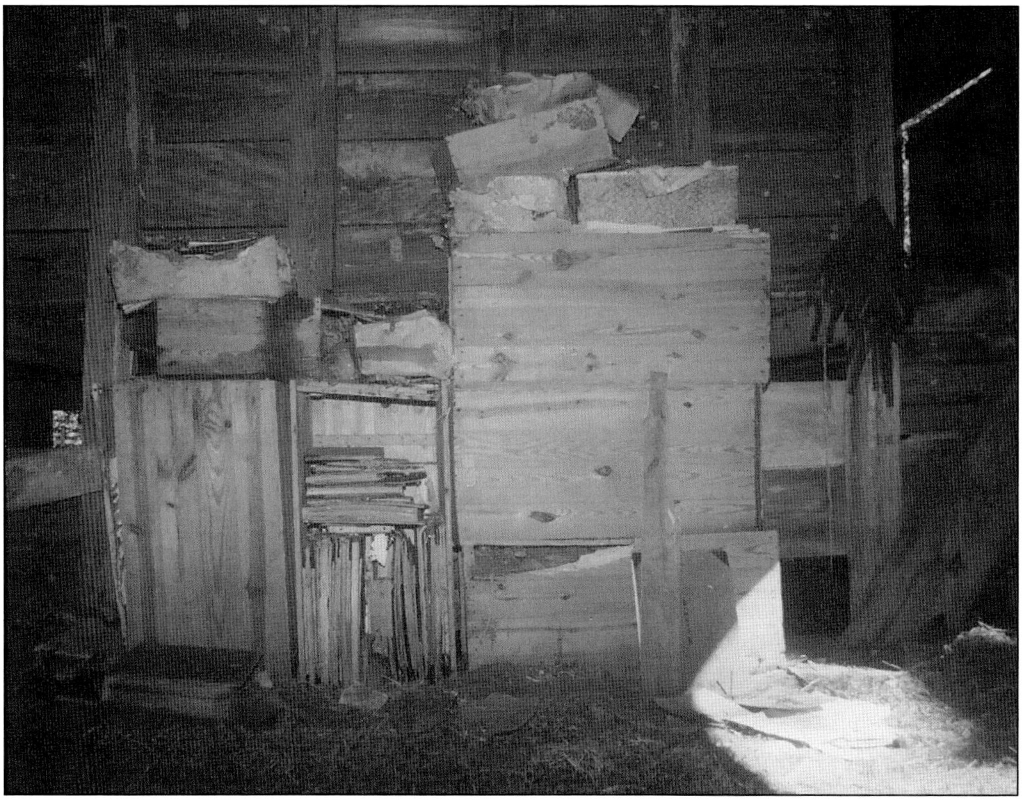

The Book Team

On June 2, 1999, this group of volunteers met with Lewis C. Forrest at the Hyde County home of Maxine Simmons for a workday to select photographs and provide accurate information for this book. Over several years, these volunteers have contributed many of the photos shared in this book. They have also assisted in locating photo collections for The Mattamuskeet Foundation's ongoing efforts to preserve historical photos pertaining to the history of New Holland, Lake Mattamuskeet, and Hyde County, North Carolina. These individuals have been invaluable in tracking down leads on historical information, individuals with ties to the lake history, and sources of related published materials.

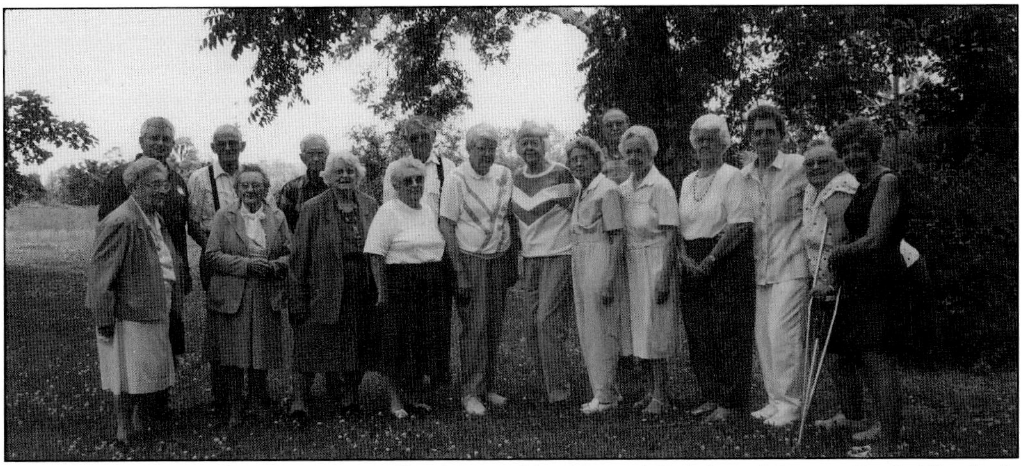

From left to right are (front row) Ercell Gibbs, Mildred Swindell Askew, Virginia Pugh, Elizabeth Butt, Iberia R. Tunnell, Mary-Louise Swindell McGee, Lizzie Mae Credle Britton, Dorothy Dudley, Willie Murl Bonner, Janie Cutrell Swindell, Maxine Simmons, and Bea Simmons; (second row) Lewis C. Forrest, Leonard T. Pugh Sr., Leon Ballance, Edward Cuthrell, and Alfred J. Schmitt Jr. The group was photographed by Harold Simmons.

Special credits go to Louis Van Camp of Coastal Images, Washington, North Carolina, and the Photo Section of the North Carolina Division of Archives and History, who provided professional assistance in copying original photographs for The Mattamuskeet Foundation's Photo Collection.

The Mattamuskeet Foundation, Inc.

The Mattamuskeet Foundation is a 501(c)(3) nonprofit organization with the mission of engaging in research and educational activities to preserve, publish, and otherwise tell the stories of the rich history and ecology of Lake Mattamuskeet and the surrounding areas of eastern North Carolina.

For more information about the foundation, contact:
The Mattamuskeet Foundation, Inc.
Lewis C. Forrest Jr., Ed.D., Executive Director
4377 Lewis Lane Road, Ayden, NC 28513 USA

Toll-free: 1-888-MAT-LAKE
Phone: 252-746-4221 Fax: 252-746-4698
E-Mail: mat-lake@coastalnet.com
Website: *http://www.mattamuskeet.org*

All proceeds from the sale of this book go to support the mission of The Mattamuskeet Foundation, Inc.